LEVERAGING CONSTRAINTS FOR INNOVATION: NEW PRODUCT DEVELOPMENT ESSENTIALS FROM THE PDMA

LEVERAGING CONSTRAINTS FOR INNOVATION: NEW PRODUCT DEVELOPMENT ESSENTIALS FROM THE PDMA

Sebastian Gurtner

Jelena Spanjol

Abbie Griffin

WILEY

Published by John Wiley & Sons, Inc., Hoboken, New Jersey
Published simultaneously in Canada

For general information about our other products and services, please contact our Customer Care Department within the United States at (800) 762-2974, outside the United States at (317) 572-3993 or fax (317) 572-4002.

Wiley publishes in a variety of print and electronic formats and by print-on-demand. Some material included with standard print versions of this book may not be included in e-books or in print-on-demand. If this book refers to media such as a CD or DVD that is not included in the version you purchased, you may download this material at http://booksupport.wiley.com. For more information about Wiley products, visit www.wiley.com.

Cover Image: © Stock.com/antishock
Cover Design: Wiley

Library of Congress Cataloging-in-Publication Data

Names: Gurtner, Sebastian, editor. | Spanjol, Jelena, editor. | Griffin,
    Abbie, editor.
Title: Leveraging constraints for innovation : new product development
    essentials from the PDMA / [edited by] Sebastian Gurtner, Jelena Spanjol,
    Abbie Griffin.
Description: 1st edition. | Hoboken, NJ : Wiley, [2018] | Includes
    bibliographical references and index. |
Identifiers: LCCN 2018023888 (print) | LCCN 2018028982 (ebook) | ISBN
    9781119390282 (Adobe PDF) | ISBN 9781119390275 (ePub) | ISBN 9781119389309
    | ISBN 9781119389309 (hardcover)
Subjects: LCSH: New products—Management. | New products—Marketing. |
    Product Development & Management Association.
Classification: LCC HF5415.153 (ebook) | LCC HF5415.153 .G88 2018 (print) |
    DDC 658.8/101—dc23
LC record available at https://lccn.loc.gov/2018023888

Printed in the United States of America

V10003833_081818

CONTENTS

10 AMBIGUITY AND MISDIRECTION? BRING IT ON! LESSONS ABOUT OVERCOMING FROM WOMEN MARKET TRADERS

José Antonio Rosa
Shikha Upadhyaya

ABOUT THE EDITORS

Dr. Sebastian Gurtner joined the Bern University of Applied Sciences in 2016 as a research professor with a focus on healthcare and innovation management. He leads the team strategy and innovation at its School of Business and serves as head of the executive education program Management in Healthcare Organizations. His research focuses on the creation of value with innovation and in this context especially on low-end innovation, social innovation, and resistance against innovation. While his research tackles issues of several industries, the healthcare setting always receives special attention, as the challenges in healthcare are directly linked to the well-being of our society. He has published in a variety of peer-reviewed academic journals, such as the *Journal of Product Innovation Management, Long Range Planning*, the *Journal of Business Research, Technological Forecasting and Social Change, Medical Decision Making*, and *Health Care Management Review*.

Dr. Jelena Spanjol is professor and head of the Institute for Innovation Management at the Munich School of Management, Ludwig-Maximilians-Universität in Munich, Germany. Prior to joining LMU, she held faculty positions at the University of Illinois at Chicago and Texas A&M University. Her research examines innovation dynamics across micro-, meso-, and macro-levels. In her current work she explores how innovation is motivated by and addresses societal challenges. Her research has been published in the *Journal of Marketing, Journal of the Academy of Marketing Science, Journal of Product Innovation Management, Journal of Service Research, Journal of Public Policy and Marketing, Marketing Letters, Journal of Business Ethics, Health Psychology,* and in various book chapters. She currently serves on the Editorial Review Boards of the *Journal of Product Innovation Management* and *Creativity and Innovation Management* as well as serving as an Associate Editor for the domain of innovation at the *Journal of Business Research*.

Dr. Abbie Griffin holds the Royal L. Garff Endowed Chair in Marketing at the David Eccles School of Business at the University of Utah, where she teaches the core MBA intro Marketing Management and Undergrad Capstone Marketing courses. Professor Griffin's research investigates means for measuring and improving the process of new product development. Her research has been published in *Marketing Science*, the *Journal of Marketing Research, Management Science*, and the *Journal of Product Innovation Management*, among other journals, as well as in the book titled *Serial Innovators: How Individuals in Large Organizations Create Breakthrough New Products*. Her 1993 article titled "Voice of the Customer" was awarded both the Frank M. Bass Dissertation Paper Award and the John D.C. Little Best Paper Award by INFORMS and has been named the seventh most important article published in *Marketing Science* in the last 25 years. She was the editor of the *Journal of Product Innovation Management*, the leading academic journal in the areas of product and technology development from 1998 to 2003, and the Product Development and Management Association named her as a Crawford Fellow in 2009. She was on the Board of Directors of Navistar International, a $13 billion manufacturer of diesel engines and trucks, from 1998 to 2009. Professor Griffin is an avid quilter, hiker, and scuba diver.

INTRODUCTION

Jelena Spanjol

Professor and Head, Institute for Innovation Management, Munich School of Management, Ludwig-Maximilians-Universität, Munich, Germany

Sebastian Gurtner

Professor of Health Care Management, Strategy & Innovation, Institute for Corporate Development, Bern University of Applied Sciences, Bern, Switzerland

I.1 Why Do We Need This Book?

Since the seminal work of the SAPPHO (Rothwell et al., 1974) and NewProd (Cooper, 1979) studies in the 1970s and 1980s, much has been written about how to support and enable innovation and what factors are critical to ensure innovation success. A simple search on Google Books for "innovation success factors" results in over 197,000 hits. Despite these many writings, conclusively benchmarking a reliable set of new product success factors has become more difficult over the past two decades, as the marketplace is increasingly dynamic and global, thus turning previously differentiating success factors into basic competitive norms. In this information age where globalized co-creation and data-rich environments are on our doorstep, simply meeting current needs of existing customers no longer ensures new product market success.

Innovation failure – the flip side of success factors and enablers – while of great interest to firms, has received far less attention. The Google Books "failure" search results in fewer than half the number of hits as the success search. Moreover, our understanding of innovation challenges lacks a coherent typology or framework, which could help firms more systematically overcome them. This relatively less researched side of innovation management persists despite the importance of "failing to succeed" highlighted in management books.

In this introductory chapter, we:

- Organize innovation challenges into three categories (failures, barriers and constraints);
- Indicate why we focus on constraints to innovation and how firms can adapt their innovation processes and organizations to overcome them;
- Briefly review the "standard" innovation process firms follow;
- Outline and define the three different types of innovation constraints – individual, organizational, and market;

- Depict where different types of constraints occur in the new product development (NPD) process, where the constraints must be addressed, and where they ultimately manifest if not appropriately dealt with; and
- Overview the contents of the rest of the chapters.

In summary, the goal of this chapter is twofold: to provide the background information on "standard" NPD processes and constraints firms may run into such that this material need not be repeated in later chapters and to guide readers to the chapter(s) that may provide them the largest benefit, given their firm's current situation.

I.2 Thinking about Innovation Challenges: Failures, Barriers, and Constraints

Challenges to innovation are diverse, with each type requiring a different solution. Overall, however, innovation challenges fall into three major types: barriers, failures, and constraints (Figure I.1). Firms that stick to their standard NPD approach without managing failures, barriers, and constraints appropriately experience unsatisfactory outcomes, including increased development costs, consumer resistance, delayed adoption, and/or even regulatory interventions that entirely prevent market introduction.

Innovation failures are projects with unsatisfactory outcomes or with expectations that are not met somewhere during the NPD process (Figure I.1, top). Failures require iterating the unsatisfactory phase, with appropriate changes – in short, *redos*. For example, a product prototype that is not manufacturable must be sent back, perhaps as far back as concept development, and redesigned for manufacturability.

Slightly different are *innovation barriers*, which stop or heavily delay planned NPD processes (Figure I.1, middle). An innovation barrier requires a *work-around* or detour. Pilot manufacturing facilities that are not available in a timely manner because they are busy producing other products may require using a contract manufacturer as a work-around to keep the project on schedule.

Both failures and barriers are project-specific challenges – flaws in the process as applied (failure) or unavailable resources (barrier) prevents success *in this project*. Solutions to these challenges are one-time only and must be developed specifically to fix the problem in just this project.

Innovation constraints are a bit different, as they are challenges that apply to an entire set of NPD projects that have contextually different circumstances from "regular" projects. Innovation constraints thus restrict or limit the applicability of the planned, "regular" (i.e. standard) NPD processes in some way. Therefore, overcoming an innovation constraint necessitates a modification or *adaptation* of the standard innovation approach, as the constraint represents a nonstandard situation or context for innovation efforts (Figure I.1, bottom). However, and what differentiates constraints from failures or barriers, is that firms can put in place an adaptation to their current "regular" process to repeatedly address all projects that suffer from these constraints.

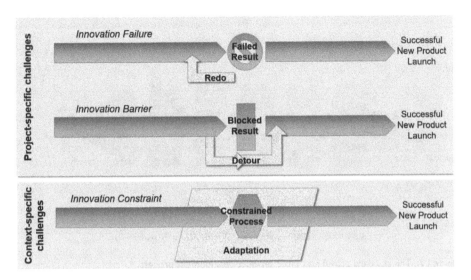

Figure I.1: Three types of challenges companies typically encounter during their innovation efforts and corresponding solution forms.

This book focuses on tools and techniques that overcome various types of innovation constraints. If done right, these adaptations can serve as catalysts to improve an organization's innovation efforts.

I.3 The Standard New Product Development Process

To fully understand what a modification entails, we briefly review the standard NPD process. A *product development process* is a "disciplined and defined set of tasks, steps, and phases that describe the normal means by which a company repetitively converts embryonic ideas into salable products or services" (see O'Connor, 2004; Watson, 2004). Key to this definition is the "repetitive" aspect of the process. To function effectively and repeatedly produce successful new products, the development process standardizes key developmental activities, processes, and structures.

Research and practice alike have long recognized that the development of new products and services should not be left to chance but actively managed. To understand how NPD works best, researchers have studied companies that most successfully manage the process from the idea for a new product up to its market launch. What the findings show – and examples of successful companies such as Procter & Gamble and 3M illustrate – is that one of the most successful ways of managing NPD is some form of cross-functional phased development process, such as the various forms of the basic Stage-Gate™ Process (Cooper, 1990; Cooper and Sommer, 2016). In this approach, the company rigorously defines and monitors NPD projects along a series of stages and gates. While generally staged and gated NPD processes can differ in how they are specifically implemented, one popular version is the Stage-Gate® process.

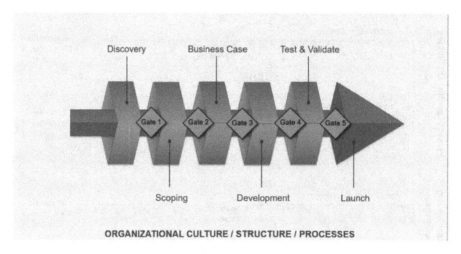

Figure I.2: The standard staged and gated product development process.

The "standard" Stage-Gate process consists of six stages and five gates, as shown in Figure I.2. The gates are the points in time when the potential of the project and progress made in a stage is judged by a defined set of evaluators according to a defined set of criteria. For example, at the gate following the stage "business case," both technical and business experts evaluate the project in terms of technical feasibility and market potential. At each gate, the firm decides whether the project will move on to the next stage, iterate some aspect of development, or be canceled. This allows companies to reduce uncertainty early in the project life cycle, constantly monitor their project portfolio, and allocate resources only to those projects that promise the highest return.

I.4 Understanding Constraints and Their Impact on the Standard Product Development Process

Recognizing, understanding, and addressing contextual constraints impacting the effectiveness of the standard product development process is more challenging than addressing project-specific failures and barriers. An innovation constraint represents two challenges: First, it is a problem that is located *outside* the NPD process. Second, where the constraint needs to be addressed, and where its negative effects bear out, may be different points in the product development process.

Innovation Constraints: Located Outside the NPD Process

The standard NPD process consists of a series of activity phases, punctuated by decision events. In essence, the development process represents a flow. This flow's momentum can be stopped by a barrier requiring circumvention. It can also take on an undesired state (i.e. failure) requiring a redo. A constraint, however, does not impact the flow of the development process directly but rather changes the circumstances of the standard flow in some manner. For example, an emerging market's cultural peculiarities (such as the hidden role of women in the economy) do not impact the development process per se but make standard market research (focus groups, surveys) less effective in the discovery stage. As a result, constraints are more diffuse, which can make pinpointing and implementing a corresponding solution more challenging.

Differently put, a misalignment exists between the standard development process as a flow of activities and constraints as contextual characteristics in which this flow is embedded. To make a solution more evident, we must first distinguish the general types of constraints that might affect the NPD process. In this volume, we distinguish among individual, organizational, and market constraints. Accordingly, the book is structured into three sections reflecting these three types.

Our definition of the three innovation constraint types reflects the scope within which these contextual factors operate:

1. *Individual constraints* are related to characteristics of important individuals in the innovation process, either people involved in the development process (e.g. managers and team members) or individual customers. For example, when individuals on an NPD team bring very different knowledge bases and perspectives to the project, it represents a possible constraint to knowledge transfer among those individuals.

2. *Organizational constraints* relate to aspects of structures, processes, and resources that firms utilize and require to develop new products and services. For example, teams that are dispersed, rather than colocated, can potentially constrain the effectiveness of the NPD process due to communication and other disruptions.

3. *Market constraints* relate to particularities of specific markets that are targeted for the new product under development. For example, cultural standards in emerging markets (such as the role of women in the economy) can constrain the discovery phase effectiveness.

Innovation Constraints: Chronological Disconnect Between Occurrence and Effect

A second challenge with innovation constraints is that they seldom present immediate negative repercussions within the development process. Instead, an innovation constraint in the ideation phase might not fully manifest its adverse effect until much later, for example, in commercialization. If the communication challenges of dispersed teams are not addressed in the discovery phase, demonstrating the business case will suffer. Similarly, if consumer attitudes and tendencies toward resisting new product adoption are not recognized and addressed in the testing and validation stage, launch performance will be diminished.

The chronological differences between constraint *occurrence* and constraint *effect* are shown in Figure I.3. When the constraint is not present, the normal activities in the

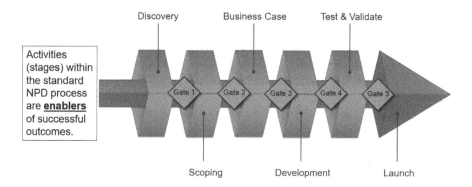

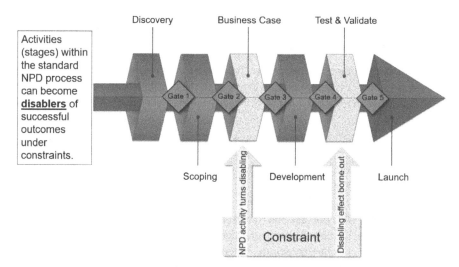

Figure I.3: How constraints turn product development process activities from enablers into disablers of NPD success.

NPD process function as *enablers* of NPD success (Figure I.3, top). When a constraint is present, the same activity can turn into a *disabling* activity, leading to lower process effectiveness and negatively affecting the output in subsequent stages (Figure I.3, bottom).

By defining where the constraint occurs and how it impacts the NPD process, a corresponding adaption (or modification) of the affected NPD process activity can be identified. More specifically, a constraint (such as the cultural standards of the targeted emerging market) can turn process activities (such as standard market research) from enabling a successful NPD outcome (by uncovering needs and opportunities) to disabling or preventing it (by leading to misleading conclusions about the target market). The full effect of the constraint might not be evident until the testing or launch phase. However, the adaptation required to address the constraint fully is needed in the discovery phase.

I.5 Mapping the Book: Where to Find Specific Constraints and Corresponding Solutions

Our goal in this book is to provide managers with actionable insights into a select set of innovation constraints and how to best deal with them. To facilitate navigation through the book, we map out the subsequent chapters in Figure I.4, identifying the constraint and where its solution must be applied in the NPD process. Note that this does not indicate where the specific constraint manifests in terms of negative consequences. A full explanation of the adverse impact from the constraints is given in each chapter. Most important, the chapters describe in detail how to adapt the standard NPD process in order to address each identified constraint.

While Figure I.4 provides a road map to the book, we also preface each section with a brief overview of the chapters in that section, for ease of referencing.

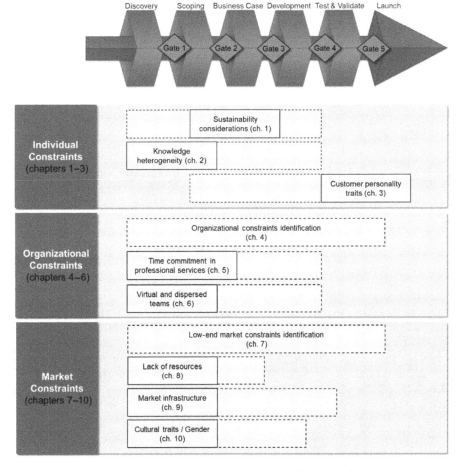

Figure I.4: Innovation constraints and corresponding solutions: Mapping the book.

References

Cooper, R. G. (1979). The dimensions of industrial new product success and failure. *Journal of Marketing* 93–103.

Cooper, R. G. (1990). Stage-gate systems: a new tool for managing new products. *Business Horizons* 33 (3): 44–54.

Cooper, R. G. and Sommer, A.F. (2016). *The agile–Stage-Gate hybrid model: a promising new approach and a new research opportunity. Journal of Product Innovation Management*, 33 (5), 513–526.

O'Connor, P. (2004). Implementing product development. In K. B. Kahn, ed., *The PDMA Handbook of New Product Development*, 2nd ed. Hoboken, NJ: John Wiley & Sons, 59–72.

Rothwell, R., Freeman, C., Horlsey, A. et al. (1974). SAPPHO updated – project SAPPHO phase II. *Research Policy* 3 (3): 258–291.

Watson, W. M. (2004). Process ownership. In K. B. Kahn, ed., *The PDMA Handbook of New Product Development*, 2nd ed. Hoboken, NJ: John Wiley & Sons, 73–80.

Part 1

INDIVIDUAL CONSTRAINTS IN NEW PRODUCT DEVELOPMENT

Individually arising innovation constraints are imposed by or come to life through individuals who effect new product development (NPD) success. Those individuals can be customers of the new product or service, employees in the company who spend their time developing new products and services, or managers within the firm who make decisions about projects or manage innovation teams. While other types of individuals also may potentially influence new product success (e.g. suppliers and other external stakeholders), internal innovation employees and customers are the most common and account for the largest part of success or failure of new products. This first part of the book focuses on overcoming individual constraints exhibited by innovation managers (Chapter 1), members of product development teams (Chapter 2), and customers (Chapter 3), as illustrated in Figure P1.1.

In the standard innovation process (see the introduction), several gates determine when and how decision makers evaluate an innovation project and decide if it will proceed to the next stage or if it will be terminated. While ideally those decisions are based on rational predetermined decision criteria, in reality decision makers frequently use intuition or rely on personal biases to make decisions, especially in situations with high uncertainty and complexity, as is the case for NPD decisions. In the end, it is the interplay among risk, uncertainty, and decision maker characteristics that influences the decision-making process and leads individuals to select one project over another.

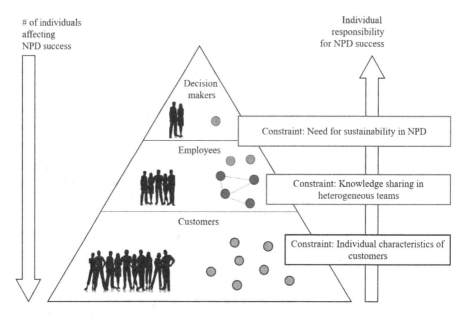

Figure P1.1: Individual constraints in NPD.

Chapter 1 in this part analyzes the role of uncertainty and creativity in decisions for NPD projects. The chapter considers constraints due to individuals in the firm and their managers who must combine knowledge and resources in new ways to create an innovation. In general, both research and practice agree that successful NPD needs highly creative and committed individuals as well as facilitation. Research highlights that individual innovative behavior in the workplace is determined by individual characteristics, exchange with and support from supervisors, and organizational commitment. It is the task of the organization to make sure that the creative potential of its employees is realized and that no constraints hinder the birth and growth of innovative projects.

Communication and knowledge-sharing boundaries are critical constraints that can prevent NPD teams from working creatively and efficiently. Chapter 2 tackles these constraints, specifically focusing on NPD teams that consist of individuals with different backgrounds and expertise. Based on a systematization of knowledge-sharing boundaries, the authors present a five-stage solution on how to make knowledge sharing work, despite the interdisciplinarity and heterogeneity of individuals on NPD teams.

Arguably the most crucial group that directly affects NPD success is *customers*, because they ultimately choose to adopt or reject an innovation. Customer constraints at the individual level differ from constraints in the market in aggregate, which are dealt with in Part 3 of this book. Chapter 3 builds on research that has found that, for individual customers, usage intensity of the product category, income, individual innovativeness, and susceptibility to normative influence determines whether an individual tries a new product or not. It is not people's demographics or position in society that drives their intention to adopt a new product or service as much as their psychographics, or values and attitudes, such as product involvement, individual innovativeness, and opinion leadership. Not all potential customers are created equal; it is their individual differences that can constrain the success of new products and services. Chapter 3 thus takes a deep dive into the personality of customers and depicts identity-related, cognitive, and emotional constraints that prevent individuals from adopting new products and services. After explaining the roots of these constraints, the author shows how to identify them and provides ideas about strategies that help to overcome those trait-based constraints.

1

FROM SUSTAINABILITY CONSTRAINTS TO CREATIVE ACTION: INCREASING MANAGERIAL INNOVATION BY SIMULTANEOUSLY SOLVING SOCIAL AND COMMERCIAL NEEDS

Goran Calic
McMaster University, Hamilton, ON, Canada

Maryam Ghasemaghaei
McMaster University, Hamilton, ON, Canada

Introduction: From Constraints to Innovation

In this chapter, we aim to advance the following proposition: Simultaneously solving social and commercial needs – *sustainability constraints* – results in greater product innovation. The common belief is that this position is false, because the simultaneous attention to both of these needs necessarily constrains the idea set, from which a manager can draw, to only those ideas that simultaneously do more good than harm to the environment and society (i.e. those that are socially sustainable) and those that are profit generating (i.e. those that are commercially successful). Such product ideas are rarer than are those that meet only the social or the commercial criteria. One would expect that this constraint would have negative consequences on product innovation by decreasing the number of opportunities available to a manager, but we argue that the opposite is true. In doing so, we present a straightforward yet counterintuitive way to enhance managerial innovation.

The marketplace for new products, with continuous changes in consumer preferences, presents managers with a constant stream of potential opportunities. Those opportunities are captured through innovations that meet specific consumer needs and wants. Yet innovation can proceed only if managers discover creative ideas (Stage 1) and subsequently implement those ideas as better procedures, processes, or products (Stage 2). Thus, new product innovation first requires discovery, then it requires action.

Before continuing, we must emphasize that enhancing product innovation may not result in better performance (e.g. greater profitability, higher market share, better solutions to problems, more benefits for managers). Innovation is inherently uncertain. Product offerings that are dramatically different from past products can result in inordinate losses or gains. How managers can reduce the likelihood of negative outcomes is briefly covered in Section 1.4 of this chapter.

Because pictures are good at conveying relationships, we rely on simple graphs to present the intuition behind the argument that simultaneously solving social and commercial needs will increase product innovation. The graphs are not only an alternative method of presenting the same arguments. They have the potential to provide the reader with insights beyond those explicit in the text.

The remainder of the chapter is organized as follows. In Section 1.1, we define innovation as a two-stage process – creativity as the first stage and implementation as the second stage. In Section 1.2, we link the two concepts and discuss their point of intersection. In Section 1.3, we present arguments supporting a positive relationship among sustainability constraints, creativity, and implementation. Here we also introduce some guiding questions managers can consider in order to include both social and commercial criteria in decision making. We introduce the corporate sustainability agenda, a strategy for turning sustainability constraints into performance, in Section 1.4. In Section 1.5, we cover situations when sustainability constraints reduce innovation. Section 1.6 concludes the chapter.

1.1 The Inherent Uncertainty of the Innovation Process

The innovation process begins with creative problem solving. A creative process generates ideas that are original and useful and have the potential to revolutionize or change the direction of a field. Such ideas are also characterized by uncertainty and nonobvious utility to the individual, as they are generally new and untested approaches. That is, the manager generating the idea is ignorant of a creative idea's utility until the idea is implemented.

Although newness is closely related to creativity, an idea does not have to be completely new to be considered creative; it must only be creative in the context to which it is applied. The application of an existing product to a new market is consistent with this conceptualization of a creative idea. In the context of business, a creative product need not be new. An imitation product can also be creative. Entrepreneurial competition involves businesspeople who follow the leader with cheaper or similar products. An entrepreneur who successfully "follows" an originator and offers a similar product still discovers an opportunity in the marketplace (e.g. better location, better price). For instance, if the follower's profits are the result of a product shortage, the manager foresaw the future fact that consumers would want more of the product than anyone, including the originator, expected. Yet creativity alone is not enough for innovation to occur.

Researchers have examined the possibility that creativity and implementation are two distinguishable elements of the innovation processes. Evidence from this line of work suggests that creative ideas are likely to be met with resistance, skepticism, and hesitation. Thus, although creative ideas may be desirable, their very nature is likely to generate reluctance about their implementation. Successful innovation requires both the generation of creative ideas and their subsequent implementation. In the next section, we discuss this interaction.

1.2 Innovation: The Tension Between Creativity and Implementation

Maximizing the conditions that increase creativity is unlikely to translate directly into a maximization of implementation. In fact, the maximization of some factors that increase creativity may result in the inhibition of implementation.

Restructuring of knowledge has been linked to creativity. Such restructuring results in a movement away from an "either/or" and toward a "both/and" way of thinking about the world. Because a movement toward a more flexible thinking style increases the availability of alternative perspectives, "right" and "wrong" are no longer fixed. When managers begin to permit the simultaneous existence of multiple perspectives, the environment can be interpreted in many more ways. Such a representation of the environment allows for the possibility of more creative solutions. However, such representations will also increase uncertainty, not necessarily in the sense that managers are less capable of implementing the creative idea but in the sense that more viable alternatives exist. More options mean much more information is sought out before a course of action is taken; and when a course of action has been taken, it is less fixed, and managers remain open to the perception that other choices may have been superior. This is the inherent tension faced by managers during the implementation process. In a quest to become more creative, people usually also become more indecisive. The relationships among creativity, uncertainty, and implementation can be represented graphically, as shown in Figure 1.1

Figure 1.1 plots the tension between creativity and implementation. The continuously increasing line, ρ, is the creativity of a generated idea in relation to its perceived uncertainty. This graph represents the fact that managers are more uncertain about creative ideas than they are about conventional ideas. The slope of the curve represents the strength of the relationship. That is, a steeper curve would mean a stronger positive

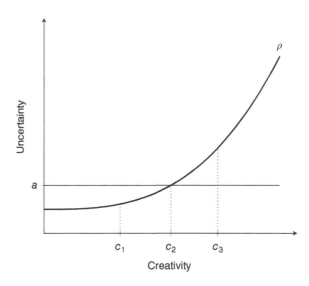

Figure 1.1: Resulting uncertainty from idea creativity levels c1, c2, and c3. Notes: A manager's uncertainty limit is represented by horizontal line at uncertainty level of a. The positive and increasing relation between creativity and uncertainty is represented by line ρ.

relation between creativity and uncertainty. The representation also demonstrates that the greater the uncertainty in an idea, the faster uncertainty tends to increase. In other words, small gains in creativity of conventional ideas increase uncertainty less than do small gains in creativity of creative ideas. The straight line at uncertainty $= a$ represents an uncertainty limit on implementation, which is the uppermost boundary of uncertainty a manager is willing to face. Uncertainty above a will preclude action. Conceptually, ideas found on or below the uncertainty limit are sufficiently close to the current way of doing things that management is willing to commit resources and take the necessary risk to implement an idea. For example, an automotive industry manager attempting to reduce carbon dioxide emissions may invest in hybrid powertrain technology (a product innovation that can be represented by c_2 in Figure 1.1) because it combines ideas that are more conventional (i.e. the internal combustion engine, which can be represented by c_1) with ideas that are more creative (i.e. full-electric powertrain, which can be represented by c_3). In this example, the hybrid technology product innovation would fall on the manager's uncertainty limit. The same manager may reject the idea of a full-electric powertrain because the idea's future success is highly uncertain and above the manager's uncertainty limit. It is important to note that we focus on the manager's cognitive process as it pertains to the generation of ideas and the decision to act on those ideas. We avoid discussion about external inhibitors of innovation, such as the firm's or consumer's reluctance to accept a novel product.

Given the graph in Figure 1.1, a manager interested in enhancing innovation could attempt to (i) increase her uncertainty limit (an upward movement of a) and/or (ii) increase average idea creativity (a rightward movement along the creativity line). Neither alone would enhance innovation. In the next section, we explore how sustainability constraints can result in increases to creativity and implementation together.

1.3 Sustainability Constraints: Enablers of Innovation

Social and commercial needs may seem desirable in isolation, but they are often contradictory when combined. The need to address these demands simultaneously leads to a risk of unintended consequences, since a solution to one criterion (social or commercial) could be detrimental to that of the other criterion. For instance, a restaurateur may choose to reduce her environmental impact by restricting food sourcing from global to local suppliers. However, profitable local sourcing can turn out to be more complex than the manager first thought. Local sourcing reduces the total number of ingredients available to a chef, which makes the production of some dishes impossible. This could result in a less appealing menu. Furthermore, local sourcing can add operational complexity by fragmenting the supply chain from one, or few, global supplies to many small, usually less managerially sophisticated, suppliers. Small suppliers are less likely to deploy total quality management (TQM) or just-in-time (JIT) systems than are large multinational firms. As such, sustainability constraints can result in a decision-making context that pushes a decision maker to think creatively and take risks. Combining interrelated yet seemingly contradictory elements, such as social and commercial needs, can increase both creativity and implementation.

Sustainability Constraints: Enablers of Creativity

Sustainability constraints may be especially effective at enabling creativity. A number of studies find that constraining a task increases the number of creative inventions generated by participants. In several studies of creative imagery, the number of creative inventions increased significantly as the task became more constrained. The greatest number of creative inventions was obtained when component parts and the interpretive categories were randomly constrained at the beginning of the experiment. In 1080 trials of the experiment, 49 objects were classified as creative when the category and parts were randomly restricted. When the participants could choose the parts, 17 creative inventions were generated; when they could choose the category, 31 creative inventions were generated. Similarly, it can be expected that a chef restricted to fewer ingredients resulting from a move to local food sourcing may produce more creative dishes. Indeed, Noma, a two-Michelin-star Danish restaurant known for its creativity, came about because of René Redzepi's desire to create the ultimate local-seasonal cuisine. Mr. Redzepi regularly dispatches his cooking staff to collect seasonally available ingredients found within a short walk or drive of the restaurant. While seasonal availability and the short distance are both factors that are in line with sustainable sourcing, they limit ingredients and impose tremendous constraints to creating a high-class menu. Furthermore, studies of entrepreneurial funding success find that entrepreneurs who adopt both a social and a commercial orientation developed more creative product ideas, which resulted in higher funding success.

The preceding examples suggest that the probability of generating a creative idea is greater whenever an individual is forced to think within constraints, as would be the case when a manager is asked to simultaneously meet both social and commercial needs. The simultaneous attention to both of these needs constrains the idea elements from which an individual can draw to only those found at the union of these two categories. It also constrains the outcome categories to those that are both profitable and socially beneficial. Such constraints increase the likelihood the manager will attempt to reframe the problem space in search of new possibilities, potentially identifying new, previously unnoticed, alternatives.

Figure 1.2 summarizes the innovation-enhancing effect of sustainability constraints. In the figure, graph (a) is the manager's status quo state of mind, with an uncertainty limit of a_1 and a creativity level c_1. Simultaneous consideration of social and commercial needs facilitates the generation of new, creative ideas. This change in creativity is represented in graph (b) by a movement along the creativity curve from point c_1 to point c_2. This alone is not enough to enhance innovation if the creativity level of the new idea

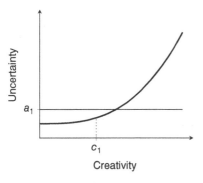
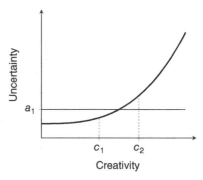

(a) Current Stable State: Mostly conventional ideas, represented by c_1, are pursued.

(b) Enhanced Inventiveness: Simultaneously attending to social and commercial needs increase managerial creativity, represented by a move from c_1 to c_2.

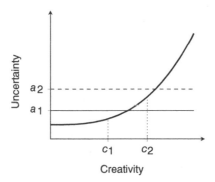

(c) Workable Certainty: Simultaneous attention to social and commercial needs does not reduce uncertainty but creates, "a more manageable mess from which managers can work", represented by an upward movement in the uncertainty limit.

Figure 1.2: Sustainability constraints as enablers of creativity and the decision to implement.

is above the manager's uncertainty limit. The idea must be acted on by the manager in order to have any organizational impact. Next, we discuss how simultaneously adopting commercial and social frames facilitates the decision to implement.

Sustainability Constraints: Enablers of Implementation

As managers attempt to make sense of a complex world, they simplify reality. Such artificial simplifications help managers make decisions in a world of near-infinite interdependencies. While simplifying reality can be useful, it can make managers shortsighted – they do not see possibilities that are not immediately obvious.

A sustainability orientation can reveal the hidden complexity of a task by encouraging the reconciliation of contradictions. For instance, introducing managers to a divergent viewpoint allows them to see an issue from a different vantage point than they did before. The new vantage point helps managers to tolerate inconsistencies in others' motives and behavior. Studies of individual creativity provide evidence for this argument. In laboratory studies exploring the effects of contradictions on creativity, participants introduced to contradictory ways of thinking (e.g. creativity is compatible with low cost) were more tolerant of novel ideas.

Simultaneously considering both social and commercial needs increases the likelihood that managers break away from existing knowledge that may prevent action on a creative idea. Breaking from existing knowledge reduces the functional fixedness or "curse of knowledge" bias. Functional fixedness is the bias that restricts a person to using an object only in the way it is traditionally used. For example, if people need a hammer but only have a frying pan, they may not see how the frying pan can be used as a hammer. By restricting the availability of existing options, a sustainability orientation can prevent existing knowledge about products, strategies, approaches from limiting which future ideas are pursued.

When managers embrace contradictions as simultaneously possible, they start thinking about ideas rather than tasks, which allows them to move toward a more workable certainty. Workable certainty is built on the idea that people can never fully grasp intricate situations. Rather than try to understand a complex world, managers must continually experiment with new ways of thinking. The restructuring of the LEGO company in the late 1990s is a case of how managers adopting contradictions as simultaneously possible became more open to novel ideas.

In 1998, LEGO, led by its chief executive officer, Kjeld Kirk Kristiansen, launched a comprehensive restructuring that changed the very nature of middle management at the company. As a result, many managers experienced an intense need to reinvent their roles according to a change they did not expect. The researchers studying the change found that managers searched for creative reinventions of their roles only when they were pushed to identify the latent contradictions (control versus autonomy) of their job. One manager who stated: "I'm stuck. I am ultimately responsible for my project leader's decisions, but I am supposed to let him, as well as everyone else, have more control over their performance. So how can I also be responsible?" (Lüscher & Lewis, 2008). The recognition that simultaneously achieving autonomy and control was required encouraged action on creative ideas. Viewing their role through this new lens helped managers to consider other perspectives, alter their assumptions, and explore issues in fundamentally different ways. Indeed, it helped managers move beyond a search for simple, local solutions to a more meaningful and actionable understanding. By embracing contradictions, managers at Lego started asking strategic questions that challenged simplistic either/or solutions and encouraged experimentation. Simultaneously attending to social and commercial needs will not eliminate uncertainty of creative ideas, but it will create "a more manageable mess from which managers can work" (ibid.).

In Figure 1.2c, workable certainty is analogous to an upward shift of the uncertainty limit from a_1 to a_2. Under workable certainty, c_2 is now considered a possibility for investment and implementation.

Emphasizing Sustainability Constraints by Asking Questions

Managers can adopt sustainability constraints during the decision-making process by asking themselves whether their current approach sufficiently meets customers' social and commercial needs. The underlying theme of the social and commercial needs, and the resulting questions managers can ask, is described in the following paragraphs, and example questions for each criterion are presented in Table 1.1. Managers should brainstorm social and commercial questions that are most relevant to their organizational context, which includes the industry's environmental and social impact and the resources available to improve commercial success and social welfare (see Section 1.5).

Table 1.1: Creating sustainability constraints			
Need	**Questions to be considered during decision making**	**Outcomes**	
Social	How does the product sustain the physical world, including the earth, biodiversity, and ecosystems? This includes intrinsic values, such as "beauties of the earth." More specific questions: How can we design buildings and workspaces that are environmentally responsible and resource efficient? How can we encourage vendors to comply with our sustainability goals and standards? How does the product sustain the complex web of relationships between sets of individuals who share norms, meanings, history, and identity? More specific questions: How does our way of business affect equal opportunity? How does our way of business result in noneconomic gains for our employees, such as education and career mobility, both within and outside our company?	CREATIVITY	WORKABLE CERTAINTY
Commercial	Does the product generate sufficient profit for reinvestment and redistribution to organizational stakeholders (employees and owners)? Does the product generate economic benefits for society? These benefits include the development of regions, institutions, and community organizations.		

Sustainability criteria can be organized into the sustainability of nature and communities. "Nature" refers to the physical world and includes the earth, biodiversity, and ecosystems. If these are not sustained, the lives of many species, including those of human beings, are threatened. For instance, studies show that exposure to green space improves human health and that the destruction of ozone has resulted in higher risk of skin cancer. The environment also serves the utilitarian purpose of providing resources and life support for humankind. If the environment is not sustained, life support for humans can be severely threatened. For instance, the reduced purification capacity of aquatic habitats due to contamination may lead to a shortage of drinking water.

The term "communities" refers to complex sets of relationships between people who share common values, norms, meanings, history, and identity. Culture, groups, and places are what make communities distinctive. Communities, from families to other larger groups, provide a sense of personal identity within large societies and are related to healthy functioning of human beings. The loss of cultural identity has been associated with alcoholism and diminished physical health and life expectancy. Places, cultures, symbols, and history serve as important community artifacts and can be threatened by commercially oriented actions.

Commercial gain is regularly seen as the counterpart to sustainability. However, it is central to the continued functioning of private organizations. The commercial perspective emphasizes the development of economic gains for the organization and society. Profitable organizations have the capacity to increase general social welfare by enriching employees and adding jobs to the economy. These commercial gains are an important goal. By enhancing the socioeconomic status of people, commercial gains can also lead to improved emotional, psychological, and physical health. This effect transcends generations, since the socioeconomic status of parents leads to enhanced childhood well-being.

Simultaneously considering questions related to social and commercial needs can enhance innovation by improving creativity and increasing the likelihood of implementation. Yet innovation may not translate to better performance. In the next section, we briefly consider the link between innovation and performance and what can be done to improve it.

1.4 From Innovation to Performance: Creating a Corporate Sustainability Agenda

Managers can obtain an innovation advantage through superior information about the future profitability of an idea. To managers, the utility of an idea is the final idea's future profit minus the cost of developing and implementing the idea. Utility is positive when future value is greater than total implementation cost. If the cost of implementing an idea is greater than the expected returns from that idea, managers will not obtain above-average industry performance. It follows that managers who have more accurate future expectations about costs and profits will be more successful. To that end, many firms have recently begun using advanced data analytics tools to estimate the benefits and costs of new ideas.

Managers can obtain information about the future value of an innovation through an environmental analysis (external analysis) or by analyzing resources they already control (internal analysis). For example, external analysis can be performed by accessing big data (click streams, videos, tweets) to extract new information and better understand markets, products, and customers. Managers increasingly view external data as a critical driver of innovation and competitive advantage. Yet, because the environment is observable by all market participants, environmental analysis cannot be assumed to improve expectations about implementation costs of some managers more than of others, and thus it cannot be a sustainable source of more accurate expectations about the ultimate value of an idea.

The analysis of internal organizational resources, which are partially unobservable to outsiders, can result in more accurate expectations about ideas. For instance, managers are privy to the costs of internal transfers, employee salaries, depreciation of equipment, ongoing research and development projects, and other costs necessary to implement an idea. Managers can use descriptive analytical tools (i.e. understanding what happened in the past), predictive tools (i.e. understanding what will happen in the future), and prescriptive tools (i.e. simulating outcomes of possible actions) to better understand unique organizational resources. Together, these internal analyses can be used to formulate superior future expectations about the utility of an idea. Considering social and commercial needs within the context of internal organizational capabilities has been referred to as formulating a corporate social agenda. Following Porter and Kramer (2006, 2011), a corporate social agenda means mapping social opportunities to organizational capabilities to solve commercial needs.

A corporate sustainability agenda deliberately leverages the organization's source of advantage. This means utilizing the organization's unique and rare capabilities. Take, for instance, Walmart's mission to reduce fossil fuel consumption through supply chain innovation, a source of advantage for Walmart. Not only did Walmart's mission have positive effects on profitability by driving costs down by $200 million, but it also reduced greenhouse gas emissions by cutting more than 100 million miles from the company's delivery routes in 2009. This new thinking revealed the benefit of utilizing Walmart's superior supply chain management to simultaneously benefit society and shareholders.

Figure 1.3 graphs the effect of a corporate sustainability agenda. As before, idea creativity is graphed against its uncertainty. The relation between creativity and uncertainty depends on how surprising the creative idea is to managers. Less surprising ideas result from leveraging resources managers are relatively familiar with. For instance, Walmart's managers have relatively more familiarity with supply chain management than do their competitors. This allowed Walmart managers to implement ideas that are relatively more innovative. Superior familiarity can be represented by a shift in the uncertainty-creativity curve from ρ_1 to ρ_2. Stated differently, leveraging existing resources should lead to an advantage unique to a manager's organization (i.e. competitors' managers will find those ideas more surprising than will the focal manager). This change in slope between the curves represents a change in perception of uncertainty. The total competitive advantage gained by better expectations can be

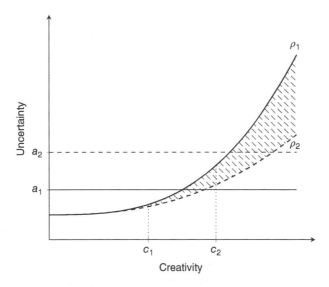

Figure 1.3: Effect of a corporate sustainability agenda on creativity and innovation. Note: Shaded area represents competitive advantage differential of better future expectations.

represented graphically as the shaded area between curves ρ_1 and ρ_2, with greater advantage accruing at higher levels of creativity.

Sustainability constraints are efficacious because they highlight the multiplicity of goals and perspectives that were previously latent. At the same time, contradictions can result in conflicts between organizational members and may result in lower performance or innovation. These dynamics are discussed in the next section.

1.5 Avoiding the Potentially Negative Effects of Adopting Sustainability Constraints

Under some circumstances, sustainability constraints may lead to behaviors of defensiveness, anxiety, and rigidity. This is most likely when managers face high degrees of external demands or threats. Under such conditions, simultaneously trying to maximize social and commercial elements in a decision may drive managers to choose only one category. In this case, an attempt to simultaneously attend to social and commercial needs could create the appearance of false trade-offs, whereby commitment to one approach reinforces the need for the other, which can further intensify the underlying contradiction and thus also the mindless commitment to one way of doing things. Such trade-off-based decision making in the face of constraints may result in lower innovation.

The likelihood of negative dynamics is greatest when a manager faces high levels of external demands – such as scarcity of resources, time pressure, and fierce competition. Evidence suggests that creative cognition occurs when individuals are free from pressure, feel safe, and experience relativity positive emotions. For instance, time pressure will increase a manager's need for a quick solution, which will reduce willingness to achieve a thorough and rich understanding of the problem – a necessary condition for successful innovation. Time pressure also reduces length of incubation time, a critical component of creative cognition. In a study of 22 work groups from 7 US companies, Amabile et al. (2002) found that deadline pressure reduced creativity, resulted in frustration with work, and led to a feeling of helplessness. For sustainability constraints to result in higher innovation, managers should be shielded from high levels of external demands and threats.

Managers facing significant time pressure, competition, or resource limitations should avoid searching for the one best solution. Instead, they should rely on rapid iteration of ideas. Rapid iteration of ideas starts with the generation of ideas that represent the smallest set of activities needed to test the viability of the product and involves gaining feedback from inside (e.g. finance, manufacturing, marketing) and outside the organization (e.g. customers, suppliers). Relying on rapid iteration emphasizes learning rather than immediate product-market fit and should bound uncertainty generated by external pressure. By bounding uncertainty, managers are less likely to exhibit behaviors of defensiveness, anxiety, and rigidity.

1.6 Conclusion

The ability to innovate is a central feature of successful managers. However, innovation presents managers with challenges: factors that increase creativity often reduce the likelihood of implementation. In this chapter, we advance the argument that simultaneously solving social and commercial needs increases the likelihood both that creative ideas will be generated and that managers will decide to implement those ideas. We also briefly discuss how innovation, particularly innovation stemming from simultaneously attending to social and commercial needs, can be leveraged to increase performance. Last, we discuss the possible negative dynamics resulting from high external demands and threats and how these can be managed by emphasizing rapid iteration of ideas and learning.

Our arguments may be true of other types of constraints. However, at least two factors make simultaneously attending to social and commercial needs most important. First, attending to social and commercial needs has received a great deal of attention from management scholars, and good evidence exists between meeting such needs and innovation performance. Second, while other types of constraints may also result in the tension necessary to spur innovation, the contradictions between social and commercial needs are nearly universally felt by managers across industrial, geographic, and cultural boundaries. As a consequence, the effects of the contradiction between social and commercial needs should apply across a broad range of contexts. This is the case because transactions by profit-seeking organizations will unavoidably produce negative externalities, which are costs suffered by third parties (i.e. those parties not involved in the transaction), and such costs are examples of the greatest market failures we have ever seen (e.g. anthropogenic climate change).

We support our arguments using research at the intersection of human cognition and management science. Relying on creative problem-solving research, we argue that sustainability constraints enhance creativity by forcing individuals to think in unconventional ways and that these constraints enhance implementation by increasing tolerance for unusual ideas. Management research suggests that superior performance can be achieved through more accurate expectations about the future utility of organizational decisions if management focuses on internal, rather than external, analysis. In line with this research, we argue that a corporate sustainability agenda will result in superior expectations about the future value of innovations and thus enhanced performance.

References

Amabile, T. M., Hadley, C. N., and Kramer, S. J. (2002). Creativity under the gun. *Harvard Business Review* 8: 52–61.

Lüscher, L. S. and Lewis, M. W. (2008). Organizational change and managerial sensemaking: working through paradox. *Academy of Management Journal* 51: 221–240.

Porter, M. E. and Kramer, M. R. (2006). The link between competitive advantage and corporate social responsibility. *Harvard Business Review* 84: 78–92.

Porter, M. E. and Kramer, M. R. (2011). Creating shared value. *Harvard Business Review* 89: 62–77.

About the Authors

DR. GORAN CALIC joined McMaster University in Hamilton, Ontario, in 2016 as a tenure-track research professor in Strategic Management, with affiliate membership in Information Systems. He holds a PhD in Strategic Management from Purdue University. Dr. Calic's research focuses on understanding why some individuals are more creative and some organizations are more innovative than others. His area of research is primarily concerned with early-stage entrepreneurship. His work on creativity in organizations was awarded the 2015 Max Henri Boisot Award. He has written in a variety of academic publications, such as the *Journal of Management Studies, Rutgers Business Review,* the *Academy of Management Learning and Education*, and the *Oxford Handbook of Organizational Citizenship Behavior*. Dr. Calic worked for four years in Osnabrück, Germany, at Georgsmarienhütte GmbH. During this time, he was involved in activities related to market research, sales, and organizational strategy.

DR. MARYAM GHASEMAGHAEI is an Assistant Professor of Information Systems at DeGroote School of Business at McMaster University, Hamilton, Ontario. Her research interests relate to technology adoption and the impact of data analytics on firm outcomes. She has published in a variety of peer-reviewed academic journals such as *MIS Quarterly, Journal of Strategic Information Systems, Information & Management, Decision Support Systems, Computers in Human Behavior, Journal of Computer Science,* and *Journal of Retailing and Consumer Services.*

2

A PRACTICE-ORIENTED APPROACH TO OVERCOME KNOWLEDGE-SHARING BOUNDARIES IN INNOVATION PROJECTS

Christiane Rau

University of Applied Sciences Upper Austria, Wels, Austria

Anne-Katrin Neyer

Martin-Luther University Halle-Wittenberg, Halle/Saale, Germany

Katja Krämer-Helmer

University of Applied Sciences Upper Austria, Wels, Austria

Introduction

Informed by the open innovation paradigm and forced by increasingly complex products and services, it is presumed that more heterogeneous people are involved in innovation projects than ever before. This heterogeneity is a constraint that calls for special attention. While the heterogeneity of development teams can push creativity, it can also lead to inefficient collaboration. Unrecognized failures of knowledge sharing in early phases of the innovation process (e.g. about different understandings of customer requirements) can lead to severe problems, such as excessive costs for rework, when discovered only in market tests.

Intuition as well as extensive scientific evidence suggests that knowledge sharing in innovation projects is important and should be supported. While this argument is nowadays trivial to state, it is not trivial to achieve. Our experience in accompanying open innovation projects over the past six years indicates that companies regularly struggle to manage knowledge sharing among diverse, interdisciplinary coworkers.

Different mental models, previously acquired competencies, and resources can impede knowledge sharing among members of heterogeneous teams and foster counterproductive behaviors that can threaten the success of innovation projects. For individuals, innovations can put their acquired competencies at stake and make resources unnecessary. They may feel that knowledge sharing might threaten their own power and status in the organization.

With the increased cognitive distance among innovation team members and high levels of novelty of the shared knowledge, boundaries of understanding and boundaries of interests are likely to emerge among interdisciplinary, diverse coworkers. Those boundaries are manifestations of the individual constraints of heterogeneous team members. Our insights from various research projects, including an interview study with 24 innovation managers in Europe and a three-year case study at a large international organization in the sporting goods industry, show how boundaries of understanding and boundaries of interests emerge and how a modification of the standard innovation process by the means of specific innovation practices can help to dissolve these boundaries.

2.1 Knowledge–Sharing Boundaries in Innovation Projects

One of the challenges associated with understanding boundaries to knowledge sharing among heterogeneous coworkers in innovation projects concerns level of complexity inherent in communication. This complexity can be conceptualized along two levels. First, from a semantic level, information needs to receive meaning through the interpretation of each coworker. Research states that this is the first boundary level to appear. The second level, which is called the pragmatic level, puts the emphasis on how communication affects both the sender and the receiver. Our interest lies in these two distinct types of knowledge-sharing boundaries: semantic and pragmatic boundaries (see Figure 2.1). Semantic boundaries represent boundaries of understanding, whereas pragmatic boundaries represent boundaries of interests.

Besides the general awareness of these two types of knowledge-sharing boundaries, it is essential to understand their relationship and interdependencies. Different types of boundaries can exist at the same time, making effective knowledge sharing even more challenging. We even found that individuals intentionally make up boundaries of understanding to mask existing boundaries of interests. For instance, we witnessed that developers pretend that misunderstandings exist to cover their unwillingness to collaborate with coworkers from other departments due to the existence of

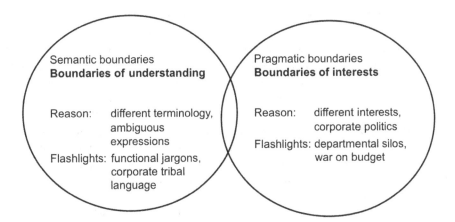

Figure 2.1: Knowledge-sharing boundaries in innovation projects.

conflicting interests in the project. Together these two boundary types form the starting point to dive deeper into the black box of human behaviors when being confronted with innovation.

Boundaries of Understanding

Boundaries of understanding might emerge in innovation projects. Why is this the case? Each of us has a very particular perspective on how things should be done. This perspective derives from specific expertise and experience, which is developed while performing distinct tasks. What is happening is that knowledge is interpreted by referring to a specific context, such as a particular field of expertise. If knowledge is shared among peers (i.e. individuals from the same field of expertise), the interpretation of information is more likely to be similar. However, beyond this context, the same information might be perceived quite differently. In this situation, boundaries of understanding emerge that hinder knowledge sharing. In innovation projects such boundaries are a crucial cost factor. For instance, consider the terminology "minimum viable product." We find extensive differences in the interpretation of this wording when comparing its use in the start-up versus corporate domain. Considering the increasing number of open innovation labs and corporate accelerators, it is crucial for corporate and start-up representatives to establish a common understanding of this terminology to ensure an effective collaboration.

Most boundaries of understanding remain unrecognized. If teams work together over longer time periods, they might participate in team building activities. As a side effect, a common understanding (in terms of terminology, jargon, etc.) among team members might but does not necessarily emerge. We rarely observed dedicated activities aimed at explicitly developing a shared understanding in practice.

So, why is it so hard for us to overcome boundaries of understanding? One answer can be found in our study with innovation managers in which we probed their experiences in running different innovation projects. What we learned is that there is not just "one" or "the" boundary of understanding but that three distinct types exist. First, coworkers might feel lost in the process of sharing knowledge. That means that they are not able to refer to tangible or familiar objects while engaging in knowledge sharing. Let's assume you have to describe an idea for a new service. You might have only a vague idea. Even if you have described the idea to the best of your knowledge, you might not be able to specify the target group, nor might you be able to explain the service delivery process in detail. This leaves a lot of room for (wrong) interpretations.

Second, team members might differ significantly in how they interpret what has been explained. We term this boundary resulting from fuzzy descriptions "fuzziness boundary." Next, coworkers might use a terminology that their counterparts are unfamiliar with or that they interpret differently. This is the "terminology boundary." Our minimum viable project example represents such a terminology boundary.

Third, coworkers have a particular mental model of their counterpart's work practices, corresponding timelines, and resources. If these assumptions are false, the so-called unbalanced mental model boundary hinders knowledge sharing. For instance, we found a product manager who tried to translate specifications for new software for information technology (IT) developers. He tried to explain the requirements in a way he thought the IT developers would understand. Unfortunately, he was not aware of the developers' programming process and complicated his explanation to a degree that the developers did not understand his purpose at all.

Boundaries of Interests

Boundaries of understanding and boundaries of interests have in common the need for the creation of a shared meaning among the coworkers. However, given the nuances of the boundary of understanding, we face the challenge to be very precise in identifying what type of boundary exists.

Loss in power and anxiety as innovation killers

Innovation projects being torpedoed due to conflicts of interests between involved parties is unfortunately not an exception. A recent study led by the German 2bAHEAD Think Tank showed that 43% of managers are concerned that innovation might lead to a loss in power (2bAHEAD, 2016). The study further provides evidence for a very common approach in practice: If the project potentially threatens a decision maker's power position, he or she tries to kill it. About one third of the respondents reported that their anxiety has stopped innovation endeavors.

In this chapter we propose an alternative approach, focusing on implementing innovation practices that support teams to deliberately alter their individual team members' interests and to create shared ones.

Boundaries of interests touch on another aspect: Individuals sometimes do not want to share their knowledge. Such intentional lack of sharing highlights the necessity to consider the divisional nature of organizations. Divisions (business groups, departments, functions, etc.) often clearly demarcate the knowledge property of a particular professional group. If new knowledge is created by one actor (e.g. in a particular department), and if this knowledge is then shared and integrated in an innovation project, then the value of the formerly leading knowledge holder in the respective domain might be perceived to be diminished. In short, one actor's knowledge affects the value of another actor's knowledge. This generates costs for the actor holding the previously unique knowledge. As Carlile states: "When interests are in conflict, the knowledge developed in one domain generates negative consequences in another" (2004, p. 559). No wonder that professionals aim at protecting their core knowledge domain from competitors. Dependencies in the face of novelty can create different interests among the actors, which might lead to knowledge-sharing resistance. As a result, so-called boundaries of interests emerge.

The findings of our study with European innovation managers further specify the concept of boundaries of interests. A "trajectory boundary" emerges when coworkers are required to gain new knowledge (or transform their existing knowledge), which generates costs and might lead to a loss of power. The term "trajectory boundary" refers to the intention of individuals to stay on the path (trajectory) chosen previously (e.g. a particular technological field of expertise), rejecting everything that would make them move outside their current trajectory of knowledge.

If coworkers whose primary task does not lie in engaging in innovation development are asked to share their knowledge for the sake of the innovation project, another type of boundary of interests emerges. We term this the "I-am-not-an-innovator boundary." We found that team members' standard approach when they are confronted with boundaries of interests is either active resistance or passive avoidance of knowledge sharing. When subordinates recognize this harmful behavior, they eventually sanction it, but mostly the behavior simply remains unrecognized and threatens the project's success.

Regardless of what type of boundary of interests emerges, the challenge is to create shared interests and to stimulate the willingness to transform "currently" applied knowledge. Our research shows that the most powerful way to do so is the implementation of a consciously designed process dedicated to solving knowledge-sharing boundaries.

2.2 Solving Knowledge–Sharing Boundaries in Five Stages

We started the chapter by pointing out that our research explores the nature of different types of knowledge-sharing boundaries in innovation projects with a diverse set of internal and external employees. In particular, we are interested to better understand how these boundaries can be dissolved by the means of innovation practices. Innovation practices are all methods, tools, strategies, and concepts that are implemented to support the progress of innovation projects.

Here is the bottom line for innovation managers (executives and employees) alike: If you want your innovation projects to be a success, you have to dive deeper into those boundaries that hinder individuals in their attempts to engage in knowledge sharing. In the following text we present our four-stage self-assessment tool, which enables those who are involved in innovation projects to efficiently and effectively identify and resolve knowledge-sharing boundaries. The tool is based on an interview study with 24 innovation managers in Europe and a three-year case study at a large international organization in the sporting goods industry. The four stages of the proposed process are listed next.

Stage 1:   Tracing hints. Learn to recognize relevant involved actor's behavior.
Stage 2:   Coming closer. Verify hints and analyze possible boundary types.
Stage 3:   Identifying "your" innovation practice.Choose an innovation practice based on your project's or company's specific context and needs.
Stage 4:   Getting to work. Implement the innovation practice and monitor effects.

While going through the self-assessment tool, users might realize that others' input is needed for some questions. Thus, an important success factor of our tool is people's openness and willingness to engage with those who are involved in the innovation project, i.e. team members, coworkers, and managers. In this process, a discussion might be initiated that can lead to an insightful 360-degree exploration of the given situation. Beyond the insights provided by the results of the self-assessment, this dialogue itself might stimulate positive changes.

Stage 1: Tracing Hints

To grasp which boundary type exists in the project, it is important to know how to interpret the behavior of the involved individuals. To gain a feeling for this, you will have to collect and analyze the behavioral patterns of individuals working at the innovation project – in other words, you need to trace hints. Please bear in mind that some of those are more obvious than others.

Let's have a closer look at the typical behaviors we found at boundaries of understanding. A first sign to recognize is whether individuals talk at cross-purposes (i.e. if two or more people talk about different subjects without realizing this and subsequently do not understand each other). Talking at cross-purposes occurs at each of the three boundaries of understanding (i.e. fuzziness boundary, terminology boundary, and unbalanced mental model boundary).

Does this situation sound familiar to you?

Situation. An interdisciplinary team interviewed buyers of cat food. Cat owners responded that their main evaluation criterion for the quality of cat food is how quickly the cat eats. After a misunderstanding of "fast/quickly," team members and customers started to talk at cross-purposes.

Manager's perspective. *"We needed to understand much better what 'quickly' meant from a consumer standpoint. ... What we actually realized was that speed for them was not necessarily the amount of cycles that it took the cat to eat. ... What the consumer is observing is how quickly the cat goes to the bowl and gets comfortable with continuous eating. Then it means it eats all or it eats very fast."*

What happened. What the team has experienced is the emergence of the terminology boundary due to the behavioral pattern "talk at cross-purposes."

Solution. The team showed a video of a cat eating food and asked the customers to describe what they see.

The importance of understanding hints in the context of a terminology boundary is also reflected in a behavior that we name "playing hide-and-seek." In this case coworkers recognize that they lack understanding of specific terms but avoid asking for clarification, as they are embarrassed to do so. For instance, one innovation manager from a German automotive company stated that colleagues only have a certain time after they became part of the company to ask about abbreviations, which are regularly used in their research and development (R&D) team. Asking about fundamental abbreviations later makes a bad impression and can even threaten an individual's status within the group. Coworkers who face this or a similar situation keep silent or circumvent certain topics to avoid situations where their peers might notice their lack of knowledge. To understand this silence, we have to bear in mind that language is a way to preserve expert status and to build cohesion within a group. If a group has developed a shared language and individuals do not understand it, they might be rejected and might lose their status within the group.

If talking at cross-purposes and playing hide-and seek are signs that can be observed to identify boundaries of understanding, then the following question arises: What behavioral hints can be found in the context of boundaries of interests?

Earlier we introduced two types of boundaries of interests - the trajectory boundary and the I-am-not-an-innovator boundary. A trajectory boundary (requiring acquisition or transformation of knowledge) can often be observed at the interface between R&D and marketing departments. R&D employees push their new solution within the organization, trying to prove its value by succeeding with the approach. In contrast, marketing employees deliberately try to find ways to stop the organization pursuing the innovation by torpedoing the project. We named these behaviors "solo attempt" and "active resistance."

Does this situation sound familiar to you?

Situation. At an automotive company, the marketing department organized lead user workshops but faced resistance from the R&D department. The R&D department was not willing to gather new knowledge necessary to work with the input they got from the lead users. The R&D department regularly found arguments not to follow up on the lead users' ideas. The marketing department, in turn, only put more effort into showing the relevance of their lead user workshops.

Retrospective view of the responsible head of marketing. "We told everybody how innovative we were, we went to trade shows, our prototypes won prizes, but we never brought a product to market. Why? Because the developers never recognized the necessity to cope with these topics."

What happened. The company experienced a trajectory boundary. While the marketing department tried to pursue the approach by itself, the R&D department showed active resistance and was reluctant to leave its technological path.

Solution. There was no solution, and the conflict finally escalated.

In recent years, a trend to open up the closed process of product and service development to other people within and outside the organization has been observed. While this certainly provides new impulses for innovation, it can also lead to negative organizational consequences. Highly skilled and knowledgeable employees are often asked to contribute to innovation projects. The sheer number of requests can be overwhelming, especially if innovation managers or supervisors expect this contribution on top of employees' usual work without any compensation (or reduction of other tasks). In response, we found that people facing the I-am-not-an-innovator boundary do not react when being invited to join an innovation project; rather, they simply play possum. For instance, a service role-playing workshop was planned with the aim to act out and improve a new service at a large company in the sporting goods industry. The workshop had to be canceled twice, because all employees from a particular department did not respond to the invitation or canceled at short notice. The responsible innovation project manager speculated: "It's not related to the present core business, so it's at the very end of their task list." Figure 2.2 summarizes which behaviors can provide hints regarding which knowledge-sharing boundary can occur in such heterogeneous team settings.

While looking for hints and reflecting on the behaviors and the corresponding boundaries in a specific innovation project, it will become obvious that some are more difficult to identify than others. Hidden behavioral patterns are the following: talking at cross-purposes, playing hide-and-seek, and playing possum. In contrast, the behavioral patterns active resistance and solo attempt are easier to identify and are referred to as

Hints for boundaries of understanding	Hints for boundaries of interests
Fuzziness boundary > Talking at cross-purposes Terminology boundary > Talking at cross-purposes > Playing hide-and-seek Unbalanced mental model boundary > Talking at cross-purposes	Terminology boundary > Solo attempt > Active resistance I-am-not-an-innovator boundary > Playing possum

Figure 2.2: Hints for knowledge-sharing boundaries.

"open" behavioral patterns. Regardless of the open or hidden nature of the behavioral pattern, you have to keep in mind that individuals at a boundary do not necessarily show these behavioral patterns. Therefore, an in-depth understanding of the dynamics is necessary. In addition, sensitivity is needed, as some behavioral patterns can be the result of multiple boundary types. Boundaries of understanding and boundaries of interests can exist in parallel. For example, the existence of conflicts of interests can even motivate coworkers to set up boundaries of understanding to sabotage the project.

The questions in Table 2.1 will support you in identifying hints from both hidden and open behavioral patterns in your innovation project.[1]

Table 2.1: Self-assessment reflection questions (Stage 1).

Stage 1: Tracing hints

	Yes	No
1. Could you observe that coworkers talk at cross-purposes?	☐	☐
2. Do involved coworkers try to evade questions or circumvent certain topics?	☐	☐
3. Do they circumvent topics related to specialized terminology?	☐	☐
4. Do particular actors argue against pursuing the project?	☐	☐
5. Do particular actors work to find evidence against pursuing the project?	☐	☐
6. Do particular actors try to forge alliances with people who might want to stop the project?	☐	☐
7. Is there an open conflict between two parties?	☐	☐
8. Does one actor/party push a new approach (e.g. open innovation) while another heavily questions its usefulness?	☐	☐
9. Can you observe that argumentation/confrontation between the coworkers is getting increasingly fierce?	☐	☐
10. Do coworkers repeatedly fail to show up to meetings?	☐	☐
11. Do coworkers not answer emails or telephone calls?	☐	☐

The explanation of how to analyze the answers can be found in the appendix.

[1] Please note: An earlier version of the self-assessment questionnaire (Tables 2.1 and 2.2) is included in the dissertation project of the first author but has not yet been commercially published.

Stage 2: Coming Closer

By tracing hints and analyzing the involved individuals' behaviors, you have been able to get a first understanding of what type(s) of knowledge-sharing boundary exist in the innovation project. As a next step, we provide a set of questions in Table 2.2 that will help you to verify the knowledge sharing boundary type(s). Why is this important? Only when you know what type of knowledge-sharing boundary is influencing the success or failure of your project can you identify and implement needed innovation practices, which act as enablers for dissolving the boundary.

Stage 3: Identifying "Your" Innovation Practice

Innovation practices are a suitable means to solve boundaries of understanding and boundaries of interests. Why is this the case? We conducted a systematic literature review of about 100 publications on innovation practices and have shown that they

Table 2.2: Self-assessment reflection questions (Stage 2).		
Stage 2: Coming closer		
	Yes	No
Boundaries of understanding		
1. Fuzziness boundary		
1.1 Did the boundary emerge early in an innovation project?	☐	☐
1.2 Are the ideas and concepts still rough and fuzzy?	☐	☐
1.3 Do the coworkers share ideas and concepts on intangible issues, e.g. services?	☐	☐
1.4 Does the team work with representations to share knowledge?*	☐	☐
2. Terminology boundary		
2.1 Do the coworkers use different terms? Can you observe that variations in their language exist?	☐	☐
2.2 Can you observe that a domain-specific language is used by one of the parties at the given boundary?	☐	☐
2.3 Did the parties work side by side and exchange knowledge regularly?*	☐	☐
3. Unbalanced mental model boundary		
3.1 Are the coworkers aware of their counterparts' work processes and the settings they work in?*	☐	☐
3.2 Did coworkers review each other's work processes, timelines and resources? Was there a kind of "reality check"?*	☐	☐
Boundaries of interests		
1. Trajectory boundary		
1.1 Does pursuing the innovation lead to additional effort for one of the actors, e.g. because the actor has to acquire new capabilities?	☐	☐
1.2 Does the relevance of actors' existing knowledge decrease with pursuing the innovation?	☐	☐
1.3 Might the actor face negative consequences (e.g. loss of power) if the innovation will be implemented?	☐	☐
2. I-am-not-an-innovator boundary		
1.1 Is there evidence that actors perceive knowledge sharing enabling innovation projects as not being one of their legitimate tasks?	☐	☐
1.2 Do the actors feel responsible for the project they should share knowledge for?*	☐	☐
1.3 Is the actor asked to integrate his/her knowledge (not doing it on own initiative)?	☐	☐
1.4 Do the actors face time pressures in doing their predefined core tasks?	☐	☐

*Reverse question: Please count if you clicked "no."
If you have clicked the box "yes" at a particular boundary twice or more (or "no" at a reverse question [*]), the existence of the respective boundary is likely. Now we need to identify a suitable innovation practice to overcome the given boundary.

use a distinct set of boundary-crossing mechanisms to help teams to overcome their knowledge-sharing boundaries (Rau et al., 2012). But what are these mechanisms? To learn more about this, we observed the use of innovation practices in three innovation projects at a large international organization in the sporting goods industry over a period of three years.

Figure 2.3 presents an overview of which boundary-crossing mechanisms proved successful to overcome specific boundary types. Next we show why particular innovation practices are promising for distinct types of knowledge-sharing boundaries and what type of mechanisms they use. Furthermore, we provide exemplary innovation practices for each boundary-crossing mechanism.

In the early phase of the innovation process, uncertainty and ambiguity are omnipresent. Are the ideas technically feasible? Which customer segments and which customer needs do they address? How will the implementation affect roles, work processes, organizational structures? Over time these ideas will mature and be transformed into concrete concepts, but at the beginning when they are rather vague, potential consequences are not likely to be clear to the project team. In this phase, the fuzziness boundary is often discovered among team members. We have witnessed the fuzziness boundary often in ideation workshops with introverted employees. The reluctance to communicate can increase the likelihood of the persistence of fuzziness boundaries. Whenever we encountered a fuzziness boundary, we used an interactive digital wall with a special application to combine collaborative work on a screen with individual paper-based work. The paper-based application enables participants to sketch their ideas on a special sheet of paper and to transfer it easily to a large interactive wall. On the wall, sketches can be compared and interactively refined. By working with these representations, team members can communicate their understanding and validate it with their counterparts. We found this mechanism of using representations to validate understandings and develop shared meanings regularly in innovation practices. We termed this boundary-crossing mechanism "developing a mutually understood language." Other innovation practices based on the same mechanism include acting out scenarios or conducting user games.

In the innovation practice acting out scenarios, the matter of knowledge sharing is represented in a scenario, which the actors depict in a role-playing approach. In their play, the actors present their understanding of the situation, and the counterparts are able to relate to it. The actors are free to propose alternative interpretations and iteratively change the scenario.

Actors participating in user games create a web of interrelated stories about prospective users of a new technology. The game consists of sign cards, labeling the stories, and moment cards. An RFID-tag is attached to each moment card. When a person holds the cards next to an RFID reader, a 30-second video sequence is played. The videos consist of ethnographic field data. Actors lay out the stories one after another. After the first story, stories have to intersect and, thus, actors have to share cards. Gradually, a crosswordlike structure emerges. The game terminates when the actors agree that the new stories would no longer enhance the actors' image of the users (Brandt and Messeter, 2004).

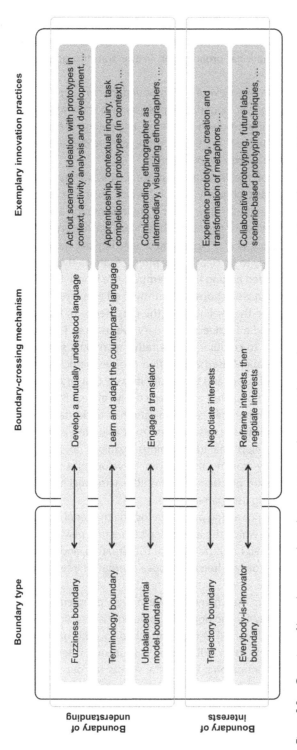

Figure 2.3: Overview of boundary types, boundary-crossing mechanisms and exemplary innovation practices. Adapted from Rau (2012).

If team members face a terminology boundary, for instance, the innovation practice "apprenticeship" can be implemented. At one large organization, a team member who was responsible for setting up a new lab overcame the terminology boundary between him and his colleagues from production by applying this innovation practice. He asked the production workers to teach him how to manufacture sports shoes. By learning their daily work processes, he also learned their specific vocabulary and was later able to utilize his colleagues' language. As a result, he was better able to communicate empathically and thus more efficiently in this heterogeneous team setting. We found innovation practices using the boundary-crossing mechanism learn and adapt the counterpart's language to be useful. Team members overcome the boundary as they observe their counterparts' behavior and learn about the particular context. More and more they gain the ability to understand and share their knowledge in their counterparts' language. Innovation practices using this boundary-crossing mechanism are, for instance, contextual inquiries or the completion of tasks with prototypes in the counterpart's context.

In contextual inquiries, team members conduct interviews in the environment of their knowledgeable counterparts to learn their language. Task completion with pro-totypes (in context) can also be applied to enhance knowledge sharing and overcome the boundary of understanding. Team members' understanding of their counterparts' perspective is enhanced as they observe the counterparts completing a task with a pro-totype. In addition, the counterparts are motivated to verbalize their thoughts.

If an unbalanced mental model boundary appears, we found innovation practices helpful in which an intermediary translates the knowledge between the team members either verbally or using visualizations. For instance, a graphical facilitator in a workshop or an ethnographer who visualizes customer insights using video collages can fulfill this role. Innovation practices of this category include the boundary-crossing mechanism engage a translator.

If a team faces a trajectory boundary, for instance, the innovation practice collab-orative prototyping can be implemented. At a large company, we faced a persistent trajectory boundary between individuals of two groups in a project to design a new service for top athletes. While one newly formed group was in charge of designing the new service, the other group had previously been in charge of handling the services with the sponsored top athletes. Launching the new service would lead to significant changes in the work processes of the latter group and alter their role. In the workshop, employees of both groups applied collaborative prototyping to model the new service offering with LEGO Serious Play™. As they built the model together, both groups contributed alike. In the process, discussions emerged that were grounded in the LEGO representation at hand. In a negotiation process, the roles of the groups were clarified and a shared understanding of the service could be developed. When the service was implemented, the new group took the role of the technical experts, while the other group took on the role of masters of ceremony guiding the sponsored athletes through the process. We find that a team can solve trajectory boundaries most effectively if representations are available that can be changed cooperatively and iteratively to communicate and subsequently incorporate the boundary-crossing mechanism negotiate interests. On one hand, representations are strong stimuli to express interests; on the other hand, we observed that representations ground the discussion in a tangible object and thus focus the discussion on the issue itself. Thereby they reduce the negative influence of relationship conflicts and emotional reactions in discussions. Another innovation practice that can be used to support the negotiation of interests is the application of systems like Caretta.

Caretta is a system implemented to enable multiple actors to include their ideas in representations. Therefore, actors surround a shared space on which an object to be designed is visualized (e.g. for city planning tasks, a map of the respective city). Each actor is equipped with a personal digital assistant (PDA) that shows a representation of the object displayed in the shared space. Using the PDA, actors change the representation according to their ideas. Afterward, they initiate a data transfer from their PDA to the system controlling the shared space. The system runs a simulation visualizing the actors' changes overlaid onto the space. The visualization can be discussed and if consensus on the representation is reached, actors inform the system to replacing the former version (Sugimoto et al., 2004).

We observed the I-am-not-an-innovator boundary often when employees who are external to the core team and responsible for a new development are asked to contribute to the project. We found that it is necessary to first change the way actors perceive interests toward a perception that is more congruous with their counterparts' interests. We termed that boundary-crossing mechanism "reframe interests." For instance, we observed an innovation project in which service staff members were reluctant to share their in-depth knowledge about customers. In the early phase, they saw the innovation project as not being part of their responsibility and presumably were afraid of imposed changes to their service process. Over the course of the project, the manager in charge was able to convey the understanding that the service staff members have an interest in engaging in the project, as this is where their future service will be designed. We did interviews with different members of the service staff and could see, over the course of the project, how their interests changed toward an understanding that they are now designing their own new service. This change subsequently led to more willingness to share knowledge. It is crucial to reframe the interests to make sure that people open up to a degree that they are willing to negotiate interests. We found that reframing interests can take place when assumptions are challenged or when team members internalize a shared vision. Otherwise, due to the playing possum behavioral pattern, team members are not available for any activities in which a negotiation would be possible. For instance, workshops are canceled on short notice. We suggest combining methods to reframe interests with those to negotiate interests.

Teams can apply the innovation practices ethnography or telling narrative vignettes to reframe interests. If team members do an ethnography in their counterparts' context, their assumptions about their counterparts might be challenged and their perspectives might change. Narrative vignettes can be told to share knowledge about relevant aspects of the offering, customer needs, etc. By telling narratives, team members can share how they make sense of the particular knowledge and create new visions about the future.

Given that a multitude of innovation practices are available for each boundary type, innovation practices must be chosen carefully. Often organizations prefer and apply certain practices highlighted by partners or at conferences without considering the appropriateness of those practices for their own specific situation. This often leads to a gap between the desired results and the delivered results. Organizations should focus on a set of factors to evaluate the appropriateness of an innovation practice rather than blindly applying it. Organizations need to identify and evaluate organizational as well as project-related conditions, such as resources, social factors, and the fit with existing organizational culture.

First, organizations need to consider the *amount of resources* required to apply a certain innovation practice. Organizations should first analyze whether they have the in-house competence to apply an innovation practice or if they need to collaborate with a suitable service provider. For the latter, organizations need to be aware of the growing service provider landscape. Thus, they should carefully screen different providers regarding their costs, expertise, and existing clients. Furthermore, organizations should also think about their own methodological expertise needed to apply the innovation practice. For instance, if the service provider supports an organization only during the method application, the organization still needs the in-house competence for the implementation of the results.

In an ideal case, organizations apply innovation practices to overcome existing knowledge-sharing boundaries for the longer term. Therefore, organizations also need to consider the "hidden" costs to guarantee the implementation of the results and the transfer in the organizational DNA. We know several examples where organizations dedicate a certain budget not only for the application of the innovation practice itself but for implementation of the results. For instance, not only do they include costs for the lead user workshops in their budgetary plans; they also commit a specific amount of the budget to transfer the results of such a workshop into concrete products or services. Innovation managers report that if the importance of the project is communicated to coworkers right from the project start, their willingness to be involved and to cooperate is higher.

Additionally, organizations should create a time schedule and milestone plan that covers the time and milestones before, during, and after the innovation practice application. If an innovation practice and the transfer of the results takes too long or crashes with existing timelines, an alternative innovation practice might be considered. If the innovation practice is going to be integrated for the longer term, organizations need to analyze whether this integration can target the core processes of the organization and, if so, what training is necessary to ensure an effective application. For instance, prototyping practices that are used to establish a shared understanding in heterogeneous teams could become a standard part of a company's innovation process at the fuzzy front end. If collaborative prototyping is then used in all heterogeneous teams, it is highly advisable to train the teams in the application of the specific methods, such as LEGO Serious Play.

However, the required resources are not the only issues that need to be considered. We recommend that organizations should further focus on their organizational culture and, in particular, the mind-set of the team members involved in the innovation practice. Will they accept and trust the designated innovation practice? Collaborative prototyping with LEGO Serious Play, for instance, is a very playful method. Organizations need to consider whether the organizational culture and the mind-set of involved employees is open-minded toward these playful approaches. Not every innovation practice is suitable for every organizational (innovation) culture. Ideally actors working in the innovation project are included in the choice of innovation practices. In that way, actors develop realistic expectations and their resistance during implementation can be decreased.

Stage 4: Getting to Work

Implementing an appropriate innovation practice is a crucial step in dissolving a knowledge boundary, but it isn't sufficient unto itself. Innovation project managers who want innovation practices to be a reliable, effective element of their boundary management practice need to make sure that these innovation practices deliver the expected results. Hence, the effects of implementation have to be monitored.

To determine whether the implemented innovation practices are successful in dissolving the identified knowledge-sharing boundaries and support knowledge sharing, innovation project managers might want to ask the self-reflection questions provided in stage 2 recurrently. In that way, they will be able to recognize if the boundaries were dissolved or if new boundaries emerged.

Ideally, experience gained by applying the innovation practices will guide the future choice of innovation practices. For instance, we proposed LEGO as a means to prototype a complex service process with a heterogeneous team that faced several challenges in their development journey over the course of about two years. At first, the responsible innovation manager was quite reluctant to try such a playful method, fearing negative gossip in the company. He agreed to utilize the method but instructed the facilitators to keep the workshop room closed and to close all shutters to the corridor. The workshop was a success. Team members stressed how this method helped them to interact constructively and to finally understand the other parties' contributions. Having experienced how the team appreciated this playful method led to more openness for future choices of innovation practices.

2.3 Conclusion

Companies struggle with the individual constraint of heterogeneity in their development teams. They frequently fail to manage knowledge sharing in innovation projects. Because such projects are increasingly complex, they are characterized by the work of a diverse, interdisciplinary group of individuals. In sharing one's knowledge with others, each individual is confronted with questions such as: Will I still be the expert if I share my knowledge? What will happen to my job if external innovators are seen as the upcoming experts? Do I really want to engage with people from different knowledge areas? How do I then have to adapt my knowledge so that others will understand it? Every innovation project manager will from time to time witness the emergence of knowledge-sharing boundaries in these settings. As mirrors of the individual constraints of team members, knowledge-sharing boundaries sometimes can be intuitively solved with moderation skills and sensitivity, but not always. Including innovation practices as a modification of the standard innovation process can provide meaningful support in dissolving these boundaries. Such innovation practices can alter destructive patterns of communication at a given boundary, refocus attention, or simply structure knowledge sharing in a way different from what employees at the boundary are used to.

In this chapter, we offer innovation project managers a five-stage self-assessment questionnaire that allows them to identify and resolve knowledge-sharing boundaries within project teams. The self-assessment questionnaire may be applied in a normative way because it helps users to decipher observed behavior and boundary types. It should be used as a basis for actively influencing the attitudes of individuals in innovation projects. It provides insights that help project teams to avoid systematic mistakes due to knowledge-sharing boundaries in innovation projects by pointing to nonideal tendencies and indicating corrective actions. This is particularly important against the background of increasing knowledge sharing among interdisciplinary individuals in today's innovation projects.

References

2bAHEAD (2016). *Der Trend Index 2016.1*. Available from: http://izz.sfu.ac.at/files/Executive%20Summary%20TrendIndex%202016.pdf

Brandt, E. and Messeter, J. (2004). Facilitating collaboration through design games. In: *PDC 04 Proceedings of the eighth conference on Participatory design: Artful integration: Interweaving media, materials and practices*, ed. Andrew Clement and Peter van den Besslaar, pp. 121–131. New York: ACM.

Carlile, P. R. (2004). Transferring, translating, and transforming: an integrative framework for managing knowledge across boundaries. *Organization Science* 15 (5): 555–568.

Rau, C. (2012). *Innovation practices: Dissolving knowledge boundaries in innovation projects*. PhD.: University of Erlangen-Nuremberg.

Rau, C., Neyer, A. -K., and Möslein, K. M. (2012). Innovation practices and their boundary-crossing mechanisms: a review and proposals for the future. *Technology Analysis & Strategic Management* 24 (2): 181–217.

Sugimoto, M., Hosoi, K. and Hiromichi, H. (2004). Caretta: A system for supporting face-to-face collaboration by integrating personal and shared spaces. In: *Proceedings of the 2004 Conference on Human Factors in Computing Systems, CHI 2004, Vienna, Austria, 24–29 April 2004, ed. E. Dykstra-Erickson and M. Tscheligi, pp. 41–48. New York: ACM.* https://dl.acm.org/citation.cfm?id=98592

Appendix

Stage 2: Analyzing Answers to the Self-Assessment Reflection Questions

A positive answer to a particular question provides a hint to the following behavioral pattern.

Behavioral pattern	Questions (see Table 2.1)
Talking at cross-purposes	1
Playing hide-and-seek	2, 3
Playing hide-and-seek	4
Active resistance	5, 6, 7, 8, 9
Playing possum	10, 11

The behavioral patterns you observed in your innovation project:

_____

_____

_____

_____

_____

About the Authors

DR. CHRISTIANE RAU is Professor of Innovation Management and Organizational Behavior at the University of Applied Sciences Upper Austria, School of Engineering. Currently, she serves as Head of Department of Innovation Management, Design, and Marketing. She is active in research, teaching, and consultancy in the fields of strategic innovation management, open innovation, and design thinking. Her research has been published in journals such as the *Journal of Product Innovation Management*, *R&D Management*, *Creativity and Innovation Management*, and *Research Technology Management*. She has a background in industrial engineering.

DR. ANNE-KATRIN NEYER is Professor of Human Resources Management and Business Governance at the Martin-Luther University of Halle-Wittenberg in Germany, where she directs the master's program in Human Resources Management. Her major research interests are in the field of human resource-oriented business governance for value creation. Currently, her research focuses on the impact of social interactions, organizational design, and human resource strategies on boundaryless cooperation and innovation in private and public organizations. Dr. Neyer holds a PhD from the Vienna University of Economics and Business Administration in Austria and received her postdoctoral lecture qualification from the University of Erlangen-Nuremberg in Germany. She was a postdoctoral research fellow at the UK's Advanced Institute of Management Research at the London Business School.

DR. KATJA KRÄMER-HELMER is an expert on strategic innovation management and user-centered research in the fields of digital products and services. She is a dedicated innovation professional who gained practical insights working for companies such as HYVE Innovation Research, Sky Germany, and adidas, all in Germany. Her research interests are in the field of collaborative work environments, open innovation, and corresponding capabilities. Dr. Krämer is a lecturer at the University of Applied Sciences of Upper Austria and holds a PhD from the University of Erlangen-Nuremberg in Germany.

3

THE CONSUMER AS THE LAST CONSTRAINT: ADDRESSING PSYCHOLOGICAL CONSTRAINTS IN NEW PRODUCT DEVELOPMENT

Nadine Hietschold

University of Zurich, Zurich, Switzerland

Introduction

New products fail at rates of approximately 40%, and a major reason for the flop of almost half of the new products is relatively simple: *Consumers resist purchasing and using the innovation*. In times of increasing availability of best-practice tools in management and marketing, new product failure rates are still surprisingly high. Although innovations usually possess an objective advantage over existing substitutes, companies still often fail to attract a large consumer group beyond some eager early adopters.

3.1 The Consumer as Constraint: Why Firms Manage Consumers Insufficiently

Why do so many innovations fail on the market despite the tremendous efforts of companies to understand their customers? The main reason is that most current market research methods focus on consumer needs but ignore the fact that *consumers' personalities and the way they make purchase decisions substantially differ.* The decision-making process of individuals is determined by their personality traits (i.e. psychological characteristics), such as the follower tendency (i.e. the tendency to conform to others instead of diverging from others). Such personality traits can have a negative effect on adoption and constrain innovation success. For example, if a company launches an innovative smartwatch that is targeted at young women and that looks very different from conventional round-shaped watches, it would likely encounter very slow adoption and low sales volume. The reason behind this consumer resistance is the personality characteristics of the target group. Younger individuals, and especially women, tend to conform to the mainstream in order to be part of the in-group. Therefore, younger women often refrain from trendsetting and buy products that have the same look and feel as those of their peers. Driven by various psychological constraints, consumers may prefer the status quo, overvalue their current possessions, or be overly concerned about the innovation's potential malfunction, physical risks, affordability, and social acceptance.

Transforming potential consumers into actual customers requires understanding psychological constraints and addressing them during product development and market launch. While marketers recognize that consumers generally have concerns and might hesitate to switch to the company's innovation, marketers often do not know what causes this resistant behavior and, therefore, how it can be addressed early in new product development (NPD).

Pepsi experienced the results from psychological constraints firsthand when it launched Crystal Pepsi in 1992. Crystal Pepsi was a clear cola, in stark contrast to brown cola expectations that differed slightly in flavor. Consumers did not accept these unfamiliar changes, and Crystal Pepsi was withdrawn from the market the following year (Jhang et al., 2012). Had Pepsi considered clarity-seeking dispositions (i.e. the tendency to perceive ambiguous situations as undesirable), a dominant psychological constraint of their target group, the company might have been able to prevent this failure.

Just as each person's DNA is unique, so are their psychological constraints. However, research has found that individuals with the similar demographic profiles (e.g. age, gender, education) often share similar patterns of psychological constraints. To prevent innovation failure, companies need to identify the patterns of psychological constraints in their target consumer groups and address them during NPD and launch. This is a challenging endeavor.

In the next section, psychological constraints are first introduced in greater detail. Then this chapter focuses on different clusters of psychological constraints (identity-related "how I am" constraints, cognitive "how I think" constraints, and emotional "how I feel" constraints) and provides advice on how companies can modify their standard NPD process to address these constraints adequately.

3.2 What Are Psychological Constraints?

When describing another person, we tend to refer to characteristics such as whether the person is extroverted or introverted, patient or impatient, accurate or messy, cordial or grumpy. The characteristics we refer to are usually *personality traits*, defined as an inherent set of individual psychological characteristics (individual differences in patterns of thoughts, feelings, and actions) (McCrae and Costa, 1995) that are largely context-independent and are stable over a long period of time. Although personality can evolve – we may become calmer as we get older – such traits are hard to influence in the short term. Personality traits influence both the way we think about products (attitude) and the way we make decisions (behavior). For example, before purchasing an innovation, an insecure consumer will listen to friends and family and rely on their recommendations, whereas a confident consumer will likely make a decision without consulting others.

While psychological characteristics can have a positive influence on innovation adoption (e.g. impulsiveness and confidence), some characteristics are much more likely to prevent an individual from buying or using an innovation. We refer to these psychological characteristics as psychological constraints. Table 3.1 summarizes the three categories of psychological constraints: how I am, how I think, and how I feel.

Subsequent paragraphs detail the eight psychological traits within the three constraint clusters: (i) demonstrating why they constrain innovation adoption, (ii) giving examples from practice, (iii) showing which consumers are especially prone to these constraints, and finally (iv) explaining how firms should address these constraints.

3.3 Being Constrained by "How I Am"

Individuals have a certain perception of themselves – a self-identity that directs how they act and consume in accordance with how they want to be perceived by others.

Table 3.1: Psychological constraints to innovation adoption.

Clusters of constraint	Definition	Trait	Example
How I am	Consumers' *self-identity*: How they position themselves in relation to others, how they perceive themselves, and what they believe	Follower tendency Prevention focus Attribute association	*Conforming*: Consumers are less likely to adopt unique new products
How I think	Consumers' *thinking*: How they acquire information from the environment, how they process information, and how they evaluate information	Pigeonhole thinking Clarity seeking Low self-efficacy	*Slightly open-minded*: Consumers are more skeptical about new products
How I feel	Consumers' *emotions*: To what extent they feel emotions and to what extent they rely on emotions in decision-making processes	Trait anxiety Emotional reliance	*Easily stressed*: Consumers are more easily overstrained by complex new products

For example, buying organic or vegan food is an expression of a sustainable and health conscious self-identity, whereas driving a Porsche corresponds to a materialistic self-identity. This self-identity helps consumers differentiate themselves from undesired others, the out-group, but also to conform to the values and behaviors of the social group to which they belong, the in-group. The products individuals consume (e.g. clothes, food, and furniture) help them express their identity. Only when consumers see a match between their own identity and the company's or innovation's identity will they adopt the product.

However, focusing on self-identities alone is not enough for companies to get their products sold. Self-identities are subject to trends (e.g. veganism) and are context-dependent (e.g. being a manager at the office and a motorcyclist in your free time). However, personality characteristics that are responsible for the effects of self-identity are much more fixed. For example, having the personality of a follower instead of a trendsetter determines whether a consumer will jump on the bandwagon of food trends such as wellness food (follower) or whether they are the first to purchase a smartwatch (trendsetter). Table 3.2 and the following sections introduce three types of "How I am" constraints: follower tendency, prevention focus, and attribute association.

Follower Tendency

The general need to either conform to the in-group (follower) or diverge from the out-group (trendsetter) is a fixed personality characteristic that strongly affects purchase decisions. Trendsetters with a high need for differentiation focus on their own uniqueness. In particular, when trendsetters consider the large mass market the out-group, it leads them to more unconventional, innovative choices and the avoidance of commonly purchased brands and products. In contrast to these trendsetters, followers rely on their social environment and make purchases that reflect their need to conform to their environment. Followers define the mass market as their in-group and will not risk social acceptance by buying a very new and different product.

Underestimating the follower tendency is one reason why Google Glass failed. NPD professionals often underestimate the tendency of their target audience to conform to subjective social standards. Google Glass just differed too much from the norm. The follower tendency is especially present among female and among younger consumers.

When facing "How I am" constraints, managers, and marketers have to make sure that the innovation fits consumers' self-identity. Individuals with a follower tendency want to be part of the in-group, and they make conventional mass product choices. Therefore, companies addressing customers with a follower tendency should adhere to four rules.

1. Avoid emphasizing uniqueness. Companies should develop one recognizable product version that attracts a large in-group. Ideally, the innovation shares the look and feel of previous versions or substitutes to enable consumers to continue to conform to their in-group.

2. Innovations should make clear to what in-group the consumer is conforming. Consumers put more weight on information about identity when they are reminded about it. For example, Motorola released the smartwatch Moto 360 that has a round shape and looks like a traditional watch. Wearing a watch is an

Table 3.2: Types of "How I am" constraints to innovation adoption.

Types of "How I am" constraints	Definition	Example of innovations affected by constraint	Typical consumers	Modification needed in NPD	Modification needed in marketing
Follower tendency	Tendency to conform to others instead of diverging from others	Smartwatches that do not look like traditional watches	Female Younger	Put no emphasis on uniqueness but on similarity to established substitute Enable community building through integration of social media and other sharing mechanisms	Communicate innovation popularity Link the new product to the in-group and the competitors to the out-group Create critical mass through low introductory prices, 2-for-1 promotions, and "refer a friend" programs
Prevention focus	Tendency to avoid negative outcomes instead of striving for positive outcomes	New cars that focus on speed instead of safety	Older	Focus on product usefulness instead of status aspects Focus on specific features instead of abstract emotional aspects Put emphasis on features that relate to safety and the efficient use of products	Communicate performance and safety information Describe the product as established
Attribute association	Tendency to relate two objectively independent product attributes	A new medicine that tastes good instead of bad as expected	Older	Develop in congruence with the "positive" attribute association dimension Develop products together with knowledgeable consumers in the product category	Prime the prevalent attribute associations and address them Make the consumer consider the opposite to dissolve associations

important part of identity expression. As many consumers want to remain in their in-group as owners of traditional watches, they tend to buy a Motorola rather than a nontraditional-looking squared smartwatch such as the Apple Watch. Similarly, for the new PlayStation 4, Sony uses the slogan "This Is for the Players," which clearly defines the in-group as players.

3. New products should communicate popularity and the fact that many other consumers have already adopted the innovation (e.g. best-sellers). If consumers perceive the innovation and the company as an element of their in-group, they will also act in favor of it and defend it.

4. Companies should define the boundaries of the out-group. Apple, for example, manages the differentiation between in-group and out-group well. In 2006, Apple launched the "Get a Mac" campaign. In the campaign, a young and hip spokesman claimed "I'm a Mac," while a middle-aged formal spokesman represented his opponent, the PC. In a dispute that followed, the Mac compared its features and capabilities against the worse-performing PC. By making the Mac identity salient and establishing a sense of unity, consumers identified with the young and hip in-group. Apple is so successful at establishing the "we are what we buy" connection that people even place Apple stickers on other products (e.g. cars) to express their belonging to the Apple in-group.

Prevention Focus

All individuals seek to obtain gains and to avoid losses. However, individuals differ in their approach to these goals. Some strive for positive outcomes more and focus on their aspirations and accomplishments (promotion focus), whereas others seek to avoid negative outcomes by focusing on responsibilities and safety issues (prevention focus) (Wang and Lee 2006). For example, some people work out to become the fastest and fittest (i.e. promotion focus), whereas others work out to avoid gaining weight (i.e. prevention focus). Prevention-focused consumers are less likely to purchase the newest high-tech products because they have more salient performance concerns about new technologies. Research shows that older individuals are especially subject to a strong prevention focus. This might explain why e-cigarette use is higher among young consumers. E-cigarettes are a new technology, and the risks and benefits are uncertain. Additionally, advertisements by large companies are dominantly promotion-focused (e.g. "Take Back Your Freedom" from blu brand e-cigarettes), which mainly attract youths. Messages are more successful when they fit the consumer's goal orientation. For example, a promotion-focused message would address social approval (e.g. gaining acknowledgment through the use of innovative technologies), while a prevention-focused message would focus on the fact that continuing to smoke traditionally would result in social disapproval (e.g. losing friends).

Consumers with a prevention focus prefer the status quo; they are safety-oriented and frequently have performance concerns. Companies should consider these needs by following four rules:

1. Prevention-focused consumers prefer utility-oriented products to pleasure-oriented products.

Utilitarian products offer functional benefits and solve problems. In contrast, hedonic products are meant to create pleasure and entertainment. When facing prevention-focused consumers, companies should focus on developing utilitarian products.

2. Prevention-focused consumers are interested in feasibility and concrete, risk-minimizing features instead of abstract emotional value. Hence, companies should emphasize functional features instead of design or social aspects. For example, in the case of electric cars, Tesla tried to address consumer concerns and introduced a resale warranty for its electric cars. Tesla ensures customers who buy the Model S a resale value after three years that is higher than any sedans from companies such as BMW or Jaguar. Similarly, several diesel car manufacturers are trying to address the risk that European cities might ban diesel cars due to their emissions by offering a three-year money-back guarantee.

3. The utilitarian safety focus is also important for marketing. Aspects that are compatible with the goals of consumers are more convincing and relevant to them and should be communicated. For example, the automobile producer Volkswagen used safety-oriented slogans such as "You cannot have your eyes everywhere. But your car can" in Germany to promote a new pedestrian detection system. In addition, the controversial electronic cigarette might cause the same risks as traditional cigarettes, and e-cigarette manufacturers sometimes try to address these consumer concerns. For example, the e-cigarette company Steamz uses the following slogan to address the safety orientation of consumers: "If you can't stop smoking, cancer will. But, smoke with Steamz E Cigarette, cancer will not."

4. A final marketing strategy is to describe the product as already established ("More than 10 000 consumers have relied for years on the product.") in order to reduce uncertainties and the perception of risks.

Attribute Association

Another personality trait determines if consumers recognize objectively independent product attributes as being independent or related. Examples where one product attribute influences the perception of another are found across a variety of product categories. Examples include: high price means high quality; a medicine's bad taste implies that it is effective; organic products have fewer calories; healthier food is less tasty. In general, attribute association is useful to consumers because consumers rarely have complete information. Attribute associations require low cognitive effort but are also rarely based on scientific truth. However, a consumer's personality determines the degree of belief in such attribute associations. In some cases, the associations can be so strong that people even rely on them when presented with objective, contrary information.

Consumers' attribute association can directly affect the success of new products. For example, a strong belief in the price-quality relationship or in bargain hunting as a low-status behavior prevents many consumers from buying at discounters such as Walmart. The webpage "People at Walmart" shows consumers with embarrassing clothes at Walmart and strengthens the negative image of the store. Lidl and Target are examples of European and US discounters that are aware of the negative influence of such beliefs. They offer a "Deluxe" line (Lidl) and a high-end meat line "Sutton & Dodge" (Target) to suggest the higher quality and status of their products. Strong beliefs regarding attribute associations are a challenge not only to innovative firms but also to general well-being. For example, the association of natural and traditional as being good and artificial as being bad can lead to the rejection of new vaccinations or to the reliance on natural healing when conventional medicine would be more effective. In general, researchers believe that attribute association develops in childhood. Therefore, adolescents are less likely to held traditional attribute associations than adults.

If well understood by companies, attribute associations can benefit new products. Companies can use the following four strategies.

1. Activate the association and subsequently promote the associated product attribute. For example, in one research study where participants were primed with quality ("Remember that price is a first indicator of quality"), the subsequent product evaluation was much more positive when the product was described as having a high versus a low price (Deval et al., 2013). Hence, when launching high-priced innovations, priming activates the price-quality relationship and higher quality becomes a justifiable reason for a higher price.

2. Address attribute associations during development, and adjust products to the "positive" bias dimension. For example, a common attribute association is that whatever is unhealthy tastes good and whatever is healthy does not. The medicine manufacturer Buckley successfully relies on this common belief and offers a bad-tasting cough mixture accompanied with slogans such as "It tastes awful. And it works," "People swear by it. And at it," or "Wait until your cold gets a taste of this." These slogans all rely on the belief that without pain there is no gain and that an effective medicine has to taste awful.

3. Avoid consumers with a high reliance on attribute association. Consumers with high knowledge of a product category are less likely to rely on attribute association mechanism because they have other criteria and rules to evaluate a product. If possible, companies should develop innovations in a product category where the target consumer group is high in expertise and a great deal of information is available and used.

4. Marketers can try to dissolve the attribute association and ask consumers to consider the opposite. For example, consumers have the naive belief that healthy food has fewer calories. In one study, consumers estimated that sandwiches from Subway (i.e. the healthy provider) had up to 35% fewer calories than sandwiches from McDonald's (i.e. the unhealthy provider). However, when researchers asked consumers to consider the opposite (i.e. consumers should question the validity of the health claim or consider evidence inconsistent with the health claim), the attribute association was eliminated. Marketers can launch educational campaigns that critically question claims and common beliefs (Chandon and Wansink, 2007).

3.4 Being Constrained by "How I Think"

Individuals differ in how they acquire information from their environment and how they make sense of it. For example, some people soak up all the information they can find, while others just want to know the basics; some are very rational when judging or making decisions, while others rely more intuitively on their gut feeling. The tendencies for a specific method of information acquisition and information assessment are anchored in personality. Some of these tendencies explicitly foster or impede innovation adoption. For example, some individuals are by nature less open-minded and thus also less willing and able to adjust to new situations and change. The next sections demonstrate how the personality characteristics of pigeonhole thinking, clarity seeking, and low self-efficacy constrain innovation adoption (See Table 3.3).

Pigeonhole Thinking

A disposition to pigeonhole thinking instead of systematic information processing can constrain consumers in buying new products. Although our preferences differ, and we might enjoy acquiring information actively in one domain (e.g. searching for a bargain flight for our next holiday) but hate it in another (e.g. searching for tax law paragraphs in order to maximize a tax return), individuals differ by disposition in how thoroughly they search for and process information in general. Individuals who enjoy effortful cognitive activities seek out more information and process the information more systematically. They are more open and curious about new information and innovations. Others have a lower need for systematic thinking and rely on pigeonhole thinking. Pigeonhole thinkers use simple decision rules that make judgments faster and more efficiently as they involve less effortful in-depth thinking (e.g. buying the familiar brand instead of an unknown brand).

Financial products, for example, are often too complex for consumers and financial investment innovations often fail. The broker platform Ayondo Markets uses consumers' lack of systematic information processing in its favor. Ayondo Markets offers social trading where customers simply follow selected top traders, and the investment transactions are copied automatically to the customers' accounts. In addition, the consumer heuristic to buy known brands often comes into play when companies engage in rebranding. When a well-known company changes its name and logos, it risks losing brand awareness. For instance, this was the case when the US retailer Overstock.com attempted to rename its brand O.co. Consumers could hardly identify the brand, and Overstock.com returned to its old name only a few months later. Research shows that a low need for cognition is related to a lower educational level. In addition, men tend to be more likely to engage in pigeonhole thinking than women.

Consumers prone to pigeonhole thinking rely on simple shortcuts, and companies face the risk that these consumers do not thoroughly understand the innovation's benefits. However, individuals who form an attitude on the basis of pigeonhole thinking are easier to influence in favor of the innovation than individuals with a well-grounded attitude. Companies should follow three rules.

Table 3.3: Types of "How I think" constraints to innovation adoption.

Types of "How I think" constraints	Definition	Example of innovations affected by constraint	Typical consumers	Modulation in new product development	Modulation in marketing
Pigeonhole thinking	Tendency to rely on heuristic cues instead of in-depth information processing	Financial innovations that require in-depth understanding	Male Lower education	Create simple-to-use products with low complexity and easy-to-grasp instructions	Communicate easy-to-capture benefits Use counterintuitive advertisements and competitor comparisons
Clarity seeking	Tendency to perceive ambiguous situations as undesirable	New food products with unnatural colors	Male Younger	Fulfill product category expectations Avoid incongruent features of the innovation compared to the product category norms	Provide a benefit rationale
Low self-efficacy	Tendency to assess one's abilities to perform a behavior as low	Mobile banking apps that require computer literacy	Female Younger Lower education	Stimulate user involvement and coproduction Conduct usability tests during testing and prototyping	Use mental simulations of usage Persuade the consumers verbally of their skills

1. Clearly communicate the benefit of an innovation in very few key points. Easy-to-capture (nonverbal) communication measures such as visual or audio appeals are helpful.

2. Use counterintuitive messages to capture the attention of pigeonhole thinkers. Interesting inconsistent information can stimulate thinking because people stop trusting their heuristics when something is completely new. Pepsi succeeded in applying this strategy when it started the "Pepsi Challenge" in the 1970s. The Pepsi Challenge aimed to take over some market share of Coca-Cola. In a blind test, consumers compared Pepsi and Coke and, surprisingly, consumers preferred Pepsi to Coca-Cola. Pepsi aggressively marketed these inconsistent results, and although Pepsi does not beat Coca-Cola in market share, it is now the second largest carbonated soft drink producer.

3. Design innovations in a way that usage is easy and does not involve high cognitive effort, because pigeonhole thinkers do not consider usage instructions thoroughly. For example, the cookbook *Picture Cook: See. Make. Eat.* by Katie Shelly uses drawings instead of written information to explain how the different ingredients are mixed. Similarly, the media company BuzzFeed launched the video series "Tasty" for social media channels, which uses time-lapse short films to show how food is prepared.

Clarity Seeking

Clarity seeking (i.e. the tendency to perceive ambiguous situations as undesirable) hinders the purchase of innovations because innovations are always accompanied by ambiguity. Whereas pigeonhole thinking can impede innovation awareness, clarity seeking can hinder the development of positive attitudes to new products. Ambiguous situations are unfamiliar, complex, and sometimes contradictory. For example, a traditional mobile phone user who is confronted with a smartphone for the first time might experience the situation as highly ambiguous because he or she is not familiar with how it operates, and therefore it is unclear whether the phone fulfills the job it is supposed to. In this case, clarity-seeking customers would probably refrain from purchasing the innovation. When individuals have a high clarity-seeking tendency, they try to avoid everything that is unfamiliar, more complex, and contradictory, leading them to reject most innovations.

Research shows some initial evidence that men are more clarity seeking than women. Individuals want to solve ambiguity quickly, and, therefore, they rely on information that is quickly accessible without studying the innovation in detail. Hence, companies should not leave consumers with unresolved ambiguity. For example, in 2000, Heinz launched the EZ Squirt bottles, which included ketchup in different colors, such as purple, blue, or green. The ketchup bottles were a nice gimmick for children and were an initial success. However, in the long term, parents could not get comfortable with nonred ketchup and the product was withdrawn from the market in 2006.

The best strategy for firms in dealing with clarity-seeking customers is to reduce the novelty perception of the innovation.

1. Make sure that the innovation fulfills the expectations consumers have toward the product with regard to its look and feel as well as functionality. When Amazon launched the Kindle e-book reader in 2007, many other e-book readers had already failed on the market. One reason for the success of the Kindle reader is that, in contrast to previous e-book readers, it fulfills all expectations of the product category of books. The Amazon Kindle mimics book letters with a special E Ink technology, but most important, it is a stand-alone device that, in contrast to its predecessors, does not need a computer connection.

2. Try to avoid implementing features of the innovation that are in strong contrast to the expected product category norms. Since the color brown is a major characteristic of cola and red is a major characteristic of ketchup, both Crystal Pepsi (the transparent cola) and Heinz EZ Squirt (the colorful ketchup) did not fulfill category norms. When innovations are incongruent, consumers often do not understand their benefits, as they cannot rely on existing product category knowledge.

3. Utilize a benefit rationale to help consumers understand the innovation's reason for being. For example, instead of communicating uniqueness and modernity, which is no benefit per se, Crystal Pepsi could have communicated that the transparent cola does not have artificial color additives. Apple is a company that deliberately introduces radical innovations but rarely fails. For example, Apple decided to remove the headphone jacks from the new iPhone 7. However, consumers accept these changes because Apple provides them with a vision of progress: The removal paves the way for the future of wireless Bluetooth earphones.

Low Self-Efficacy

Self-efficacy is the individual's assessment of his or her ability to perform a task. Consumers who have low self-efficacy have less confidence in their ability to use an innovation. If consumers think they do not have the ability to handle the change and learning processes associated with an innovation, they will continue using the alternative they can already operate or choose an alternative that seems less difficult. Although empirical evidence is not always clear, men seem to have higher self-efficacy than women. In addition, self-efficacy usually increases with age (up to a certain point) and is higher for people with a higher education. Hence, female consumers as well as very young or very old consumers generally have lower self-efficacy and should be considered in particular when designing and marketing complex products.

Low user self-efficacy was the reason Microsoft launched the operating system Microsoft Bob in 1995. Microsoft Bob was designed to have an easier interface than the Windows 95 operating system. Instead of a desktop, the user navigates in a room where known objects correspond to programs (e.g. a wall calendar to a calendar program and pen and paper to a word processor program). However, Microsoft Bob was not more intuitive for users but rather confusing. For example, the virtual room also contained several decorative items that lacked function. Although the idea of physical analogies was great, the actual realization to address consumers low in self-efficacy failed.

Low self-efficacy discourages consumers from purchasing and using innovations. Companies can address low self-efficacy in four ways.

1. Undertake extensive usability testing throughout the product development process to identify issues that decrease the ease of use of products and might lead customers to feel incapable of using the product. Usability is so important that specific consulting agencies, such as Designaffairs, specialize in human-machine interfaces and advise companies on how to design new products so that the user experience is particularly smooth and pleasant.

2. Aid consumers in imagining how they would use the innovation with a mental simulation of the usage process. This is the easiest way to boost self-efficacy. Very new products require learning, as usage differs from previous products. For example, companies can show customers how to use their innovation easily in advertisements. The website builder Wix.com shows within seconds how easy it is to create one's own website with only a few clicks by using templates, drag-and-drop features, and customizations without any HTML codes.

3. Strengthen consumers' confidence in their abilities by verbally persuading them of their skills. For example, the DIY store chain Hornbach in Germany launched the campaign "Women at Work" that includes workshops for women as well as humorous advertisements. In a parody of a women's magazine showing the slogan "Colors of Hornbach," a model presented her colorful wounds from handicraft activities (such as a blue thumbnail) instead of colorful clothes. Hornbach announced that it succeeded in engaging more than 10 000 women for handicraft activities in workshops in 2015.

4. Involve users in the actual manufacturing process (i.e. coproduction) to increase their self-efficacy as they are guided in using the innovation and can gather knowledge. As a result of extensive testing and a focus on visual instructions, for example, IKEA makes it easy for consumers to build their furniture at home using premanufactured components.

3.5 Being Constrained by "How I Feel"

Emotions ("How I feel") can guide our behavior and decisions more strongly than can our thinking. For example, individuals consume chocolate when feeling sad, although they know that this behavior is unhealthy. Emotions often emerge as temporary mood stages, but some individuals feel certain emotions more often and more strongly than others. Being emotional can prevent potential customers from adopting an innovation. For example, consumers who feel easily stressed are less likely to handle technically demanding products and therefore are also less likely to buy and use them. In terms of emotions, two personality characteristics constitute especially relevant constraints to innovation adoption: trait anxiety and emotional reliance (see Table 3.4).

Table 3.4: Types of "How I feel" constraints to innovation adoption.

Types of "How I feel" constraints	Definition	Example of innovations affected by constraint	Typical consumers	Modulation in new product development	Modulation in marketing
Trait anxiety	Tendency to be anxious and favor threat-related information	Nanotechnology products associated with unknown risks	Female Younger	Identify sources of fear and threat during testing and prototyping Include stress relievers in new product design	Use fear appeals (e.g. threat of not using the innovation) Communicate the calmness, simplicity, and security of the innovation with facts
Emotional reliance	Tendency to rely on emotions instead of information	New medical drugs that are associated with disgust	Female Older	Address positive emotions in product design Elicit positive emotions during the usage experience	Prime positive affect with ads Communicate with negative emotions such as shame and guilt

Trait Anxiety

Individuals with high trait anxiety are more prone to anxiety and are more likely to focus their attention on threat-related information but also on sources of safety that help them cope with the threat. For example, in the context of car purchases, individuals with high trait anxiety focus on the availability of airbags or other safety features, in contrast to driving pleasure or design. Trait anxiety impedes the adoption of innovations, as individuals mainly focus on the risks instead of the benefits. Additionally, usage of the innovation is a potential source of stress for consumers with trait anxiety, which they try to avoid. For example, research shows that consumers with high trait anxiety are less satisfied with self-service technologies and less prone to repeated usage (Meuter et al., 2003).

The more radical the innovation, the more trait anxiety blocks adoption. For example, research shows that consumers fear the risks of gene technology and exhibit much higher levels of concern about genetically modified food than regular food (Laros and Steenkamp, 2004). To stop the diffusion of genetically modified food, consumers founded the "March against Monsanto," repeating protests across cities all over the world. As consumers' trait anxiety can affect firms very negatively, it is valuable to know which consumers are likely to have this constraint. Women generally score higher on trait anxiety than men. In addition, aging tends to increase emotional stability; therefore, trait anxiety will decrease with age. Hence, product categories that are targeted at young and middle-aged women in particular (e.g. health and food) could be at risk of being constrained by consumers' trait anxiety.

Consumers with high trait anxiety experience stress intensively and focus on threats as well as safety issues. Companies can use the next four strategies to better address consumers with trait anxiety.

1. Identify sources of stress (e.g. usage complexity and unpleasant design) early in NPD.

    To identify stress triggers, companies can invite consumers with high trait anxiety to test the innovation and monitor which features or usage actions lead to stress (e.g. with the think-aloud method).

2. Reduce stress triggers and include stress relievers.

    For example, the design consultancy company mPath developed a tool that combines electronic sensors to measure skin conductance and observations to identify stress triggers. LEGO used this tool during innovation development. LEGO developed a tablet app for LEGO Technic that included animated instructions about how the LEGO pieces should fit together. With the stress-detecting tool, mPath identified that adding animation to the virtual page overwhelmed the children. Stress was also triggered when children realized that they had made a mistake and had to go back to the instructions. Including checkpoints during the building process would ensure that a step was completed correctly before moving on to the next one.

3. Use fear appeals in marketing.

    For example, in South Africa, a seat belt ad was launched to enhance compliance with using seat belts. The emotional campaign named "First Kiss" describes the romance of a young couple who met at a party but who never experienced their first kiss because they died in a car accident on the way home from the party. Six weeks after the launch of the ad, seat belt compliance increased by 11%.

4. Address threat concerns directly, for example, with specific statistics that show how reliable the product is.

    People with high trait anxiety are less likely to rely on their emotions when instructed to make determinations on the basis of facts. Hence, ads that recommend that consumers rely on safety statistics can reduce the influence of anxiety on the decision.

Emotional Reliance

Emotions are part of our everyday lives, but some of us rely more heavily on emotions than others when making decisions and tend to experience emotions with a higher intensity. Using emotional cues, such as sounds or colors, is sometimes easier and faster and can be more efficient than in-depth thinking. However, emotional reliance stands in the way of openly considering other sources of information about new products and services. Emotional reliance is thus a type of decision heuristic because individuals use cues to judge an innovation. However, in contrast to pigeonhole thinking, individuals high in emotional reliance can process information systematically but in the end weight emotional aspects more. Emotions influence consumer judgment and decision making more strongly than other aspects, such as factual information. In general, older people use heuristics more often and focus more on emotional information than younger people. In addition, women have been reported to be more emotional than men.

In general, if consumers have a negative feeling about an innovation, they judge risks as high and benefits low. For example, during the mad cow disease crisis, consumers generally avoided products containing beef, although the likelihood of falling ill was very low for humans. How consumers actually evaluated beef products depended very much on the specific terminology used in the news media. In one study, participants exposed to the phrase "mad cow diseases" relied on emotions in their subsequent decision to consume meat. When the phrases "bovine spongiform encephalitis" or "Creutzfeld-Jacob disease" were used, participants relied instead on objective risk judgments in subsequent purchase behavior (Sinaceur et al., 2005). Emotional reliance was also at work during the product recall of the new Samsung smartphone Galaxy Note 7 in 2016. The probability of an overheated battery catching fire was very low, but since consumers overestimated the risks, Samsung had to recall the entire product line.

Individuals high in emotional reliance assign a higher importance to information that is in line with their emotions. Companies can use the following strategies to stimulate desirable emotions toward the new product.

1. Adhere to design principles that promote positive emotions.

    For example, harmony and balance in design objects are perceived as pleasant. Moreover, communicating the right product category can also influence emotions toward an innovation. Smartwatches, for example, when considered as part of the product category of technical devices, might induce negative emotions among consumers such as anxiety related to technology. However, when understood as part of the category of watches, they might induce passion in consumers who are fond of watches.

2. Consider the specific emotions that are elicited after purchase and during usage.

   Those emotions depend on consumers' previous expectations, usage difficulty, and perceived benefits of usage. The usage experience starts after the purchase with unpacking the new product. "Unboxing" as a joyful event has even become a trend with people recording videos of unpacking new products and uploading the videos on YouTube. Apple, for example, tests potential package designs over and over to optimize the positive experience. The thoughtful packaging design is simple, the components are accurately arranged, and opening is easy.

3. Trigger positive emotions to tempt consumers to engage in (impulsive) buying behavior.

   For example, Coca-Cola directly primes positive emotions with slogans such as "Open happiness" or "Taste the feeling," which are supported with happy music. Audi uses its logo of four overlapping circles cleverly to promote that "Jooooy finally has meaning."

4. Communicate guilt or shame for not using the innovation, as consumers with high emotional reliance are also persuaded by negative emotions.

   For example, the company Juicy Juice shows a picture of a bike-riding child and says "You check his helmet. You check his training wheels. Shouldn't you check the label on his juice?" Another controversially discussed ad is the "Are you beach body ready?" ad by Protein World, which shows a woman with a perfect body. The ad tries to stimulate guilt and shame for not have lost enough weight before the summer comes. Although body-shaming campaigners protested against the ad, the emotion elicitation was successful as the ad increased sales enormously.

3.6 Uncovering Psychological Constraints

How can a company determine if a specific target group is prone to psychological constraints? Companies can uncover the psychological constraints of consumers by either a rough or an in-detail target market study. In contrast to current market research methods that focus on the needs of consumers and the desired features of innovations, these approaches focus on consumers' individual characteristics.

Companies often address consumers who will benefit the most from the innovation as their target audience. Considering the smartphone market, BlackBerry used to target business customers, Apple targets young and hip consumers, and Fairphone aims for consumers with high ethical consciousness. The particularities of the most attractive consumer group are identified by market research. Target groups are usually studied according to sociodemographic variables, such as age, gender, income, and place of residence, or according to psychographic variables, such as attitude, values, and lifestyle. Traditional market research efforts do not always result in success. For example, psychographic segmentation according to the greenness of consumers (i.e. how environmentally conscious they are) has resulted in product failure for many companies. For instance, the cleaning products producer Clorox launched the "Green Works" product line for its environmentally conscious consumers. However, the new products simply did not fit the identity of the consumers, because environmentally conscious customers were not willing to buy products of brands with superficial green efforts. Uncovering psychological constraints adds an important puzzle piece in understanding the relevant target group as well as designing and communicating innovations. Uncovering psychological constraints may require a more in-detail study of their target consumer group.

Companies can measure psychological constraints through a detailed survey of a representative sample of the target consumer group. An example of questions that reliably measure psychological constraints can be found in Table 3.5. Consumers read the questions and indicate on a nine-point scale ranging from 1 (strongly disagree)

Table 3.5: Survey instrument for the in-detail market study.	
Psychological constraint	**Examples of measurement questions**
"How I am" constraints	
Follower tendency	1. I actively avoid wearing clothes that are not in style. 2. At parties I usually try to behave in a manner that makes me fit in. 3. When I am uncertain how to act in a social situation, I look to the behavior of others for cues.
Prevention focus	1. I usually obeyed rules and regulations that were established by my parents. 2. I worry about making mistakes. 3. I frequently think about how I can prevent failures in my life.
Attribute association	1. The price of a product is a good indicator of its quality. 2. When a product is scarce, it is usually more valuable than others. 3. Organic products are healthier than conventional products.
"How I think" constraints	
Pigeonhole thinking	1. I do not like to have to do much thinking. 2. I try to avoid situations that require thinking in depth about something. 3. I believe in trusting my hunches.
Clarity seeking	1. A person who leads an even, regular life in which few surprises or unexpected happenings arise really has much to be grateful for. 2. I like parties where I know most of the people more than parties where all or most of the people are complete strangers. 3. A good job is one where what is to be done and how it is to be done are always clear.
Low self-efficacy	1. One of my problems is that I cannot get down to work when I should. 2. I avoid trying learning new things when they look too difficult for me. 3. I feel insecure about my ability to do things.
"How I feel" constraints	
Trait anxiety	1. I worry too much over something that really does not matter. 2. I feel nervous and restless. 3. I get in a state of tension or turmoil as I think over my recent concerns and interests.
Emotional reliance	1. When I recall a situation, I usually recall the emotional aspects of the situation. 2. I make decisions with my heart. 3. I often get too emotionally involved.

References for each scale are available from the author upon request.

to 9 (strongly agree) how prone they are to the constraints. Companies then form an average value for each psychological constraint across all consumers to get an impression of how prevalent the constraint is among their target consumer group. Companies should become alert if the mean of a psychological constraint exceeds a value of 5, which indicates that most consumers in their target have an inclination to this constraint (i.e. absolute average method). Companies should also calculate the average value across all constraints – in other words, the overarching mean of all the means of the psychological constraints – and then detect which psychological constraints exceed this overarching average value (i.e. relative average method).

If companies discover only one or two constraints above average, they can simply stick to the modifications suggested in the previous sections. However, if they discover multiple psychological constraints, companies need to determine if the modulation approaches suggest contradictory actions. If so, companies might have to decide to address only one of the contradictory constraints. For example, a target group with a prevention focus would require the company to focus on concrete information in marketing and utilitarian features in NPD. If the same target group also scores high on emotional reliance, the company would prefer a focus on hedonic and positive emotional appeals. In such a situation, the company should pragmatically look at the number of consumers that score high on each of the psychological constraints and address the constraint that is more prevalent in the target group.

References

Chandon, P. and Wansink, B. (2007). The biasing health halos of fast-food restaurant health claims: Lower calorie estimates and higher side-dish consumption intentions. *Journal of Consumer Research* 34 (3): 301–314.

Deval, H., Mantel, S. P., Kardes, F. R., and Posavac, S. S. (2013). How naïve theories drive opposing inferences from the same information. *Journal of Consumer Research* 39 (6): 1185–1201.

Jhang, J. H., Grant, S. J., and Campbell, M. C. (2012). Get it? Got it. Good! Enhancing new product acceptance by facilitating resolution of extreme incongruity. *Journal of Marketing Research* 49 (2): 247–259.

Laros, F. J. and Steenkamp, J. B. E. (2004). Importance of fear in the case of genetically modified food. *Psychology & Marketing* 21 (11): 889–908.

McCrae, R. R. and Costa, P. T. (1995). Trait explanations in personality psychology. *European Journal of Personality* 9 (4): 231–252.

Meuter, M. L., Ostrom, A. L., Bitner, M. J., and Roundtree, R. (2003). The influence of technology anxiety on consumer use and experiences with self-service technologies. *Journal of Business Research* 56 (11): 899–906.

Sinaceur, M., Heath, C., and Cole, S. (2005). Emotional and deliberative reactions to a public crisis mad cow disease in France. *Psychological Science* 16 (3): 247–254.

Wang, J. and Lee, A. Y. (2006). The role of regulatory focus in preference construction. *Journal of Marketing Research* 43 (1): 28–38.

About the Author

DR. NADINE HIETSCHOLD is a postdoctoral researcher at University of Zurich, Switzerland, where she currently works in an externally funded research project on social innovators. She graduated from Technische Universität Dresden, Germany, in 2017 with her dissertation work on the subject of consumer resistance toward innovations. In her research, she is dedicated to the microfoundations of innovations. Specifically, she studies individuals' (negative) perceptions, emotions, and behaviors toward innovations as well as antecedents of individuals' (social) innovative behavior. She has published in peer-reviewed academic journals such as *R&D Management*, the *International Journal of Production Research,* and *Health Services Management Research.*

Part 2

ORGANIZATIONAL
CONSTRAINTS

The chapters in Part 2 propose solutions to organizational constraints, which we define as relating to aspects of structures, processes, and resources that firms utilize and require to develop new products and services.

Chapter 4, by Katharina Hölzle, Tanja Reimer, and Hans-Georg Gemünden, provides a diagnostic framework to identify the symptoms and causes underlying organizational constraints that reduce the effectiveness of the standard innovation process. The chapter explores four combinations of symptoms and causes in more depth. The authors outline a holistic approach to addressing these constraints and provide an illustration of the solution within a specific organization.

The remaining chapters in this part examine more specific organizational constraints to innovation: the challenges that come with using virtual teams and the time constraints experienced by service professionals in pursuing innovation. Chapter 5, by Floortje Blindenbach-Driessen, develops a framework that delineates the dual roles service professionals play in their firms' innovation efforts. The chapter highlights the three issues of motivation, efficiency, and project selection as critical to address and provides concrete steps on how to get started in doing so.

The part is closed out by a discussion on constraints that arise from virtual teams in NPD. Chapter 6, by Donovan Hardenbrook and Teresa Jurgens-Kowal, breaks down the problem of dispersed virtual teams by contrasting the standard innovation process with a proposed virtual team-based innovation process. As companies increasingly engage and rely on multicultural, global, dispersed teams, this chapter provides important guidance to managers on how to implement and manage virtual new product development teams. The authors identify five distinct dimensions of virtual team-based innovation and discuss concrete steps for implementing the adaptation.

4

IDENTIFYING AND OVERCOMING ORGANIZATIONAL INNOVATION CONSTRAINTS

Katharina Hölzle
University of Potsdam, Potsdam, Germany

Tanja Reimer
Europe University of Flensburg, Flensburg, Germany

Hans Georg Gemünden
BI Norwegian Business School, Oslo, Norway

Introduction

As identified in Chapter 1, innovation challenges can be thought of as barriers, failures, or constraints. In order to control and take appropriate actions to overcome organizational innovation constraints, it is necessary to be able to identify them. In this chapter, we provide an approach to systematically identify symptoms and causes of organizational constraints. We also present one solution approach for training and enabling employees how to overcome organizational constraints: the "Innovation Think Tank." In this chapter, we categorize and explain four different innovation constraints that we have identified in our research. Details about our research are presented in "About Our Research."

About Our Research

To effectively identify and analyze dominant causes that lead to common symptoms and to derive a specification of innovation constraints, we conducted a large-scale empirical investigation: a total of 142 interviews with product development project managers and team members across three multinational German companies (company A, B, and C respectively). Two of these companies (B and C) have independent business units that have a high heterogeneity with respect to the markets they serve. Consequently, these business units have unique processes, structures, and cultures and can be considered as independent organizations for this study (named B1–B4 and C1–C3). Consequently, we have a total of eight organizations from Germany (GER), Switzerland (CH), Great Britain (GB), and the United States (USA), all based in the manufacturing sector (see Table 4.1). All organizations have a high need for innovation, which makes them an ideal fit for this study. We selected projects in different phases in the innovation process to maximize diversity; thus, we looked at exploratory research and technology projects in the early stage of the innovation process but also at incremental development projects right before market introduction. Another selection criterion was the formal status of the project with one full-time project leader and at least one or more full-time project members. Overall, we looked at 42 projects with an average length of two years and team sizes from between 2 and 25 members. We conducted interviews with 142 individuals across these product development projects. The respondents were either team leaders or team members of a new product development team and had an average tenure of 12.8 years with a range from 2 to 28 years in their respective organization. Seventy-six percent of our respondents were male and 24% were female. Ninety percent of our respondents held one or more academic degree(s), 70% from science or engineering, 25% from business or social science, and 5% from other. Each project member described multiple experiences with innovation challenges resulting in a total of 580 experience descriptions. For more details of our sample, please see Table 4.1.

Table 4.1: Overview of empirical study

Organization	A	B1	B2	B3	B4	C1	C2	C3	Σ
Country	GER	GER	GER	GER	CH	GER	GB	USA	8
# projects	6	6	7	5	3	2	8	5	42
# interviews	26	23	24	15	12	4	27	11	142
# innovation challenges	104	98	95	57	51	14	114	47	580

GER = German business unit; CH = Swiss business unit; USA = or American business unit of the respective companies A, B, and C.

For a full report of the original research in German, please see Mirow (2010) and Reimer (2014).

4.1 Systematic Identification of Organizational Innovation Constraints

In the literature, various factors are described as organizational constraints to innovation although they might either be the triggers or the effects of a true constraint. We therefore start with a multidimensional concept for innovation constraints. An innovation constraint can be characterized by a *visible* symptom and its underlying (often *hidden*) cause. The symptom is usually easily observed and manifests in arguments against pursuing a particular innovation project (e.g. high development costs, uncertain sales). Constraint symptoms are triggered by hidden causes such as misdirected resources or insufficient knowledge. By combining the symptom and its cause(s), innovation constraints can not only be better identified but also can be more clearly explained with a manageable number of symptoms and causes.

As Figure 4.1 shows, it is possible for an innovation constraint to have several causes that together lead to a symptom that is visible and recognized by members of the organization. The combination of the cause(s) with the symptom is the innovation constraint. A useful analogy for this is the medical field. A patient shows identifiable symptoms of an illness (limping) that may have multiple causes (sore muscles, broken bones). Causes and symptoms together lead to a constraint (can't go for a run) that hinders the patient from pursuing a particular goal (stay or become fit).

Recognizing Innovation Constraint Symptoms

In order to overcome an innovation constraint, we have to tackle the roots of the problem. As these roots are often not or only barely detectable, we need to clearly understand how the constraint is expressed by its symptom(s). When project members and leaders are asked what hinders the optimal course of the innovation development process, they usually have an array of different descriptions (constraints) that must be linked to the respective symptoms in order to understand the underlying causes and tackle them in turn. Next we describe the five main symptoms that we have found in our research. The description of these symptoms will help the reader to diagnose what the problem is. Then we explain some root causes of these symptoms and then discuss solutions to solve the causes in order to overcome the innovation constraint.

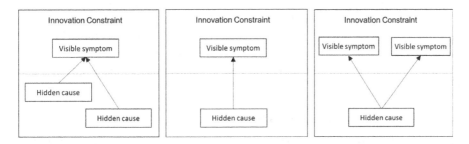

Figure 4.1: Structure of an innovation constraint.

The five main symptoms we have found are:

1. Lack of internal cooperation
2. Lack of external cooperation
3. Shortcomings in goal setting
4. Lack of adequate infrastructure
5. Restriction of innovative action

Lack of Internal Cooperation

Internal cooperation is crucial in the product development process. It includes members of the project team as well as organizational members outside the team with whom team members work. For example, an innovation constraint symptom may be too little communication within the project team or the fact that essential information is not made available to the team by individuals outside of the team. Similarly, a detectable symptom might be the insufficient level of support provided by colleagues within and outside the team. Finally, another visible symptom is that project members must expend a very high level of effort in their immediate work environment. In other words, team members express perceptions that they cannot work satisfactorily with their colleagues.

Lack of External Cooperation

The lack of external cooperation symptom describes problems in the organization's collaboration with suppliers and customers, thus explicitly focusing on the interface of the innovation project with the company's external environment. A detectable symptom can be missing, incomplete, or not shared information or insufficient communication from the external partner. Furthermore, team members express the feeling that involved employees from the supplier's or customer's organization do not support the cooperation or recognize its value.

Shortcomings in Goal Setting

The symptom of shortcomings in goal setting is expressed by uncertainty and disagreement about the project's goals from the involved parties, i.e. management, partners, and project members. It includes uncertainties about the actual problem structure as well as future goals. Often project goals are changed over the course of a project and are not adequately reflected in a change project structure or alignment of the project with its environment. The project might be stopped for an undefined period of time and/or important decisions for continuing the project may not be made. Another frequent problem is caused by changing project objectives that also entail a change in the task within the project framework. Furthermore, unclear responsibilities contribute to a lack of a clear definition of involved internal partners tasks,' responsibilities, and timelines.

Lack of Adequate Infrastructure

The term "lack of adequate infrastructure" for an innovation project refers exclusively to tangible resources, such as personnel, financial resources, and operational resources.

A personnel shortage is characterized by inadequate staffing with professional staff. A financial shortage prevents, for example, the purchase of materials or machines. In regard to operational resources, unsuitability of existing equipment and software slows down the development work. Another crucial point is the support of project members through deliverables from outside of the project, such as construction and prototypes. This deficiency is outside the project team's area of responsibility and inhibits the progress of the project due to exceeding time limits or insufficient quality.

Restriction of Innovative Action

The restriction of innovative action symptom describes the lack of individual capacities identified by the innovators themselves. This means that innovators within the project do not have enough time to get involved in their innovation project. The symptom is visible in the fact that employees cannot fulfill their project tasks due to insufficient capacities or cannot develop new ideas freely. Hence the creative potential of the innovators cannot be fully exploited, which ultimately has a negative impact on the innovative nature of the project. Again, this symptom is the individual-perceived deficit of his or her own resources.

Understanding the Causes of Innovation Constraint

The symptoms just described can be triggered by one or more causes. In our research, the respondents gave us at least one cause for every symptom. From the perspective of the people involved in the innovation process, there are four main causes of innovation constraints:

1. Lack of skills
2. Lack of motivation
3. Strategic restrictions
4. Operational restrictions

We would like to point out that these are the causes that our respondents *perceived*. Although some causes obviously have some deeper and far-reaching reasons, we have decided to stay on this level of explanation because these were the causes respondents associated with each symptom. This is important as these perceived causes need to be remedied and addressed in the eyes of the project team. Even if there are broader structural causes at play (and upper management should of course address these), the perceptions of team members is critical for recognizing and then actively overcoming the constraint.

Lack of Skills

Lack of skills means that the existing knowledge at the company is not sufficient to solve the tasks at hand. This is due to the fact that either the individual and/or the organization lacks the knowledge to carry out the tasks of the innovation project. Organizational knowledge is missing if individual knowledge is not available and/or successfully transformed into organizational knowledge. The know-how and experience required for the innovation can also be missing in the company if projects are outside the core competencies of a particular department or if the innovation concept has been developed outside the company and the necessary skills are not available in the organizat ion are not available. Furthermore, often innovation projects are associated with very high technical requirements and, depending on the state of knowledge, high to very high decision-making risks. While a lack of skills can be associated with a not-well-planned human resources policy or shortcomings in the hiring process, this is a rather long-term aspect of human resource planning that we have not been addressing with this research.

Lack of Motivation

Lack of motivation describes the individual rejection of the innovation project. To be innovative, individuals need to be willing to spend time on and be dedicated to the innovation project and have a certain risk tolerance for it. A lack of motivation leads to an insufficient willingness to support the innovation; in its enhanced form, lack of motivation can even lead to active action and conscious decisions against the innovation. Furthermore, risk-averse behavior – i.e. the lack of willingness to take an increased risk and an adherence to known experiences – is particularly restrictive, since it is associated with the lack of motivation to learn new and to change habitual behaviors. Individuals need an intrinsic drive for change to become innovative and to actively support innovation. However, if they have had prior bad experiences with innovation, their motivation for engaging in innovative behavior will be rather low.

Strategic Restrictions

Strategic restrictions occur when the strategic direction of the company or a department is not consistent with the objectives of the innovation project. This can lead to conflicts if departments are overloaded or if overlapping areas of responsibilities lead to competency disputes. Furthermore, unclear task guidelines and poor project support delay the development progress. Often an innovation is desired but will be accepted only if innovators prefinance the project out of their own departmental budgets. Unclear decision-making powers are manifested by restricted access to external information, either because a third party is intervening or due to restrictive guidelines of the company. Furthermore, if project managers have a low degree of autonomy, they will also not be able to make decisions needed for the project. This is particularly evident if the relationship between the line and the project is not clearly defined or if the matrix organization is not correctly set up.

Operational Restrictions

Operational restrictions occur when strongly formalized or inflexible processes hinder the project. These routines are mostly set up to facilitate day-to-day operations and to perform standard tasks effectively and efficiently. They can make innovation easier if they leave room for flexibility and change but can hinder projects if they are too formalized. However, the other extreme is also possible: that there are no defined processes or only internal information flows. Spatial separation of project teams or inadequate organizational knowledge management leads to undefined internal information paths. In terms of personnel policy, high employee fluctuation and the distribution of employees on too many different projects poses problems for the progress of innovation.

Dealing with Organizational Innovation Constraints: Symptom-Cause Combinations

The five symptoms and four causes can be combined in a variety of ways. As a result, there are theoretically 20 possible types for innovation constraints; however, all do not occur with high frequency. For this chapter, we focus on three innovation constraints we have found most often in our research. In the following sections, we describe these three constraints in detail by the specific manifestations of their symptoms and causes. We furthermore elaborate on organizational limitations that further enhance the innovation constraint and provide some best practices from our research for the adaptation of the innovation process (i.e. how to overcome the innovation constraint).

No Freedom for Innovative Thinking ("I Have a Dream")

In many organizations, there is no time or freedom to think outside the box or to try things out. Often employees feel that, although they are required to be creative and innovative, this is neither enabled nor rewarded. In particular, the goal-oriented achievement of project goals is rated higher than the elaboration of truly novel solutions. When project members are working to the limit of their ability in fulfilling day-to-day tasks, they no longer have the intellectual capacity to develop new ideas for innovative solutions. Furthermore, the lack of temporal freedom leads to incremental improvement and suboptimal solutions in current and future projects due to constant time pressure. Besides the operational restrictions, we also observe that a lack of motivation leads to a restriction of innovative action, as some employees told us that they tried to propose new ideas or improvements in the past and were either laughed at or were in other ways negatively associated with their "dream." And last but not least, a lack of skills and methods with respect to how to think creatively, how to take different perspectives, or how to communicate these often fuzzy ideas adequately were also identified as causes of a lack of innovative action.

Adaptation. In order to enable employees to develop innovative solutions with sufficient time and intensity, they have to be given freedom outside their day-to-day work. This freedom can be promoted by a temporary spatial separation from their workplace and/or by a methodological support of the employees. From the very beginning of the innovation project, freedom for creativity needs to be encouraged and integrated in the project plan. This means less formalism in the early stages of the innovation and a basic understanding of all participants for the innovation process and its implications. Project management must be designed based on the size of the project; i.e. reporting procedures should be reduced to a basic level where true value is created and the procedures should be considered in project planning and controlling. Furthermore, a fixed percentage of working hours could be assigned to scouting or project-relevant studies. Working in a designated space – e.g. an Innovation Think Tank – also helps project members to get in a "thinking and doing mode" that fosters creativity and innovation. Some organizations train their project teams in using creativity methods and provide external support for literature and patent research. Overall, we have found that providing designated time-outs from the operational project work and offering team members dedicated freedom for innovative thinking outside of their regular work environment helps to overcome the constraint of not enough innovative thinking. This can be done through, for example, one- to two-day Design Thinking or creativity workshops led by experts in creativity, Design Thinking, or other innovation methods. Scheduling dedicated innovation project days where experts from other departments or units are invited can also help companies look for solutions outside of the box. In later project stages, freedom for innovation can be supported by providing venture capital to develop these ideas further or providing sabbaticals for employees to pursue their ideas for a designated period of time.

Ideas Are Rejected (Being Don Quixote)

Once employees take the initiative to think outside of the box and develop a new idea, often the idea is turned down. Innovative, unfamiliar, or seemingly crazy ideas are rejected or do not get any attention. They are not included in the idea selection or prescreening process as nobody feels responsible for them. As a result, the initiator feels like Don Quixote jousting at windmills and being the only one taking a stand for the idea in order to secure the support of the department or unit on his or her own. Especially for employees who have not been with the department, unit, or organization for long, this is a major innovation constraint. The symptom for this constraint is a shortcoming in goal setting, caused by operational restrictions. While formalities and criteria for the decision-making process play an important role at product development process gates to ensure the comparability and transparency of the innovation process, they are a major obstacle for conceptual ideas as they are not suitable for evaluating them. This is particularly serious in the case of radical innovations. On one hand, such innovations are desired by the company; on the other hand, they do not find a place in the innovation process because they are so novel that they cannot be assessed with standardized criteria and thus fail at the gates.

Adaptation. If the organization is looking for ideas outside the existing business area, it has to create a way to overcome the filter "Fit to existing business or process." Already in the phase of idea generation, it should be possible to get "homeless" ideas into an idea pool and to enable an initial assessment by experts from different disciplines. In order to develop these ideas further, resources need to be provided centrally, e.g. by a central or cross-divisional research department. Depending on the size of the organization, this might be done through one designated idea scout/promotor or a team. This person/team serves as the "idea police" for radical or crazy ideas and is equipped with its own designated fund to conduct a first assessment of these ideas (involving different experts and/or external stakeholders). In their target agreement, this person/team is responsible for scouting a specific number of radical ideas per year. Furthermore, the organization might want to rethink its product development process and adjust it based on the degree of innovation; thus, shorter, more iterative, flexible, and open process might be used for radical ideas while incremental ideas follow the standard innovation process.

No Support for Innovation Projects (the Nonstarter or "We Don't Do That")

Even if the idea is evaluated positively and the innovation project is (often with a lot of expectations) kicked off, many projects become nonstarters as they are not sufficiently supported through adequate resources. For example, there is a lack of specialists for specific tasks and development steps in the project or there is a lack of technical support because there is not enough staff (e.g. technicians and designers) available for the project. The lack of financial resources for an innovation project is particularly noticeable in technological innovations. It is often very difficult to get long-term, reliable financing for these types of innovation. The causes for these symptoms can be lack of skills or strategic restrictions. If a company starts too many projects at once because of the fear of missing out on something, in most cases there are not enough available resources. If several innovation projects are running in parallel, experts need to spend their time on various projects, which leads to work overload and conflicts. Here, we often find a lack of coordination of innovation projects across the whole organization (missing innovation portfolio management). In addition, employees are often withdrawn from projects at short notice if a problem occurs in their regular field of work, resulting in a lack of personnel resources for the innovation project. The reason for insufficient long-term financial support for technological innovations is often that such projects are associated with high risks and unknown ends. When a company decides to invest in technological innovation, the commitment has to come from top management. If this is not the case, or if the commitment is only on paper, often the research and development (R&D) department has to cover the necessary expenses from its own budget and cannot sustain the innovation project in the long term, which often leads to abandoning the project on short notice.

Adaptation. It is mandatory to establish overall portfolio management and assign resources accordingly. The company needs to have central innovation portfolio planning to know exactly which projects are planned (in the early stage), which are currently running, in which stage of the innovation process they are, who is assigned on what basis to which project, and what the status of the project is. The innovation portfolio could also include those ideas they have identified with potential but that are currently in the evaluation stage. Furthermore, the planning has to ensure that experts are not allocated to too many projects at once. Personnel fluctuation and skill development need to be considered. And last but not least, the company needs to let all project team members know what comes after the current project so they don't spend time looking for the next project while the project is still running, which would lead to a lack of commitment and motivation.

If promising ideas are identified and the exact amount of resources needed is not known up front, sufficient funds and resources need to be assigned for longer than the expected project duration and permanently allocated to the project so that they cannot be withdrawn on a short-term basis. A written contract at the beginning of the innovation project confirms the organizational commitment to the project and increases the hurdles to shift resources. With respect to technological innovations, the company needs to be aware that these innovations are usually not one- to two-year commitments but rather long-term ones that need different criteria for evaluation and management of the innovation process than, for example, incremental product innovations. Providing a shared space where experts can gather to give feedback to several projects at specific times (as e.g. in the Innovation Think Tank; see Section 4.2) allows for better exploitation of scare resources.

In summary, these three examples have shown the structure of innovation challenges, consisting of observable symptom(s) and their underlying cause(s), as depicted in Figure 4.1. If the organization or the employee feels that there is an innovation constraint, the diagnostic instruments described in this chapter can help to separate the symptom from the cause. Our examples show how the constraint manifests itself and can be overcome using one or more of the described adaptations. In the next section, we present a best practice that we have developed, prototyped, tested, and evaluated together with one of our corporate partners. Many of the individual adaptation options are combined in the concept of the Innovation Think Tank.

4.2 Overcoming Innovation Constraints: The Innovation Think Tank

At one of our corporate partners, we repeatedly found two innovation constraints: no freedom for innovative thinking and no support for innovation projects. Although the organization itself is a highly innovative and technology-oriented company that praises itself for its technical and engineering competence, the employees expressed their concerns about major constraints especially in the early phases of the product development process. They felt that they not only lacked time to push the early stage of R&D projects, but they also had problems to keep a clear head for these tasks when working long hours on daily business. Furthermore, they often found that they could not get an expert's opinion on short notice because there was no project contracting due to the small size of the activities and other departments would not allow their experts to join the project. Based on our classifications and the proposed adaptations, we developed and tested the concept of an Innovation Think Tank in order to overcome the constraints of the early phase of innovation projects. The Innovation Think Tank is a space within this company where R&D employees meet to work on early-stage tasks. The Innovation Think Tank supplies them with food for thought and inspiration in order to accomplish their tasks and (early) project goals. Unlike the classic think tank that focuses on a single topic, our concept allows for simultaneous work on different topics. Common to the classic concept is the get-together of experts who help one another. The focus of the Innovation Think Tank is on the completion of concept studies (innovation projects in their early phases). Hence the Innovation Think Tank also helps to balance the importance of the early and late stages of innovation projects within the organization.

Elements of the Innovation Think Tank

The Innovation Think Tank prototype consists of four elements:

1. Space design
2. Structure of work and time
3. Effective learning
4. Networking

Space Design

The design of the Innovation Think Tank aims to provide an alternative working environment that is creativity-enhancing. Vitally important is the physical separation from the daily workplace. To meet the special requirements of early-stage tasks, it is important to create a calm and undisturbed workplace (positive isolation effect). Single-user workstations allow for independent and individual research and work. A physically separate room for intensive discussions or conference calls is available. A coffee area, a place for expert group discussions, and an information area (with access to scientific literature) are also included in the think tank.

Structure of Work and Time

The structure of work and time is flexible. The attendance at the Innovation Think Tank is voluntary. Participants are, however, requested to work on a specific and already planned task. The Innovation Think Tank was open for four weeks (starting at 8 a.m.) and employees could freely choose their time slot, though they were asked to use the Innovation Think Tank for several days with a minimum of four hours per day. The flexible structuring of work and time led to different group compositions and fostered creativity-enhancing exchange of information. A joint kick-off session every day (10–10:30) was the only compulsory interruption of the workday. Participation at expert discussions that usually took place at one o'clock was voluntary. In order to keep day-to-day business away from the Innovation Think Tank, participants were asked not to be accessible via mail and telephone to the greatest possible extent while they were using the think tank.

Effective Learning

Effective learning is reached through the systematic finishing of innovation activities and a support program. Participants experience how they can successfully handle tasks in the early phase of innovation projects. The support program is made up of speeches and expert discussions as well as methodical support concerning literature and patent searches. The methodological support is provided by the corporate information center that delegated one staff member for the term of the Innovation Think Tank (four weeks). Over the course of the four weeks, 15 expert discussions were hosted by nine corporate experts in the field of creativity techniques, technology trends, business segment strategies, and marketing.

Networking

Networking, facilitated by a moderator, is an important element of the Innovation Think Tank as it fosters communication and exchange. Finding a balance between a calm working atmosphere and an active exchange among the R&D employees is a major challenge for running the Innovation Think Tank. To solve this conflict, interpersonal exchanges were particularly promoted during expert discussions and kick-off sessions (where participants were directed to introduce themselves and their topic to the group in five minutes). Next to these directed networking offerings, participants also bonded at the coffee area – in many cases cross-departmental.

Promotion and Execution of the Innovation Think Tank

The offer to use the facilities of the Innovation Think Tank was distributed via corporate intranet. Additionally, department heads were personally informed about the concept and served as multipliers. The test phase of the Innovation Think Tank spanned four weeks and was used by more than 100 R&D employees (60 of them worked on their early-phase innovation tasks; the others attended workshops). In the first week, a simple lunch was provided for everybody interested in visiting the new facilities. The team of the Innovation Think Tank offered tours, brief stand-up workshops, and short exercises. Furthermore, top management specifically addressed middle managers to identify and invite inventors and multipliers to the think tank.

Evaluation of the Innovation Think Tank

The number, length of stay, and behavior of participants were recorded on a daily base. Additionally, the trial run of the Innovation Think Tank was accompanied by a written evaluation (conceptualized by the research team). The evaluation consisted of two parts – initial and final evaluation. The initial evaluation was based on personal interviews about an individual's motivation for participation and expectations. Main drivers for motivation were (i) the search for a calm and undisturbed work area, followed by (ii) the wish to complete the early phase of a current innovation project, (iii) to see what colleagues are working on, (iv) pure curiosity, and (v) the search for support. Participants expected a time reduction until completion of the early phase up to 50%.

The final evaluation looked at the extent to which the individual targets had been reached. Furthermore, improvement of the concept was to be derived from the evaluation of the different elements of the Innovation Think Tank. The vast majority of participants achieved a significant time reduction while working on their projects in the Innovation Think Tank. One participant stated: "It was great. [Our stay in the Innovation Think Tank] effectively reduced the processing time by several months." Results concerning the work atmosphere in the think tank also showed that the physical separation enabled a more efficient working style. Besides the small number of disruptions, the low noise level and the limited availability by phone were evaluated very favorably. Expert rounds with a strong focus on interaction got positive ratings whereas expert rounds in a "presentation style" were less appreciated. The expert rounds in the fields of patent or literature research and technology trends were valued highly while topics in the field of business segment strategies were considered least useful.

Furthermore, participants expressed their gratitude for having the freedom to "just try things out." They felt that they could openly express crazy ideas and found support (sometimes from very different departments) to exchange ideas and work on their projects. They also felt that the think tank's team provided valuable input on how to pitch their ideas in subsequent phases to obtain funding and support.

At the beginning of the test phase, the concept of the Innovation Think Tank faced a lot of skepticism in all hierarchical levels. Reluctance was particularly observed at lower and middle management levels. Consequently, the degree of capacity utilization was low during the first two weeks of the testing phase, and true collaboration did not really happen. In the second half of the test phase, the number of participants continuously rose as the Innovation Think Tank became wider known within the company due to the positive feedback of the initial users.

To sum it up, the first prototype of Innovation Think Tank was a success. Results indicate that team members could execute tasks more efficiently and with lower effort compared to their working style outside the Innovation Think Tank. Moreover, the Innovation Think Tank made it possible for participants to work on ideas that usually buried in day-to-day work. Therefore, the Innovation Think Tank could be a good tool to mitigate typical innovation challenges that occur in the early phases of innovation projects.

The positive feedback of the R&D employees who tested the prototype for four weeks provides evidence that a corporate Innovation Think Tank can be a valuable tool for handling innovation challenges, especially in early phases of innovation projects. The Innovation Think Tank is meant to support the execution of pre-studies in a quicker, more cost-efficient, and more innovative way. It provides space, freedom, and support for developing ideas and get first feedback. It aims to enable a better and more intense access to innovation projects in the early phases. Moreover, it provides guidance and support in the forefront of important gate decisions. The testing phase of our prototype revealed that the intended targets have been met. The Innovation Think Tank made it easier for R&D employees to apply successful tactics to overcome organizational constraints leading to innovation challenges: These tactics included intense discussions within the project team, having a designated team space for the innovation project, communication with experts from other teams, and having the freedom to work on alternative concepts.

References

Mirow, C. (2010). *Innovationsbarrieren*. Wiesbaden: Gabler.

Reimer, T. (2014). *Umgang mit Innovationsbarrieren – Eine empirische Analyse zum Verhalten von F&E-Mitarbeitern*. Hamburg: Verlag Dr. Kovac.

Further Reading

Amabile, T. and Kramer, S. (2011). *The progress principle*. Boston: Harvard Business Review Press.

Catmull, E. and Wallace, A. (2014). *Creativity, Inc: Overcoming the unseen forces that stand in the way of true inspiration*. New York, Random House.

Dougherty, D. and Hardy, C. (1996). Sustained product innovation in large, mature organizations: overcoming innovation-to-organization problems. *Academy of Management Journal* 39 (5): 1120–1153.

Kanter, R. M. (2006). Innovation: The classic traps. *Harvard Business Review* 84 (11): 73–83.

Loewe, P. and Dominiquini, J. (2006). Overcoming the barriers to effective innovation. *Strategy & Leadership* 34 (1): 24–31.

Wheelright, S. and Clark, K. D. (1992). *Revolutionizing Product Development*. New York: Free Press.

About the Authors

DR. KATHARINA HÖLZLE, MBA, is a tenured professor and holder of the Chair for Innovation Management and Entrepreneurship at the University of Potsdam in Germany. She is also an Associate Professor at the Hasso Plattner Institute and its School of Design Thinking in Potsdam. She is Editor in Chief of the *Creativity and Innovation Management Journal* since 2016. She has published various articles in the fields of innovative behavior, business model innovation, project management, and open innovation in leading scholarly and practitioner journals. She holds a PhD from the Technische Universität of Berlin, a diploma in business engineering from the University of Karlsruhe, and an MBA from the University of Georgia, Athens, Georgia. In her research, she looks into culture and organization of innovation, barriers to innovation, design thinking, innovation leadership, and digitalization.

DR. TANJA REIMER is a postdoctoral researcher at the University of Flensburg in Germany (Dr. Werner Jackstädt-Zentrum für Unternehmertum und Mittelstand). Her research interests are in the field of innovation/entrepreneurship, strategic leadership, and corporate governance. Dr. Reimer obtained her PhD from the Technical University of Berlin, where she also worked as a research assistant (2008–2011) at the Institute of Technology and Innovation Management. From 2012 to 2014 she was a member of the Center for Controlling and Management at the Otto Beisheim School of Management in Vallendar, Germany, and worked on projects about volatility and innovation topics in the field of management accounting.

DR. HANS GEORG GEMÜNDEN held the Chair of Technology and Innovation Management at Technische Universität in Berlin from 2000 to 2015 and is currently Professor of Project Management at the BI - Norwegian Business School. He has published several books and a great number of articles in the field of technology and innovation management, corporate management, organization, marketing, human resource management, and accounting. Professor Gemünden's specific areas of interest currently are the research of radical innovations and innovation networks, service innovations, particularly in the field of telemedicine, entrepreneurship, and strategic project management, as well as lead users and lead markets.

5

NEW SERVICE DEVELOPMENT FOR PROFESSIONAL SERVICES: TIME COMMITMENT AS THE SCARCEST RESOURCE

Floortje Blindenbach-Driessen

Organizing for Innovation LLC, Tyson's Corner, VA, USA

Introduction

Professional service organizations (such as law firms, hospitals, and consultancies) are organizations whose primary asset is a highly educated professional workforce and whose outputs are intangible services encoded with complex knowledge. As a result, these organizations differ significantly from manufacturing firms in their organizational structure, employee composition, and decision-making processes (Von Nordenflycht, 2010). The most valuable asset of professional service organizations is their pool of talented professionals. Given the pivotal role of these professionals in the day-to-day operations and innovation efforts, their time commitment is a scarce resource that significantly impacts the management and organization of new service development.

5.1 The Peculiarities of Innovating in Professional Services

Time Commitment as a Major Constraint

In theory, there are few differences between the development of a service and a product. It is difficult to differentiate between the two, and the process from idea to implementation is similar for both. In practice, however, there are significant differences. In this chapter, I argue that professional service organizations face a unique innovation constraint: i.e. time commitment. Therefore, they need to organize and embed the innovation process differently from the standard approach described in Chapter 1 of this volume. Specifically, professional service organizations require an innovation support function.

The Need for New Service Development

Companies seeking to thrive need to focus both on their current business and prepare for client demands of tomorrow. For most companies, this is a very challenging balancing act in which many ultimately fail, which explains why so few Fortune 500 companies remain on that list for more than 20 years.

In contrast, most of the American top 100 law firms have been in existence for over a century. The Big Four accounting firms were established more than a century ago. With the exception of a few notorious examples, such as Arthur Andersen and Dewey & LeBoeuf, professional services firms were beacons of stability in the past. Now the future of those firms is threatened by changes in technology.

The first, second, and third industrial revolutions, driven respectively by the power of steam, electricity, and information systems, did not bring much change to professional services. Computers introduced electronic record keeping, making the lives of professionals easier. However, computers did not significantly alter the way professionals interacted with their clients until recently. The World Economic Forum labels the current era the fourth industrial revolution, fueled by unprecedented technological change due to artificial intelligence and connectivity. This fourth industrial revolution is disrupting professional services. Take, for instance, the opportunities telehealth offers. Patients can now monitor their own health, make their own differential diagnoses, and interact with specialists anywhere on the globe. In short, the current technological opportunities not only make clients more proficient, they also alter how professionals and clients interact.

The pressure to improve and implement innovative models of professional services is mounting across industries. In healthcare, changes in regulations and demands for better care at lower costs are major driving forces. Accounting and financial services companies are being challenged by technology companies that serve clients faster, better, and cheaper. While demand for change is rising, professional service firms have been struggling to adopt effective and efficient practices to develop new services that address these challenges and opportunities. As McKinsey chairman Dominic Barton stated, "I think we're very good at telling our clients what they should do, what medicine to take. But we don't like taking it ourselves" (Knowledge@Wharton, 2015).

The Key Role of Professionals in the Innovation Process

In professional services, the success of new service development efforts depends on the involvement of an expert professional to champion the innovation endeavor. This key role of professionals as innovation champions – as drivers of their innovation projects – is confirmed in several research studies (Anand et al., 2007; Blindenbach-Driessen and van den Ende, 2010). There are three main reasons for this (see also Figure 5.1).

Diversity of Expertise

Professional services organizations are conglomerates of highly specialized experts. Because of the deep expertise required for new service development, it is almost impossible to adequately staff a dedicated, separate innovation unit. The high cost of service professionals; the need for continually updated, state-of-the-art knowledge (generated by practicing the profession); and the breadth and depth of the expertise domains that need to be covered make such dedicated innovation unit staff choices impracticable.

Lack of Scalability

Most professionals service only a few clients. For that reason, generating substantial returns on investment from any new service is challenging. Consequently, it is important to keep development costs down. Since man-hours are often the largest cost in

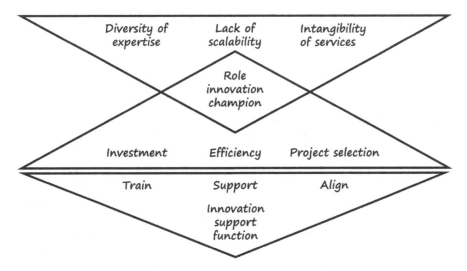

Figure 5.1: The key role of innovation champions in professional services.

new service projects, it is important to execute development projects in a timely and efficient manner to minimize the overall investment and ensure that a return can be generated, in spite of the limited scalability.

Intangibility of Services

Professionals deliver intangible services encoded with complex knowledge. This makes it essential for professionals to identify, develop, and implement new services themselves, because it is difficult to transfer this (often tacit) knowledge to others.

Vendors certainly play an important role in the innovation process of professional service organizations. Their products can help providers work more effectively and efficiently. Yet, given the complexity of professional services, even such prepackaged innovative solutions still leave professionals with the task of incorporating these products and technologies into their practices and fitting them into their workflows. As a result, even when technology can be purchased, it requires the time of a professional to turn it into a service offering that clients will value.

In summary, opportunities to innovate are abundant, but professional service providers need to play a pivotal role in the new service development process. Given the challenges just laid out, service professionals are the bottleneck for bringing innovative ideas into practice. Simply stated, most professionals are too busy providing today's services to be able to focus on developing tomorrow's services as innovation champions.

In other words, the organizational context – defined by the diversity of expertise, lack of scalability, and intangibility of services of the professional services – puts top-down pressure on the role of innovation champions. To change the game for their organization or profession, they will have to roll up their sleeves (see Figure 5.1).

5.2 Understanding Time as an Innovation Constraint in Professional Services

Time devoted to new service development does not generate direct revenues, but it does impose opportunity costs. As such, many innovation champions in professional services are under pressure to engage in new service development efforts and make up for the invested time by being more productive in the hours they dedicate to day-to-day operations. This scenario is clearly not sustainable (Kornacki and Silversin, 2015).

Usually when time is discussed in the new product development literature, it concerns time to market – that is, how fast an organization can transform ideas into practical solutions. In the context of this chapter, time constraints relate to the limits on time commitment professionals encounter when engaging in new service development activities.

Certainly, time is a scarce resource anywhere, and time spent on new service development activities never generates immediate revenue. However, time commitment poses special challenges in professional services, because opportunity costs need to be taken into account. Generating revenue and billing hours are key performance indicators for most professionals. While time is money, decision making regarding time and budget allocation in professional services is very different from that in the manufacturing sector. Optimizing for limited available funds is a top-down decision, made by those who have budget ownership and accountability. Optimizing for scarcely available time is a bottom-up decision made by individuals, especially in professional services, where individuals have autonomy over their own actions.

To overcome this time constraint, I start by addressing three intertwined issues:

1. *Investment.* How to stimulate busy professionals to take on dual roles and invest time in delivering today's and tomorrow's revenues successfully and sustainably
2. *Efficiency.* How to develop new services in the most efficient and timely fashion in professional service organizations
3. *Project selection.* How to ensure professionals work on the most promising projects only, eliminate less promising initiatives in a timely manner, and remain aligned with the organization's strategy

In other words, innovation champions efforts face pressure from the bottom up, when investment, efficiency, and project selection are not properly addressed (see Figure 5.1).

Time Investment

It seems paradoxical that in order to alleviate the time-commitment constraint, busy professionals have to invest time and develop new services themselves. Getting professionals to engage in new service development will happen only when there is proof that this time investment actually pays off – in other words, that the rewards are worth the effort and risk both for the innovation champion and the organization.

Historically, when professionals engaged in research or development endeavors, the benefits were for the profession as a whole (e.g. research papers) and the individual (e.g. personal development and reputation). These research projects were funded by various sources, with no clear expectations of a return. However, new service development is geared toward advancing the organization by offering its clients higher-value services. This, in turn, creates a shift in the risk and reward balance from the individual to the organization.

The FISHstep case shows how one legal service professional was able to successfully launch a new service offering. The case illustrates that considerable personal risks were incurred, and substantial investment of personal time was required.

FISHstep

Phyllis Kristal, principal at Fish & Richardson P.C., developed FISHstep – a program to help start-up companies prepare and file patent applications with deferred billing arrangements in exchange for an equity stake.

What led Kristal to initiate FISHstep? After years of hard work, Kristal achieved her ambition and became principal. Then she wondered, "What

(continued)

next?" The more time Kristal spent pondering this question, the more certain she became that it was time to change her way of doing business. There were too many entrepreneurs out there that needed her help yet could not afford her services.

Engaging with the local Washington, DC, entrepreneurial community confirmed her observation. There was indeed a large need among start-up firms for legal advice related to intellectual property. Depending on the complexity of the matter, legal fees typically ranged anywhere between $10,000 and $100,000; for international patents, they could rise even higher. Since most start-ups were cash-constrained, obtaining intellectual property protection represented a daunting hurdle for entrepreneurs eager to move forward.

Kristal's supervisor was initially not too enthusiastic about her proposal to address the needs of the local cash-strapped entrepreneurial community. Yet he did not stop her from exploring the opportunity further.

More than a year after Kristal started her adventure, FISHstep was launched. Kristal is the first to admit that she would never have envisioned the current shape and format of this service. What remained from the original proposal was the goal of helping cash-strapped entrepreneurs protect their intellectual property while creating a new revenue stream for Fish & Richardson.

Clearly, Kristal was the driver behind the FISHstep initiative. Less evident is that most of the effort, especially during the proposal phase, was expended outside her professional service hours. In other words, Kristal made a significant personal time investment – time over which the company has no control and for which it provides no payment.

Kristal spent a lot of time acquainting herself with how to write the business case for the initiative. She had not yet been in a leadership position long enough to have experience with the business and management side of running a law firm. Training and guidance in this area could have saved Kristal a lot of time.

While Kristal was successful, few organizations take into account that most new service initiatives fail and don't deliver any tangible results. Simply encouraging participation in new service development activities is thus insufficient to stimulate professionals to invest personal time in these activities.

Failure – or, more accurately, "finding dead ends" – is an intrinsic part of the innovation process. Few organizations cope well with apparent failure. Failure is typically blamed on the team or even more specifically on the team leader. That is problematic.

First, blaming failure on the individual makes it even riskier for employees to stick out their necks and participate in innovation efforts. After all, the chance of success in innovation is small. If failure is blamed on the innovator personally, the consequences of failure will be detrimental to the person's career. This turns investing time in innovation efforts into a career killer instead of a career advancer.

Second, forces beyond the individual leading the innovation effort affect the outcome of a project. The market or technology may not be ready, or the required problem-benefit balance may not exist. In other words, there are often issues beyond the scope of control of anyone involved. Therefore, teams should be lauded for finding out quickly that the opportunity is not worth pursuing further, as this saves the organization time and money while creating room for investments in other, more promising endeavors to advance.

To conclude, to motivate professionals to take on dual roles and invest time in both day-to-day and innovation activities, they need to be helped with the execution of their innovation projects to ensure a return of investment from innovation activities. Time committed to new service development should be spent well and increase the likelihood of success of the project. As most initiatives will not be successful, incentives that encourage participation only are insufficient. With too many initiatives in the pipeline, all efforts are doomed to fail. Instead, incentives should aim to make professionals follow best practices in service development. Best practices are those that speed up execution, help identify and stop less promising endeavors, and only advance the most promising initiatives. At the end of this chapter, I discuss how this can be accomplished with the adaptation of an innovation support function.

Efficiency

Bringing structure to innovation activities is paramount to ensure efficient and effective execution. Innovating in an ad hoc manner (while still common in the professionals services industry [Leiponen, 2006]) is not an effective or efficient way to innovate (Barczak et al., 2009).

Among other factors, an appropriate innovation structure is needed to ensure that the scarcest resource of all – the time commitment of professional service providers – is spent wisely and actually delivers results. This is not a given, because the decisions to commit time are made by individuals, not at the organizational level. Without some overarching structure, there is no way to ensure that the sum is greater than its parts.

The importance of creating an appropriate innovation structure can be illustrated in the healthcare domain. A survey among 121 healthcare providers, including 83 hospitals (as part of the 2015 Institute for Healthcare Improvement annual conference session on innovation management; Trimble et al., 2015) shows that 39% of the participants stated that no innovation infrastructure existed in their organization, and only 12% stated that they had access to a dedicated innovation lab. Given existing and developing healthcare challenges and the ever-increasing demands on clinicians' time, it is surprising how few healthcare organizations have a structured new service development process and structure in place.

It is possible that the lack of structure is due to a persistent myth that structuring an innovation process (such as new service development) limits creativity. Because professionals are used to defining and following their own processes, following a structured innovation process might be challenging. Or perhaps, bringing structure to the process is deemed expensive. Whatever the reasons, having a structured approach is a more effective and efficient way to transform ideas into reality (Barczak et al., 2009).

The George Washington University Telemedicine case illustrates how structure and guidance can help advance new service development in a simple and effective way. The program participants (all full-time working professionals) developed proposals and testable concepts in six weeks. Each participant spent on average three hours per week on the program. In comparison, in most professional service organizations, it takes six to eight months to run an idea up the management chain and 40 to 80 hours to develop a detailed proposal. In other words, by using a structured approach, more was accomplished in less time and resulted in better outcomes.

George Washington University Telemedicine Course

In July 2016, 14 participants started a six-week online Innovations in Telemedicine summer course, facilitated by an online new service training and support platform. The participants were all busy professionals; four were practicing clinicians.

In the first assignment, participants learned how to brainstorm, and each submitted 10 or more telemedicine ideas. This assignment took less than 10 minutes to complete. Next, participants were tasked with initiating projects around predefined telemedicine needs. The software matched each project with ideas and potentially interested team members.

This project initiation and team formation phase took just one week. During this phase, six projects were initiated, with 36 invitations sent to the 14 participants. As a result, most participants had multiple projects to choose from. Within a week, everyone joined a team, with each team consisting of at least three team members with different backgrounds (engineering, healthcare, health policy, management). These diverse teams would later be characterized by several participants as the "best team I ever worked in."

In the next five weeks, participants received weekly assignments that addressed several topics, from end users, stakeholders, value propositions, to business models and others. The training modules explained the topics. The assignments enabled teams to apply the concepts to their project, identify associated uncertainties, and explicate their assumptions. Together, the assignments formed the core of the teams' proposals. Because topics were taught in complementary fashion, each team was able to present a testable new service concept.

Weekly progress reports from the online learning system and feedback from coaches kept the teams on task. The progress reports enabled teams and coaches to identify relative weak areas that needed strengthening. By the end of the course, four testable concepts were presented, with each concept substantiated by data.

Streamlining the ideation process saved participants time. Aligned tasks and motivated team members helped the teams to be successful in their innovation endeavors.

The telemedicine case shows that by providing structure, training, and coaching, it is possible to guide busy professionals through the new service development process and help them be effective and efficient in their innovation endeavors.

The training, support, and assignments that were part of the system taught the teams how to generate ideas, vet ideas, and validate their own solutions. The structured approach – the exercises that enabled teams to focus on the most relevant topics; the feedback that enabled prioritization of efforts on the weakest and most uncertain aspects; the methodology that forced teams to provide proof for the assumptions underlying their new service concepts – ensured that very little time was wasted. As a result, all the professionals were enabled to combine ideation activities with their full-time jobs.

Two of the four teams realized that pursuing their ideas beyond these six weeks was not worth their time, a finding that shows that when teams are given the opportunity, they are able to evaluate their own progress and likelihood of being successful and are capable of timely stopping unpromising endeavors.

Without a structured approach, bottlenecks that significantly frustrate and hinder the progress of innovation projects are not always recognized for two reasons: (1) because these organizations don't keep track, they don't have the data to identify and address the inefficiencies in their innovation process; and (2) without structure, organizations will not be able to recognize the pattern of failure that may exist or be able to address the cause. An example illustrates this dynamic: In one of the intrapreneurial programs I taught, all the teams faltered about one year into the program. Concurrently, most team leads left the organization, each of them providing a reason for their departure unrelated to their project (e.g. moving because of a spouse's job, moving back to the home country, taking on another job opportunity, etc.). Yet because I was mentoring the teams, I knew that the intellectual property policy of the organization had been tremendously frustrating and hindered the teams' ability to attract collaborators and outside capital. As a result, their promising projects were stuck. Given their ambitions, these talented innovators were not going to sit around and waste their time in an organization that did not truly support their innovation efforts. Had their projects not been frustrated, they probably would have made different personal and career choices. In the absence of success, the organization canceled the intrapreneurial program and failed to address the issues that caused the participating teams to falter.

The innovation support function, as I explain later, is an effective, low-cost solution to execute new service development efficiently in professional service organizations.

Project Selection

To sustain a pipeline of new service development initiatives, rigorous vetting is required so that only the most promising projects are fully supported. Deciding what the most promising projects are in an unbiased and objective manner is a major challenge in any organization, but especially in professional services ones due to typically flat hierarchies and the fact that there are as many specialty areas as there are leaders.

How can these organizations validate and vet projects to ensure that the scarce available resources to execute innovation endeavors are spent only on the most promising projects? The Innovation Institute case illustrates how challenging project selection can be in a professional service organization.

The Innovation Institute

A hospital received a large grant to improve the surgical experience of pediatric patients. It used these funds to create a new innovation institute.

The moment the initiative was announced, proposals for projects started pouring in. While funding seemed abundant, it clearly was impossible to support all these efforts. Would the strategic guidelines on which the institute was founded be sufficient to effectively select excellent projects and weed out mediocre proposals?

The leaders of the institute, five physicians, convened in the meeting room early on a Friday morning to review the submitted proposals. Clearly, each team had put in substantial time and effort to create its proposal. As a result, in front of the leaders was a large stack with 40 proposals, each 10 pages long with many appendices. On average, there were 10 proposals for each of the four strategic goals and two projects from each principal investigator. Even the newly hired principal investigator had submitted a proposal, a novel way to address brain cancer by making it possible to biopsy the tumors.

The five physicians looked at each other. Everyone had read at least 16 proposals. All were of excellent quality. They were by now well aware that selecting a few projects to fund among these 40 was going to be an impossible task.

The projects covered topics from anesthesia, biopsies, cancer diagnostics, devices compatible with magnetic resonance imaging, and pain management programs, to using DNA sequencing for personalized treatments. While selected for their expertise, none of the committee members had the knowledge to assess the tremendously broad set of opportunities in front of them.

Each proposal came from the hospital's expert in the area. What could the committee members challenge these experts on in their proposals, except for obvious flaws in methodology, which seemed to be absent?

To make matters worse, *not* funding their proposals would mean these investigators would not have any funds to sustain their research endeavors. Without funding from the institute, these principal investigators would have to go back to 100% clinical work, which was not an ideal outcome as many had been eager to join the hospital because of the research opportunities available.

Yet the pile of proposals exceeded the year's budget nearly twice over.

After a long day of discussing the proposals over and over again, it was decided to fund 25 of the 40 projects. There was no way to justify prioritizing one project that improved the life expectancy of children with a rare brain cancer over another project that promised to improve the comfort of thousands of children undergoing anesthesia. All of these projects sought to improve the surgical experience of pediatric patients.

To bring the funds available in line with the funds needed to support these 25 projects, all investigators were asked to do more with less. The expenses were spread over multiple years. This tactic continued until the institute ran out of money and no funds were left to support any of its projects.

The result? After five years of hard work, none of the projects had been able to make significant progress. The only tangible results were several

> publications and awards – rewards that advanced the profession and individuals' careers. However, for the organization and its patients, these results had no benefit. None of the teams had been adequately funded to implement results in practice, let alone to create a return on investment for the organization.

As demonstrated by the Innovation Institute case, without effective ways to select projects, too many projects remain in the pipeline, making new service development a very frustrating process for everyone involved. No project will have sufficient funding to accomplish anything.

In most organizations, a selection committee has the authority and the ability to select and prioritize innovation projects. However, because of the diversity in expertise and the intangibility of the service provided, even the most accomplished and senior professionals lack the insights to vet projects that cover the expertise and domains of all experts in the organization. In addition, while such committees may have a say in how funds are allocated, they typically don't have the authority to dictate how each professional should allocate their time.

The Innovations in Telemedicine course discussed earlier shows that teams can stop unfruitful endeavors in a timely manner. "Timely," in this context, means not giving up too early or continuing too long. It is in the interest of the innovation champion to stop unpromising initiatives in a timely way, due to the opportunity costs involved. Clearly, stopping unfruitful endeavors is important to prevent clogging of the innovation pipeline. With just a few of the most promising projects in the pipeline, these projects can receive full support and be executed swiftly. Simply relying on self-selection, as showcased in the telemedicine case, however, may not be sufficient. I discuss later in this chapter how the innovation support function can further facilitate project selection.

5.3 Resolving Time as an Innovation Constraint in Professional Services: The Innovation Support Function

Having addressed the three intertwined issues of investment, efficiency, and project selection, it is time to propose a solution that alleviates the time constraint in professional service organizations.

In the *standard approach to new product development* (see Figure 5.2), management is responsible for defining the strategy. Innovation units are tasked with identifying opportunities and developing an organization's innovation activities to execute upon this strategy. The unit is held accountable for the number of innovation projects in the pipeline, the number of new services introduced in the market, and the success of these new services in terms of revenue and profit. The market introduction and

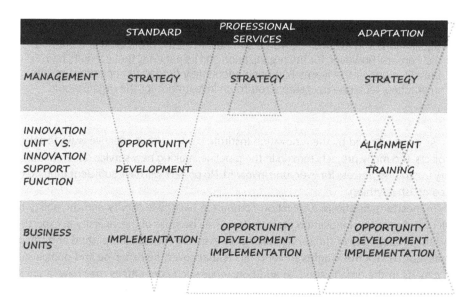

	STANDARD	PROFESSIONAL SERVICES	ADAPTATION
MANAGEMENT	STRATEGY	STRATEGY	STRATEGY
INNOVATION UNIT VS. INNOVATION SUPPORT FUNCTION	OPPORTUNITY DEVELOPMENT		ALIGNMENT TRAINING
BUSINESS UNITS	IMPLEMENTATION	OPPORTUNITY DEVELOPMENT IMPLEMENTATION	OPPORTUNITY DEVELOPMENT IMPLEMENTATION

Figure 5.2: The standard approach versus the adaptation.

outcomes are often responsibilities shared with the business unit delivering these new services. In other words, an innovation unit executes the innovation process and has the budget, staff, capabilities, and expertise needed to transform ideas into practical applications. Needless to say, setting up such an innovation unit is a costly endeavor due to employee costs, among others. Over time, the results of the innovation efforts should create sufficient return on investment to cover these costs.

In *professional services*, management also defines the strategy. However, the standard model to execute on this strategy does not work, because in service firms in general, having an innovation unit in general does not generate more revenues as it does in manufacturing firms (Blindenbach-Driessen and van den Ende, 2014). This lack of result may explain why few service firms have an innovation or research and development unit.

Without an innovation unit, identifying opportunities and acting on them is often left to the business unit or the professionals within the business unit. Without any accountability for development activities, there is a void between the strategic intent of management and the new service development activities that are initiated by professionals and that take place throughout the organization. This was the case for Kristal who developed FISHstep.

The *adaptation* of the standard innovation process model proposed here includes the following: Instead of having an innovation unit execute innovation activities on behalf of the organization or having no such unit, professional service firms should implement an innovation support function that is responsible for providing support, training, and guidance to the new service development process. It is a support function, because the innovation activities are executed by professionals, which (as discussed earlier) is key to the success of these endeavors.

To ensure efficient and effective execution of new service development activities by these innovation champions, the innovation support function should provide training and coaching. As showcased by the Innovations in Telemedicine course, such training can also help with project selection and is effective in eliminating the least promising endeavors.

Let's contrast responsibilities of the innovation support function with those of a traditional innovation unit. Instead of being accountable for execution, the innovation support function can be held accountable for the courses taught, number of professionals engaged, survival rates or projects, and life span of unsuccessful efforts. Other metrics that are effective in keeping track of the effectiveness and efficiency of the new service development efforts are those that measure the performance of the training program. That is, does the training program provide teams adequate insight in the value and chance of success of the project they are pursuing? Does it help teams focus on the critical activities that support go/no-go decisions? By assessing the results of the training activities in terms of self-selection and average project duration, the innovation unit can support and be held accountable for preserving the scarcest resource in professional service organizations, professional time commitment to new service development activities.

Alleviating the Time Constraint

To innovate successfully, professional service organizations need to engage their busy professionals in the innovation process. Having someone else innovate on their behalf is not effective, because professional services are complex and labor intensive and involve tacit knowledge and expertise. It is difficult to transfer state-of-the-art frontline knowledge and expertise to an innovation unit and have innovation professionals develop novel new services (Leiponen, 2006). Professional services are typically not very scalable either, as they are highly dependent on the service provider. Because of these considerations, it is more practical and economical to engage the workforce in new service development activities than to have a dedicated innovation unit execute these activities (Blindenbach-Driessen and van den Ende 2006, 2014). However, this engagement creates significant constraints on the time commitment of professionals who step forward as innovation champions.

These professionals, who are not skilled or familiar with innovation activities, need to be supported in the innovation task. They need to be able to evaluate which opportunities are worth investing personal time in. These professionals, who are not skilled or familiar with innovation activities, need to be supported in the innovation task. They need to be able to evaluate which opportunities are worth investing personal time in. Providing organizational support to all innovation endeavors brought up in the organization is not feasible or sustainable. There needs to be some form of selection. Putting a lot of money into funding the innovation process is not the solution because, among other reasons, it will be very challenging to recoup these investments due to the limited scalability addressed earlier.

To reduce the burden of time constraints and facilitate efficient and effective execution of new service development projects, the innovation support function must provide

GETTING STARTED	INNOVATION SUPPORT FUNCTION ROLE	IMPACT ON TIME CONSTRAINT ISSUES
1. ARTICULATE THE STRATEGIC GOALS OF THE ORGANIZATION TOGETHER WITH YOUR PROFESSIONALS (MANAGEMENT, BUSINESS UNITS)	ALIGN	INVESTMENT, PROJECT SELECTION
2. BUILD THE INNOVATION SUPPORT FUNCTION TO SUPPORT THE NEW SERVICE DEVELOPMENT PROCESS (INNOVATION SUPPORT FUNCTION)	TRAIN, SUPPORT, ALIGN	INVESTMENT, EFFICIENCY
3. DEFINE THE PROCESS YOUR PROFESSIONALS MUST FOLLOW TO TRANSFORM IDEAS INTO REALITY (INNOVATION SUPPORT FUNCTION)	TRAIN, SUPPORT, ALIGN	EFFICIENCY, PROJECT SELECTION
4. TRACK AND TRACE THE PERFORMANCE OF THESE NEW SERVICE DEVELOPMENT ACTIVITIES (INNOVATION SUPPORT FUNCTION)	SUPPORT, ALIGN	INVESTMENT, PROJECT SELECTION
5. INCENTIVIZE DESIRED BEHAVIOR (MANAGEMENT, BUSINESS UNITS)	ALIGN	INVESTMENT

Figure 5.3: Steps to create an innovation support function.

structure to the new service development process through alignment and training that delivers:

- Guidance as to which projects to pursue
- Insights that enable teams to self-select more from less promising endeavors
- Actionable data that enables management to identify and prioritize the most promising projects

Getting Started

The innovation support function enables professional service organizations to explore many opportunities yet leaves the organization with just a few, fully vetted projects to support in the more expensive and time-consuming development and implementation phases of the new service development process.

The next five steps will help professional service organizations build their innovation support function. (See Figure 5.3.)

Step 1: Articulate the strategic goals of the organization together with your professionals.

When management – in collaboration with business units – articulates the strategic goals, the objectives of the new service development program become clear. This clarity will motivate professionals to know in which initiatives it will be worthwhile to invest personal time. Articulating the strategic goals also contributes to project selection, as it provides guidance as to which areas to focus on. A law firm shouldn't be interested in 100 projects executed by each of its 100 partners that cover 100 different directions. Instead, it is more valuable for the firm and its clients to gear the innovation efforts toward the same objective, such as being recognized as the leader in Brexit services. Because the firm focuses innovation efforts, interested partners can together figure out how to best help clients who struggle with Brexit-related questions. Such an endeavor, if successful, will benefit all partners, including those not involved in the particular initiative because new services bring in new clients, enable the organization to retain top talent, and increase the innovation capabilities of the organization as a whole.

From Kornacki and Silversin's (2015) work with hospitals, it is clear that telling professionals what to develop rarely works. Quite the contrary, it often results in friction and behavior that undermines the organization's goals. Instead, having physicians and management formulate the strategic mission together creates commitment.

The role of the innovation support function is to facilitate this process of establishing strategic goals by, for example, organizing a strategy alignment workshop. Another role is to make sure that all innovation champions are aware of these strategic goals and can articulate how their projects contribute to achieving them.

Step 2: Build the innovation support function to support the new service development process.

Once the strategic goals are defined, it is clear that someone in the organization needs to orchestrate the process of achieving these goals. As explained earlier, the innovation support function should not be involved in the execution of innovation activities. Instead, it focuses on creating alignment, building support, providing the necessary training to enable the workforce to innovate, and reporting on the progress of the new service development activities.

In this respect, professional service organizations can learn a lot from the entrepreneurial community. No one tells entrepreneurs to start or quit their start-up or how much personal time to invest. Intrinsic motivation drives their behavior. Training programs such as I-Corps provide budding entrepreneurs insight in the efforts necessary to translate their idea into a company (https://www.nsf.gov/news/special_reports/i-corps/). Such accelerators are effective in terms of time to market and profitability if they provide training, connections, and support for start-ups. The innovation support function should take on the same role as accelerator programs and facilitate the new service development process within the walls of a professional service organization.

The innovation support function is thus truly the support function of the new service development process.

Step 3: Define the process professionals must follow to transform ideas into reality.

The innovation process – from idea generation, development, and implementation to diffusion – is a value chain, with the weakest link determining the overall outcome. In other words, if the organization excels at idea generation but is weak in implementation, the excellence in idea generation is not going to benefit the organization as long as this is not accompanied by the ability to also implement these innovations.

To save time, professionals need to know what process to follow and what expectations there are when they attempt to transform their ideas to practice. The telemedicine example shows how training can be used to provide structure and advance new service development activities efficiently. This example also shows that building feedback mechanisms into the education program enables teams to self-identify and self-select the opportunities that are worth the investment for them and their organization.

The innovation support function is not only responsible for creating, supporting, guiding, and overseeing the innovation process. It is also responsible for training those who partake in this process and providing coaching and other support to advance promising projects. In line with this responsibility is the task to identify and alleviate organizational bottlenecks that hinder innovation projects' progress and that may cause professionals to spend more time on new service development than is strictly necessary.

Step 4: Track and trace the performance of the new service development activities.

New service development activities are to sustain the future revenue stream and profitability of the professional service organization. The innovation support function should develop metrics that show whether the organization is on track. That is, the metrics should show that the ongoing projects enable the organization to reach its strategic goals. Since the innovation support function is not involved in the execution of new service projects, it cannot be held accountable for the success of individual projects.

More suitable metrics to keep track of are therefore related to ensuring that:

- Sufficient projects are initiated;
- Unsuccessful endeavors are stopped in a timely manner;
- Fully supported projects are executed swiftly; and
- The portfolio of innovation activities is sustainable and enables the organization to achieve its strategic goals.

Feedback on project progress, work quality, and team effort will enable teams to compare their projects and team against the pool of projects. Such feedback, as the Innovation in Telemedicine example, makes it possible for teams to self-select and quit mediocre innovation efforts with limited chance of success in a timely manner.

However, just relying on self-selection is not sufficient. Senior management still needs to make a selection among the good and great projects that remain in the pipeline and select a portfolio of projects that is aligned with the organization's strategic goals. By tracking the progress, team effort, and learning of each team in the pipeline, it is possible to compare teams with each other and identify the teams with the highest likelihood of success. These objective metrics make it possible for management to make evidence-based and data-driven decisions, instead of opining about what are potentially good ideas and projects.

Step 5: Incentivize desired behavior.

Although it is important, new service development is rarely as urgent as the daily activities that occupy professionals. Without incentives, professionals will delay or even forget to invest time in new service development activities. With a process, metrics, and the innovation support function in place, incentives can be used to stimulate desired behavior. These incentives should aim to achieve the following:

- Stimulate personal time investment in innovation initiatives.
- Encourage alignment of the innovation activities with the organization's strategy.
- Make quitting of unpromising endeavors in a timely fashion as important as pursuing success.

- Capture lessons learned of failed attempts, as these are often breeding grounds for future successes.
- Ensure that projects are executed as swiftly as possible when given support.
- Promote sharing of the findings and results of successful initiatives with others in the organization to ensure that each successful innovation endeavor delivers a maximum return on investment for the organization and creates benefits for the organization as a whole, not just for the involved professionals.
- Make receiving support for a new service development project a received privilege, awarded to the most talented and dedicated teams only.

By following these five steps, a professional service organization should be able to build an innovation support function that alleviates the time constraint of professionals involved in the innovation process. Successful outcomes motivate professionals to participate. Training and support make it possible to do so. A structured process creates alignment and efficiencies. Metrics enable self-selection and facilitate evidence-based decision making when it comes to selecting and supporting new service development project teams with the highest likelihood of success. This way, even professional service organizations – despite the diversity of expertise, lack of scalability, and the intangibility of their services – are able to bring their ideas to practice in a sustainable and profitable manner.

With an innovation support function in place, professional service firms can also start reaching for more audacious goals. The next step could be productizing the low end of their service offerings, as Legal Zoom, Littler, and Minute Clinics are currently capitalizing on. This low end represents a sizable market share that leading professional service providers of today will permanently lose if they fail to innovate and develop new service offerings.

5.4 Conclusion

The main assets of professional service organizations are their professionals. Their time commitment is the scarcest resource in these organizations. To innovate, professional service organizations will have to commit some of this time to activities that generate new revenue and address future client needs. These innovation projects need to be championed by professionals to be successful. An innovation unit that executes projects on behalf of service professionals will be unable to deliver the desired results because it will lack the critical insights that only service professionals themselves possess, such as expertise diversity, full understanding of intangibility, and recognition of difficulty with scalability of professional services. That is, an innovation unit can create innovative project solutions, but research has shown that the projects do not result in new revenue or additional profits. An innovation support function is therefore a more effective way to assist innovation champions in their dual roles – serving today's and tomorrow's clients. The innovation support function can ensure that innovation projects are worthwhile investments – from both a personal and an organizational perspective; that the innovation process itself is efficient and delivers results; and that performance data is available to select and prioritize the most promising innovation projects. That way, the scarcest resource of professional service organizations – time commitment of their professionals – is invested in the most promising projects only and delivers a maximum return when it comes to innovation and new service development.

References

Anand, N., Gardner, H. K., and Morris, T. (2007). Knowledge-based innovation: Emergence and embedding of new practice areas in management consulting firms. *Academy of Management Journal* 50 (2): 406–428.

Barczak, G., Griffin, A., and Kahn, K. B. (2009). Perspective: Trends and drivers of success in NPD practices: Results of the 2003 PDMA best practices study. *Journal of Product Innovation Management* 26 (1): 3–23.

Blindenbach-Driessen, F. and Van den Ende, J (2006). Innovation in project-based firms: The context dependency of success factors. *Research Policy* 35: 545–561.

Blindenbach-Driessen, F. and Van Den Ende, J. (2010). Innovation management practices compared: The example of project-based firms. *Journal of Product Innovation Management* 27 (5): 705–724.

Blindenbach-Driessen, F. and Van Den Ende, J. (2014). The locus of innovation: The effect of a separate innovation unit on exploration, exploitation, and ambidexterity in manufacturing and service firms. *Journal of Product Innovation Management* 31 (5): 1089–1105.

Knowledge@Wharton.   http://knowledge.wharton.upenn.edu/article/mckinseys-dominic-barton-on-leadership-and-his-three-tries-to-make-partner,   September   9, 2015.

Kornacki, M. J. and Silversin, J (2015). *Aligning physician-organization expectations to transform ptient care*. Chicago, IL: Foundation of the American College of Healthcare Executives.

Leiponen, A. (2006). Managing knowledge for innovation: The case of business-to-business services. *Journal of Product Innovation Management* 23: 238–258.

Trimble, C. et al. (2015). Managing innovation in healthcare organizations. Institute for Healthcare Improvement, 27th Annual National Forum, 6–9 December 2015, Orlando, FL, Sessions D6 and E6.

Von Nordenflycht, A. (2010). What is a professional service firm? Toward a theory and taxonomy of knowledge-intensive firms. *Academy of Management Review* 35 (1): 155–174.

About the Author

DR. FLOORTJE BLINDENBACH-DRIESSEN is the Founder of Organizing4Innovation LLC, a company that offers the support and tools professional service organizations need to succeed in their innovation endeavors.

She has assisted professionals with their innovation efforts in engineering firms, system integrators, information technology firms, consultancies, law firms, research centers, healthcare, and entrepreneurship programs. Dr. Blindenbach-Driessen championed many innovation projects while working for the Fluor Corporation and for the Children's National Health System in Washington, DC. She teaches courses related to innovation management and new business development for executive education programs around the globe. Her research focuses on the innovation challenges and opportunities in the professional services and has appeared in *Research Policy, IEEE Transactions on Engineering Management,* the *Journal of Medical Practice Management,* and the *Journal of Product Innovation Management.*

6

BRIDGING COMMUNICATION GAPS IN VIRTUAL TEAMS

Donovan Hardenbrook

Littelfuse, Chicago, IL, USA

Teresa Jurgens-Kowal

Global NP Solutions, Houston, TX, USA

Introduction

New product development (NPD) projects are typically performed by colocated teams that easily communicate and share knowledge via informal means. Lean principles have evolved over time to reduce waste and, in the case of NPD, as shown in Table 6.1, to create reusable knowledge (Ward and Sobek, 2014). Lean NPD uses the best resources, regardless of geographical location, to optimize product development cycles while generating new, reusable, and transferrable knowledge. Yet capturing such tacit knowledge has typically been notoriously difficult for virtual teams,[1] which can diminish the benefits brought to the organization by team members with richly diverse skills contributing to the team's work from various worldwide perspectives. Vital, day-to-day communications are in themselves more challenging when these virtual team members are scattered in different offices across geographical boundaries and various time zones.

---

[1] Note that we use the term "virtual team" to represent NPD teams that are physically separated for the duration of the project. Others may use terms such as "dispersed teams," "global teams," "distributed organization," "virtual work groups," "globally distributed teams," or "cross-geographic teams" to indicate distance between team members and lack of face-to-face (F2F) contact within such teams. We reserve "dispersion" as a specific term describing the numbers of and distance between individual and groups of team members. However, "virtual team" is meant to represent globally dispersed team members working on a shared goal whose communication is primarily through technologically mediated channels and lacks F2F interactions.

Table 6.1: A comparison of standard and lean NPD.

Organizational structure	Standard NPD	Lean NPD
Environment	Stable conditions	Uncertain environment
	Long cycle time	Reduced cycle time
Practices	Stepwise product improvements	Customer-centric continuous improvements
	Multiple iterations	Process waste reductions
Teams and Leadership	Colocated teams	Virtual teams
	Specialized skill sets ("I-shaped" people)	Generalized/specialized skill sets ("T-shaped" people)
	Limited working hours	Anytime, anywhere connectivity
Outcomes	High development cost	Cost efficient product development
	Project-specific data	Reusable, shareable knowledge

Companies can reduce long cycle times and high development costs by taking advantage of global assets, such as reusable and repeatable knowledge of customers, markets, and technologies. Utilizing the concepts of lean NPD to improve virtual team communications can lead to increased innovation throughput and quality. In this chapter, we focus on bridging the inherent communication gaps that can plague virtual teams and reduce their overall innovation effectiveness. We describe a virtual team model (VTM) with five key elements[2] that allow a dispersed team to benefit from lean principles in creating reusable knowledge and, with implementation, make the virtual team even more competitive than traditional, colocated product development teams. Crucial to effective NPD is the capture and dissemination of innovation knowledge that is both process and product specific. Communication drives the creation of reusable, shareable knowledge.

6.1 A Lean Team Is Virtual in NPD

Traditional innovation utilizes a waterfall process implemented by a colocated, cross-functional team. In fact, the colocation of teams working on breakthrough innovations is often encouraged, suggesting that such a structure can lead to higher productivity. Yet colocation of team members may not be feasible or desirable due to cost factors and other organizational constraints. For example, product development assignments in a matrix structure represent only a fraction of a team member's workload. Furthermore, staff may be restricted geographically due to work, family, or health concerns. Thus, NPD efforts are often forced to utilize team members in different

[2]The full VTM model includes 16 operational practices to support the five key elements. Due to limited space in this chapter, we address several crucial practices to build communication among dispersed innovation team members. The VTM model is presented in full in Jurgens-Kowal (2016). Please contact her for a full description of the model and implementation guidelines.

locations. Communication is primarily via digital media with little, if any, face-to-face (F2F) contact among team members. This is what we call a *virtual team*.

In the realm of NPD, virtual teams reflect a direct implementation of lean principles. The core concept of lean manufacturing is to reduce waste and improve quality. Lean NPD reduces waste by improving knowledge sharing among and between team members to speed up cycle time as nascent ideas are converted to commercial realities. Several aspects of teamwork either help or hinder the ability of an NPD team to accomplish these goals, including how the team is formed, how it communicates, what operating protocols it follows, how knowledge is captured and shared, and which leadership styles guide and frame the team's progress toward its objectives. A virtual team embodies the lean principles, as shown in Table 6.1. Applying the VTM framework allows organizations to overcome assumed barriers introduced by dispersion and to capture the benefits of lean NPD.

6.2 The Basics of Virtual Teams

Half of all virtual teams fail to meet their goals (Connaughton and Shuffler, 2007). Failures are attributed to differences in time and space, cultural differences, poor working relationships, lack of coordination and communication, lack of trust, low accountability, ineffective organizational structures, and reliance on individual contributions. The quality of work produced by a virtual team declines as the degree of dispersion increases (Monalisa et al., 2008). *Dispersion* is measured by the number of miles or time zones between team members, number of locations per team, percentage of isolated team members, and unevenness of team members (Siebdrat et al. 2009). Unevenness is demonstrated, for example, by having five team members at one site and only one or two team members at other sites.

Various sources define virtual teams differently. It is perhaps illustrative to define a colocated team that is traditionally used for NPD work and contrast it with the virtual team. Members of conventional colocated NPD teams work near one another – geographically, temporally, and culturally. These teams use informal communication methods and build social relationships through close interactions among team members. Social sharing further builds trust, which leads to greater collaboration and creativity. These traits are desirable for efficient innovation by a team of cross-functional professionals.

Virtual teams, in contrast, are more cost-effective than traditional teams, and a virtual team can advantageously tap into local markets for knowledge sharing across the team, the product line, and the global organization. Virtual teams can be described as "work arrangements in which a group of people share responsibility for goals that must be accomplished in the total, or near total, absence of face-to-face contact" (Zofi, 2012, p. 1). Unfortunately, many organizations have soured on virtual teams because of poor practices, inadequate communication among team members, and failure to deliver promised outcomes. Resorting to traditional colocated development teams, however, can drive up the cost of design and development, slow time to market, and limit creativity.

The Challenges of a Virtual Team as an Organizational Constraint

Note that dispersion of team members becomes a communication constraint whenever electronic communication replaces F2F conversations. For instance, team members located on different floors of the same building encounter some degree of physical dispersion resulting in communication and coordination challenges nearly as great as teams located in different countries (Siebdrat et al., 2009). As physical distance increases, team affiliation declines due to a lack of social or F2F interactions.

Because of dispersion, most communication within a virtual team is technologically mediated, meaning that the team's work is supported primarily by various information technologies. Unlike a traditional team that develops normalized practices by sharing a common work space, virtual teams are separated by time, space, organizational function, and culture. Pure F2F NPD rarely exists in today's globally competitive environment, where time to market for new products is critical and in which developers must consider a worldview in designing new products or services.

A Model for Effective Virtual Teams

As gleaned from our own experiences and those of other virtual teams, we have framed a model for virtual teams that drives knowledge sharing and active communication to support efficient product and process development. The model presented in this chapter is built from the authors' firsthand experiences, observations, research, and implementation of work practices. The model was refined based on application to different real-life virtual teams as well as literature and management case studies, as indicated in the "Driving Virtual Team Improvements" box.

Driving Virtual Team Improvements

A virtual team was tasked to improve a petrochemical procedure to treat a proprietary material. Team members were located in three different cities in Texas and New Jersey, while vendor and customer sites spanned the globe (Asia, Europe, and North America). To overcome the challenges to effective communication in such a dispersed team, the team agreed on a common goal and frequently revisited the project objectives to anchor efforts. This shared goal allowed the team to effectively work with customers to codevelop quality standards and product specifications. These quality and performance standards were reiterated at each team meeting (VTM: Initiation and Structure). To facilitate full sharing of information, email was used as the primary communication vehicle within the team and with customers, and quality standards were developed collaboratively among the team and customers (VTM: Communication Practices). Lessons learned during trials at each vendor site were shared among all team members via both synchronous communication and asynchronous messaging (VTM: Meetings and Protocols).

This practice supported knowledge transfer for the existing as well as future teams (VTM: Knowledge Management). Finally, core team leaders visited each company and each customer site, pairing team members for additional site visits. These actions demonstrated unique leadership skills (VTM: Leadership). Whereas similar projects had previously dragged on for years with few results, the combined practices from the VTM framework allowed this team to deliver a successful product within a few months.

Specifically, the key elements in the VTM are:

- Initiation and Structure
- Communication Practices
- Meetings and Protocols
- Knowledge Management
- Leadership

Each element of the VTM is accompanied by several supporting practices that have been revised and refined over the years as application of the VTM evolved and improved. An NPD team can immediately realize enhanced communication pathways by implementing any of the elements or practices in whole or part. However, the VTM is most successful for NPD teams that establish the practices within each element and apply the model universally since the elements and practices intertwine with one another in the complex relationships necessary for successful NPD (see Figure 6.1).

The first element, Initiation and Structure, addresses team member characteristics, team formation, and goal-setting. The next elements, Communication Practices and Meetings and Protocols, define practices that help virtual teams overcome the natural barriers faced by people working outside of informal, F2F relationships. Of course, to

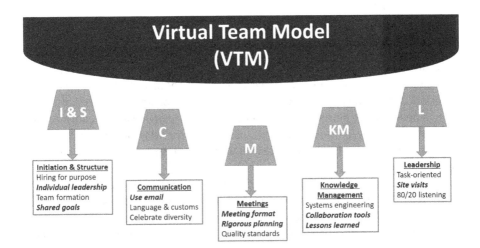

Figure 6.1: A lean NPD virtual team model (VTM).

meet the objective of a lean NPD team, virtual teams must find efficient and effective ways to share knowledge. Systems and best practices for Knowledge Management are presented in the next element of the VTM. Finally, no team can be successful without effective Leadership, and this last element of the VTM includes three practices that support unique skills to lead a virtual team. In this chapter, we highlight a subset of the practices to implement for successful innovation projects. An example application of the VTM is provided in the appendix to this chapter.

6.3 Initiation and Structure

Initiating a team and designing the proper organizational structure is even more important in a virtual team than in a traditional, colocated team. Leaders must select team members based on interpersonal skills in addition to technical expertise. Effective virtual teams start with hiring for purpose in which team members are vitally connected to the mission and overall goals of the NPD effort.

Because team members are often isolated from other designers and developers, hiring for purpose requires a more extensive skill set match as well as identification of personal characteristics, such as individual leadership, that will enhance virtual team communications over the product development life cycle. Firms can screen for both staff and project positions based on connections to their mission before interviewing candidates, thereby prepopulating the potential pool of virtual team members with devoted and enthusiastic people. An organic food and beverage company, for example, may hire for purpose by screening applicants for their commitment to family nutrition and the environment. A fitness center may screen applicants for their commitment to a healthy lifestyle and service to others. A private school may screen applicants based on their dedication to values and knowledge transfer. Virtual teams require participants who are strongly committed to the values and mission of the firm to represent the company and the project effort.

Individual Leadership

Conventional colocated NPD project team members are usually selected for project work based on functional ability and availability. While these are important characteristics of virtual team members as well, the successful initiation and structuring of a virtual team depends on the personal motivation and leadership of individual team members. Self-motivation serves not only to drive passion for the NPD project goals but also supports other elements and practices within the VTM, such as communication and individual leadership.

However, individual leadership goes beyond self-motivation and self-direction. Virtual team members with individual leadership carry out project tasks independently and value cross-functional relationships with other team members. While conventional team members participate in project teams as specialists, virtual team members cross the boundaries and fill roles of "generalist/specialist" as shown in Table 6.1 to support lean principles of knowledge transfer. Isolated team members direct their own work and do not necessarily need a strong central leader. (The role of the virtual team leader is discussed later in this chapter.) Individuals are frequently assigned project activities that leverage their strongest skill sets, such as planning, designing, or analyzing. Virtual team members demonstrating individual leadership work to complete their own tasks within their specialization but can support the team as a generalist as necessary ("T-shaped" people). For example, a team member in Japan may be a specialist in fluid flow but can represent the local customer's need to the rest of the NPD team in a general way. As such, the generalist-specialist capability deployment helps to reuse knowledge and communication to drive the project goals.

Individual leadership on a virtual team is contrasted with task-oriented membership in a traditional team. Colocated NPD team members tend to act as subject matter experts working piecemeal on a project. Traditional teamwork includes bounded hand-offs between functions while team members represent a single skill set ("I-shaped" people). Project inquiries are referred to the project manager who represents the overall team. Virtual team members serve multiple functional roles and represent the whole project within their geographical region or market sector. This requires both breadth and depth of product knowledge rather than solely functional expertise.

Of course, a team leader will consider individual leadership during team formation, and individual leadership is interwoven throughout the other elements of the VTM. In particular, we see how individual leadership helps to build broad communication pathways and creates efficient Knowledge Management systems. Further, individual leadership establishes the foundation for knowledge transfer when the virtual team disbands and transitions to new roles on other projects.

Shared Goals Initiate Virtual Team Communications

Choosing the correct team members with appropriate characteristics is crucially important for the success of a virtual team. Virtual teams must be even more proactive, deliberate, and disciplined in their interactions than traditional colocated teams. Therefore, team formation must include team member selection to represent all areas of technical expertise required to complete the project as well as evaluation of personalities and abilities for individual contributors, such as self-discipline, motivation, and leadership. Forming the team is an exercise that brings together the diverse team members from around the world to join in a common cause. The mission of the NPD team is reviewed and revised through the practice of *team formation* in the VTM.

Technology

Technologically mediated communication is less rich than F2F interactions. It can lead to a source of confusion and misunderstanding that negatively impacts the virtual team. However, the use of technology allows an organization to realize the benefits of distributed workers to identify local customer needs and bring a global perspective to the product development project. We suggest a few team collaboration tools later in this chapter.

Any technologies that will be used for team collaboration, communication, or knowledge management should be introduced at the project kick-off meeting. Adequate training on new tools and expected usage of these technologies should also be provided at the kick-off meeting. To increase productivity of team members, this same tool set should be utilized continually throughout the project. New or improved software should not be introduced during the project unless all team members have received training and have agreed on communication protocols to utilize the new technology.

Communication standards and meeting protocols are critical for success of a virtual team and are established up front for a virtual team. Team operating rules set expectations for communication and team member interactions. Again, these communication standards overlap with the second and third elements of the VTM; however, establishing general and specific expectations during the team formation process will reduce conflict during team formation and ensure later successes in team performance. For example, setting initial team protocols regarding meeting format and attendance allows every team member, regardless of his or her location, to be prepared for and responsive to group norms.

As indicated, the best members for a virtual team are self-starters who are motivated by the task and have high degrees of emotional intelligence and cultural awareness. Individual leaders will maintain a focus on customers and stakeholders throughout the project. Moreover, shared goals drive commitment to the work and is the number one measure of success for a virtual team. Establishing shared goals is a key practice in initiating and structuring a virtual team. Commitment to shared goals results in successful team performance. Shared goals should be disseminated at the kick-off meeting and reinforced frequently by the leader in order to balance work distribution and enhance team member cohesion.

According to Hoegl and Proserpio (2004), successful virtual teams focus on the shared goal by

- Open sharing of information,
- Task coordination,
- Balanced distribution of work,
- Mutual support with cohesion, and
- Task effort.

It may take more energy and time for a virtual team to initially agree on the mission and goals of the work. Yet the problem definition should occur synchronously for the virtual team to enhance commitment to the project. The team must also share a common understanding of stakeholder expectations. Maintaining a relentless focus on the customer leads to higher success rates for virtual teams and drives the lean principle of customer-centric, continuous improvement.

Initiation and Structure: Action Steps

In order to successfully meet product development and knowledge transfer objectives using a virtual team, an organization must be deliberate in initiating and structuring the

Table 6.2: Establishing a new virtual team for product development.

Scenario: You have been assigned to work as part of a virtual product development team. You are serving as the team leader and there are two other team members colocated at your site in Canada. There are three team members in different cities in the United States, one team member in Asia, and another in Italy.

Virtual team model	Standard approach	Actions for lean NPD
Initiation and Structure	Select team members based on skills and availability.	Select team members with individual leadership characteristics who are committed to the project goals.
Communication Practices	Face-to-face. Informal.	Establish communication norms being aware of time zone differences.
Meetings and Protocols	Frequent status updates. Informal water cooler conversations.	Set up predictable, routine meetings but be respectful of different time zones.
Knowledge Management	Tacit knowledge is transferred in a project of long-standing team members with specialized skills.	Establish and enforce Knowledge Management norms. Select appropriate cloud-based collaboration tools.
Leadership	Directive leadership style.	Reiterate common purpose and expected outcomes. Conduct one-on-one site meetings with each team member.

team. The VTM includes several practices demonstrated to establish team characteristics and behaviors for successful NPD project execution. The first element, Initiation and Structure, is perhaps the most important element of the VTM because errors and omissions in setting up the team are not easily overcome later. Table 6.2 illustrates the scenario of a new team leader setting up a lean, virtual team for product development work, focusing on the Initiation and Structure of the team. As the elements of the VTM naturally overlap, you will begin to recognize the value of the other elements – Communication Practices, Meetings and Protocols, Knowledge Management, and Leadership – and their influence on the Initiation and Structure of the virtual team up front, as discussed later in this chapter.

6.4 Communication Practices

Not surprisingly, communication can make or break a virtual team because communication is critical for any relationship to succeed. The term "communication" includes both what we say and how we say it. More than 70% of communication is nonverbal (Aguanno, 2005) involving visual cues and body language. Obviously, virtual teams can lose a lot of the message when they use primarily asynchronous, technology-assisted means of communication. Yet, with the right approach to communication, virtual teams can be successful. We recommend a three-pronged approach addressing method (email), language, and cultural differences. (See Figure 6.2)

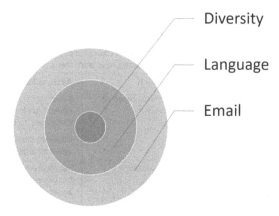

Figure 6.2: VTM practices for improved communication.

Email as a Primary Communication Tool

Virtual team members typically work in different time zones around the globe. One team member may be just logging onto the computer for the first time that day while another is shutting down to head home. Texting and instant messaging are common tools for communication today but can be disruptive for virtual teams. Nothing can be more frustrating than answering a "beep" on one's cell phone in the middle of the night and finding a simple, nonurgent message such as "Thx for sending the docs."

Therefore, we agree with experts in recommending email as a primary communication tool for virtual teams. First, email is asynchronous and does not demand an instant response like a phone call or a text message. Second, email is inexpensive and can easily link group members together. Training is not required regardless of geographical location. Next, users normally are more careful in composing an email message, paying greater attention to grammar, spelling, and punctuation in order to clarify the message. An email can be composed, reviewed, and corrected before sending. Moreover, email can be organized in project folders to enhance knowledge sharing – a goal of lean NPD.

While it seems a good idea to include all team members on all communications, some issues will involve only a couple of team members. A best practice for virtual teams is to include names in the "To:" list that need to take action on the message while the "cc:" list is reserved for information only. "Reply to all" must be used with extreme caution. Moreover, it is crucial to include an appropriate subject line. Sometimes email chains grow and the conversation morphs from one topic to another. Because the team should not lose historical conversation threads, a best practice is to simply update the subject line. For example, if the original topic was the project schedule, but the conversation has changed, the subject line should now read "Subject: Construction Materials (re: Schedule)." This alerts receivers to the change in topic and preserves its relation to prior conversations. (Please see an example of email best practices in the box.)

> ## Virtual Team Communication Best Practice for Email
>
> Marvin (based in Cleveland) sends an email to the team requesting specific completion dates for each of the new product subsystems. Product development team members in Singapore (Wei Lu), Barcelona (Alejandro), and Portland (Lisa) reply to all on the email with expected completion dates of March 12, April 22, and May 16 for the transmitter, encoder, and network security patch for the new product. Wei Lu also notes that she needs inputs from Lisa to complete her portion of the work for a final prototype by May 30. With a three-week testing period, Lisa responds to all explaining limitations in her subsystem development. Marvin adapts the subject line to "Prototype Testing (re: Schedule)" and leaves Wei Lu and Lisa as addressees ("To:"), while he puts Alejandro's address as "cc:" since his role is not crucial to completion of this subsystem prototype. In this way, the whole team is kept informed of interactions and ongoing developments that drive the product completion, yet actions are required only of the key team members involved in the specific task. Virtual team communications are recorded for knowledge sharing but streamlined to a need-to-know basis.

Virtual Teams Use Language and Diversity to Build Creative Solutions

Team members must be proficient in the common language of the project. They must be able to both speak and write in that chosen language. As we've seen, written communications dominate in virtual teams, so writing skills will slightly outweigh verbal skills. Regardless of the team's selected language, it is important for colocated team members to use the common language in all communications. For instance, virtual team members will quickly become disengaged during a teleconference if team members at another location begin conversing in their native tongue.

Because email is the primary communication tool for a virtual team, team members need to be tolerant of odd sentence structure or peculiar phrasing. Nonnative English speakers, for instance, may translate their idea from a Romance language to English, resulting in longer sentences with a lot of descriptive clauses. Words may appear out of order (e.g. "coat blue" instead of "a blue coat"). All of us need to have patience with team members who may struggle to communicate in a different language. We also need to be receptive to clarifying meaning and intent if we are not as familiar with the written language.

Furthermore, emails and other communications should remain task-oriented. It is hard enough for friends and family to recognize humor in a text message. Trying to convey humor across cultures in an email message can result in misunderstandings and lead to unnecessary conflict. It is a best practice to keep communications succinct, focused on tasks, and action-oriented.

While emails may not be the right place to share humor or personal stories, a virtual team *should* celebrate their differences and build on the inherent positive aspects of their diversity. A fundamental benefit of a virtual team is the opportunity to tap into local market knowledge and practices and to use cultural differences to benefit the outcome of the project. Virtual team members of different educational, national, and cultural backgrounds bring different perspectives to a project; and they bring the viewpoint of multiple customers to ensure world-class design.

Cultural differences can sometimes be a challenge to virtual teams, just as language and humor are. Instead of trying to force the culture of the corporation's headquarters onto the virtual team, virtual teams establish their own culture and climate. Team members learn from the different cultures represented, and these differences will drive creativity for NPD. Product usage under various conditions found across the world will enhance the development of simple features that serve the needs of a wide customer base. Different mind-sets and backgrounds introduce more and varied solutions to problems. As team members share and build on one another's ideas, unique customer-oriented concepts evolve.

It is important for team members in a colocated, traditional team to adopt a single culture, and it is normally one that reflects the organization's broader culture. Virtual teams, in contrast, will celebrate their differences and adopt a unique culture and climate that builds on their own purpose in that time and space. A characteristic of successful teams establishes strong cohesion among team members. Open dialog and meetings in which knowledge is shared build trust and common understanding regardless of native culture.

Because team members in a virtual setting don't know what someone else knows (or doesn't know), it is critical for members to share their professional backgrounds and work experience. While discussion forums are usually underutilized to share work in progress or opinions, a discussion forum is a great place to share team member biographies. These biographies include information to build trust and enhance sharing.

For example, Marvin posts a photo of himself decked out in Cleveland Cavaliers basketball gear. He writes that he obtained his degree in mechanical engineering from The Ohio State University and has three kids. He also notes that he worked at two other companies prior to this job and has 10 years' experience in the telecom industry, of which one year was in management training.

Similarly, Wei Lu posts her biographical information as in Figure 6.3. Because Marvin and Wei Lu both love the same sport, they instantly build social trust. Moreover, Martin feels free to use sports analogies in meetings since he is assured that team members will understand a culturally narrow reference. What's different in this situation versus a noncommunicative virtual team is that the team members have intentionally shared professional and personal information to build trust and establish professional competency. Discussion forums and collaboration tools offer means of knowledge sharing and cooperative communication that build trust to support common project goals.

Synchronous meetings for virtual teams start with a few minutes for members to share something about themselves to continue to build camaraderie. A good conversation starter will include questions about national holidays or sporting events. Another way to celebrate cultural differences is to ask one team member per meeting to share his/her biography in depth. Even without body language clues, other team members will be able to pick up a person's passions and energies.

ABC's Project X Open Discussion Forum

- Education: BS in Economics, University of Houston (2014)
- Office location: Singapore
- Project experience: 2 years technical support on Project Bluebird
- Phone: 65-1111-4444
- email: wei.lu@abc.x.com
- Best time to reach me: 4-6 pm Time Zone
- Something unique about me: I like to watch basketball on television
- Hobbies: Cooking

Figure 6.3: Example of dispersed NPD project forum.

6.5 Meetings and Protocols

Virtual teams are successful when there is a strong commitment to a shared goal and team communication focuses on achievement. Team members often work independently and will have fewer check-ins with other members than in traditional, colocated teams. Such team members may exchange ideas while at the coffeepot, water cooler, or company cafeteria. Casual interactions can stimulate deeper conversations leading to solutions of outstanding project issues or other problems. Thus, team meetings tend to be uneventful and serve more to inform the team leader of ongoing activities. Of course, virtual teams lack these opportunistic contacts with other members. Therefore, team meetings, protocols, and performance standards serve as critical checkpoints for virtual teams.

Select an Appropriate Meeting Format for Virtual Teams

Naturally, F2F team meetings involve informal information sharing, problem solving, and decision making. But most of these meetings also include the social aspect of building a shared identity. Alternatively, virtual team meetings serve to clarify roles and responsibilities, verify task performance, and validate project deliverables. Meeting format best practices for a virtual team include rotating meeting times and places, varying the technology medium, soliciting active participation, and rigorous planning. Clear follow-ups also are necessary.

Rotate Meeting Times and Places

Meetings for a virtual team are important touchpoints and connections for the dispersed members. Because team members spend a great deal of time working alone on tasks, team meetings provide an opportunity to establish group consensus, commitment, and shared understanding as well as decision making. Team goals should be reiterated at each and every team meeting to emphasize the common purpose and goals of the team. The time of meetings should be varied to ensure that it is convenient for all team members. It is unfair to ask the same team member to get up in the middle of the night every week for a team meeting. Instead, vary the time of day so that everyone on the team sacrifices equally.

Vary the Technology Medium

Likewise, try to vary the type of meeting. Teleconferences can be prone to multitasking (checking email or Facebook) during long conversations, and virtual team members may disengage from the conversation. Webinars with video force attention to the meeting topics at hand. Team protocols and norms describe how the virtual team members will interact at meetings. Simple actions, such as using the mute button and identifying oneself by name when speaking, can influence the team's positive communications to derive shared knowledge. Video conference and webinars encourage higher context communication but require more bandwidth. Remote team members and those in drastically different time zones often participate in meetings via cellphone. The use of a small screen dictates another set of standards for the team. In sum, while communication media may be designed for synchronous sharing, some virtual team members will necessarily participate in meetings with less bandwidth. Do not put them at a disadvantage. Appropriate planning and consideration for each meeting can smooth live interactions for virtual team members.

Solicit Active Participation from All Virtual Team Members

Because language and location are barriers to communication in a virtual team, meetings can face periods of stagnation. Participation increases not only when the times and media for virtual team meeting are varied but when task responsibility also rotates among team members. For example, facilitation of the meeting and distribution of meeting notes by different team members encourages more active participation by remote individuals and supports the team's common, shared purpose. Task sharing to present project milestones to the rest of the team encourages peer-to-peer communication and knowledge building.

Team norms also establish meeting participation protocols. For example, do all core team members need to be present at every meeting? Can a core team member send a stand-in to the meeting? Are meetings recorded and archived for those who miss one?

Finally, active participation in a virtual team meeting requires that team members speak up to share what they are working on, what challenges they face, and how their tasks lead to project completion. A quick check-in by the facilitator, calling out each team member by name, can lead to active participation by all.

Rigorous Planning Is Necessary for Engaged Virtual Team Communications

Important to planning a virtual team meeting is ensuring that an accurate agenda is distributed in advance. For virtual teams working in multiple time zones, distributing the agenda one week before a monthly meeting or two days before a weekly meeting is acceptable. Many agenda items comprise standing reports, obligations, and information sharing as well as problem solving and decision making that require interactive team member engagement. Agenda items will vary according to the progress of the product and are flexible enough to add new items when the meeting commences. Past follow-ups are noted on the agenda to mark completion or identify issues that impact accomplishing the product design.

Distribution of the agenda in advance of a team meeting is crucial when team members are nonnative English speakers and cultures are very different. A detailed agenda allows the isolated team members time to plan their own responses and the opportunity to privately communicate concerns to the team leader or meeting facilitator as necessary.

Meetings of virtual teams tend to be more formal than those of colocated teams. Body language cues are missing from communications, and both language and culture can be barriers to successful virtual meetings. However, success of virtual teams is driven by a focus on the common, shared goal. The project objective should be repeated frequently throughout virtual team meetings to ensure task alignment. Meeting agenda items focus on task completion to deliver the new product efficiently. To help overcome language and cultural barriers, virtual team meetings start with a standing trust-building exercise to support the initiation and team formation social interactions.

Because Communication Practices and Meetings and Protocols are critical elements for long-term success of a virtual team, we emphasize and contrast the lean approach to build knowledge sharing with that of a standard approach in Table 6.3.

Table 6.3: Managing an existing virtual product development team.

Scenario: You are working on a project to add features and functionality to an existing product. The launch of the next-generation product is expected within a year. You estimate that about half of the work has been completed on the product's hardware and software elements. Unfortunately, two of the seven team members are new to the team, replacing one team member who was reassigned to another department and another person who left the company for a different job.

Virtual team model	Standard approach	Action for lean NPD
Initiation and Structure	New team members demonstrate comparable technical skills.	Use discussion boards and collaboration tools to share personal and professional biographies.
Communication Practices	New team members learn project status informally.	Welcome diversity and experience of new team members.
Meetings and Protocols	Informal welcome lunch for new team members. Casual conversations convey project status.	Use video conference to introduce new team members. Rotate meeting management to new team members and invite them to share background and experience.
Knowledge Management	Transfer of tacit knowledge is informal.	Ensure adequate tool training is available for new team members.
Leadership	Builds social interactions and manages interpersonal conflict.	Leader visits one on one with each new team member. Paired site visits between new and existing team members.

6.6 Knowledge Management

All teams depend on gathering, collecting, and evaluating information from a variety of stakeholders. Projects are initiated and planned by identifying key stakeholders and their requirements or expectations for the project. During project execution, these features and functionalities are tracked as part of the product development work. Projects should not reinvent the wheel every time a problem is encountered. In fact, lean project teams depend on learning and reusable knowledge for efficiency and productivity. Knowledge needs to be translated into explicit information to be useful to a virtual team. In addition to a successfully commercialized product or service, NPD teams should also contribute substantially to the knowledge base for future work.

Systems engineering offers many tactical and operational tools that will aid a product development team. These tools help the team ensure that technical linkages among subsystems are properly configured and designed for assembly. Version tracking and configuration management are key concepts in systems engineering. (For additional information, please see the references and contact the chapter's lead author.)

Collaboration Tools Eliminate Distance as a Barrier to Creativity

A wide variety of tools are available today to help virtual teams share information, transfer knowledge, and increase collaboration across distances. Groupware creates a common base for virtual team members and the virtual environment. New group collaboration tools are continually emerging as technologies continue to advance.

Document sharing tools, like Dropbox™, are a necessity for virtual teams to coordinate work and build shared databases and specifications for projects. Microsoft Share-Point™ is a common knowledge management tool for larger enterprises and traditional teams; however, the team should select appropriate collaboration tools based on its size and locations of team members. Other software tools assist indirect communication, like webinars and meetings. Whiteboard and desktop sharing allow virtual teams to collaborate across time and distance.

Robust project management tools are necessary for virtual innovation teams. These include traditional software tools like Microsoft Project™ to track schedule, budget, and resources. Many virtual teams opt for less expensive cloud-based project management tools such as Basecamp™, Wrike™, Asana™, productboard.com, Redmine, and the like. Software tools like Slack™, Yammer™, and I Done This (idonethis.com) engage team member communications as well as track project progress. Mindjet™, for example, provides a creative ideation tool that easily translates requirements into a Gantt chart so the team can focus on what matters most.

The advantage of cloud-based tools versus enterprise software tools lies in accessibility and maintenance of the tool(s) for the virtual team members. A team member with a home office does not have an information technology department on hand to troubleshoot software glitches. In addition to project management functionality, these cloud-based tools also provide a collaborative environment for the project team to work issues, store documents, and track email discussion threads while enhancing shared creativity, problem solving, and decision making.

The purpose of a lean innovation team is to develop a new product or service that is valued by customers around the world and to create reusable knowledge, not to learn new software. If a new tool is required by the team, it should be introduced with appropriate training at the kick-off meeting and not changed throughout the life of the project. The same technology should be used before, during, and after significant project milestones to increase productivity (Ketch and Kennedy, 2004). For instance, simply deleting the requirement for a passcode on conference calls improves accessibility for team members in remote locations or for those who are traveling outside of their home office. Communication and collaboration tools must be simple and easy for isolated team members to troubleshoot and access regardless of available technology capability. Tools and technology effectiveness are evaluated during a postproject audit. In addition to capturing specific product development information, the team should identify the most successful collaboration and knowledge management techniques.

Using Lessons Learned to Transfer Knowledge

Typically, lessons learned are collected after a project and are often discussed by a single team, then filed away with the project archives. In this common situation, lessons learned are rarely transferred between teams, and only a few outstanding items are captured by the project leader for future implementation. Traditional teams rely on word of mouth to transfer these practices and behaviors. Virtual teams, in contrast, rely on individual tacit knowledge and formal organizational practices for continuous learning.

An important goal, perhaps the number one goal, in applying lean principles to product development teams is to effectively and efficiently transfer knowledge. A company-wide shared database captures lessons learned and can be searched by anyone in the organization. Similarly, a Project Management Office or innovation department records and disseminates project learnings. The Project Management Office may sponsor a virtual project leader network encouraging free exchange of ideas and learnings during independent project activities. Reusable knowledge helps NPD teams deploy new products and services faster and with a higher degrees of success.

The use of virtual teams to accomplish these goals is mandatory in a globally competitive world. We illustrate the fourth element of the VTM, Knowledge Management, in the case study (see Appendix). Knowledge Management is key to successful lean NPD so that teams are not re-creating practices or relearning problem-solving techniques (see Tables 6.4 and 6.5).

Table 6.4: Using collaboration tools to generate reusable knowledge.

Scenario: You are a technical project team member working on a new product for the company. Some of your teammates work from home-based offices, while others are scattered across the globe. You work out of a production facility so you have access to information technology and other company services, like human resources and payroll, but many of your teammates do not have these support functions available at their locations. During a recent team meeting via video conference, the team outlined the project expectations and working norms.

Virtual team model	Standard approach	Action for lean NPD
Initiation and Structure	Team members are specialists and participate as needed.	Actively participate in all team-building activities and the project kick-off meeting.
Communication Practices	Knowledge transfer is informal.	Use email instead of instant messaging for project communications.
Meetings and Protocols	Little documentation on task completion, status.	Complete assigned follow-ups on time.
Knowledge Management	Enterprise systems with strong information technology support.	Shared document storage and collaboration tools utilized. Share lessons learned,
Leadership	Manage status F2F.	Enable paired site visits to expand learning and customer viewpoint for product development.

Table 6.5: Leadership for virtual team engagement.

Scenario: You have been recently appointed the leader of a new product development team. The technical team is colocated at your site, but the marketing team is located across the country in another city while other designers and developers are located in India, China, and the Netherlands. You have led some very small project efforts in the past, and this is your first chance to lead a major product development team.

Virtual team model	Standard approach	Action for lean NPD
Initiation and Structure	Available resources on site.	Share project goals and expectations.
Communication Practices	Interactive F2F messaging.	Use email to introduce yourself as new team leader.
Meetings and Protocols	Informal decisions prior to meetings.	Practice rigorous meeting planning, including updates of issues log.
Knowledge Management	F2F knowledge transfer.	Study lessons learned on this project and similar completed products.
Leadership	Command-and-control focusing on social conflicts.	Visit each team member at local site office(s).

6.7 Leadership

There is no shortage of research or literature describing what makes a great leader. However, most historical studies have focused on traditional teams, and leadership theory has evolved based on conventional, hierarchical reporting structures for management. Virtual teams are more egalitarian and leaders require a different skill set to demand success. Notably, traditional leadership has been only moderately correlated with virtual team effectiveness (Lurey and Raisinghani, 2001). Leaders for colocated teams, where conventional managers handle conflict and project status via informal mechanisms, have different roles from virtual team leaders.

Virtual team leaders, in contrast, are task-oriented, travel frequently to visit team members, and practice active listening. A directive or command-and-control style is rarely appropriate for a virtual team leader since team members are self-motivated, highly skilled technical experts. Moreover, leaders who emphasize social orientation and team cohesion above project goals are less likely to be successful on a virtual team that is more task-oriented.

Leadership training programs often fail to engage fundamental skills, like speaking, listening, and analyzing. Skills necessary for a virtual leader to be successful include flexibility, endurance, strength, self-control, and focus. Virtual teams require managers to adapt their style for each unique situation. According to Ivanaj and Bozon (2016), in a virtual setting, leaders can build trust by:

- Setting communication expectations quickly,
- Engendering a positive social environment,
- Validating rigorous meeting and team protocols, and
- Encouraging active participation for all team members.

Using Paired Site Visits for Knowledge Sharing

Because there are fewer routine and casual F2F interactions among team members, site visits are critically important for virtual teams. Certainly the leader should visit each team member at his or her local office regularly throughout the project life cycle. The leader acts as a liaison bridging communication needs for the team as a whole and reinforcing team goals.

By visiting team members locally, a virtual team leader can also better understand independent challenges facing them. Team leaders acquaint themselves with local management to improve negotiations (current and future) for materials, equipment, and workforce needs. Moreover, if the site lacks infrastructure necessary for the project, the team leader can take steps to rectify the situation. For example, one virtual team member needed to review hard copy documents for customers, but the local office only had a shared printer, which restricted her ability to access and review detailed project documents. After learning this during a site visit, the team leader acquired a personal printer for the team member, and her productivity greatly increased.

Site visits should not be restricted to the leader alone. Site visits include exchanges and are alternated among team member sites. A design team member visits the representative plant site and vice versa. The team leader facilitates these exchanges by assigning small, subprojects to pairs of team members. The benefits of site visits between team members are many. Misperceptions regarding workloads and task environments transform to reflect a common understanding among team members at the conclusion of site visits. Working side by side creates camaraderie and builds future trust for team members that extends beyond their return to their own home site. The project budget must account for these important exchanges since travel expenses are not always carefully considered as a part of the project budget for a colocated team.

6.8 Conclusion: What Makes Successful Lean Virtual Teams

NPD projects are inherently risky. Introducing a virtual team can further challenge the team's success. However, experience shows that implementing the lean VTM provides a framework to structure activities within a virtual team to achieve the dual goals of launching a new product and building transferrable, reusable knowledge.

Take action with your virtual NPD teams. Identify the largest gaps and initiate appropriate elements of the VTM. Better yet, institute the five elements and 16 practices of the VTM as the normal operating means for your teams. Check the structure of the team for shared purpose, ensure clear communication channels, and enforce team protocols. Recognize and celebrate diversity to drive creativity. Make it easy for each team member to contribute to the shared knowledge base to grow organizational learning. Encourage and facilitate paired site visits to enhance team effectiveness and achievement. Finally, recognize the benefits of a lean virtual team by speeding product development and tapping into a diversity of skills around the world.

Appendix: Case Study Application of the VTM

Adapted from Ivanaj and Bozon, 2016, pp. 238–250.

As a leading information provider in Financial and Risk, Legal, Tax and Accounting, IP Services, and Media, in 2009 Thomson Reuters implemented a new operating model to emphasize its global customer focus. The company reported over 60 000 employees in more than 100 countries with $12.5 billion in revenue in 2011. With the new operating model, Thomson Reuters recognized that virtual teams were the best way to accomplish the goal of a global focus. For example, in 2008, 50% of French employees reported to a manager abroad, and half of managers had teams spread over several countries and even different continents. About 400 people were involved in the organizational redesign to increase the global focus and improve virtual team capabilities. Success was recognized as the active transfer of knowledge, an outcome of running lean operations for virtual teams.

The Thomson Reuters global virtual team focus highlights all five elements of the VTM. First, with *Initiation and Structure*, team members were "hired" for purpose. The director of human resources at Thomson Reuters explained that a "prepared on purpose" organization is truly the only way an organization with a global customer focus – a virtual team – can succeed. Thus, virtual teams were built from those employees and staff members who demonstrated a capacity for change and management of the global client base. Team members were motivated by learning new skills beyond the restrictions of their geographic location. *Individual leadership* was emphasized by training generalists to become specialists as well as by providing additional training in personal organization and self-discipline. Next, *team formation* was utilized by structuring the teams for customer business segments: global, major accounts, trading, and investment. Finally, regardless of their geographic location, teams *shared the goal* of managing the client per specific business or product lines to drive the global customer focus.

Communication Practices is the second major element of the VTM. Thompson Reuters invested in mobile devices for all employees working on the global teams. This provided a way for all virtual team members to have access to *email as a primary communication tool* as well as other virtual collaboration technologies. Because the financial markets commonly use English for correspondence, individuals and managers at Thomson Reuters adopted English as the *language for virtual teams*. The transition was easiest in Anglo-Saxon cultures (such as United States, Canada, United Kingdom, and Nordic countries). Latin cultures (France and Italy) were less comfortable with the transition but supported English as the choice of language since account managers were often in a different country from the virtual team members.

The new globally focused client teams also *celebrated diversity* to improve trust among team members. For example, employees went to special training sessions to improve capabilities in flexibility, communication, and interpersonal competency. The group built a popular "culture wizard" website to assist staff in growing their culture and virtual intelligence. Virtual team members reported having more fun and higher individual satisfaction as a result of the new operating model accompanied by these new communication tools.

Meetings and Protocols were supported by *rigorous planning*. For example, some managers initially struggled with the discipline of holding regular online meetings, building effective agendas, and driving task completion. In response, Thomson Reuters offered logistical training to virtual team leaders on how to interact across time zones and how to run effective online meetings. The virtual teams also upheld a clear-eyed focus on the *quality standards* for their work. Maintaining and improving global client relationships was the prime objective for each virtual team.

As indicated in the VTM, effective *Knowledge Management* removes barriers to lean virtual teams, allowing them to produce results consistent with those of traditional, colocated teams. Thomson Reuters followed the practice of *systems engineering* by creating a central database and a customer relationship management system to traverse all their existing and new business processes. Further, the company invested in *collaboration tools*, such as a delivery network with document readers, video con-ferencing, and virtual presence. This allowed virtual team members access to the same information regardless of their geographical location. *Lessons learned* reviews unfortunately impacted some of the benefits realized by the virtual teams serving global customers. Some travel costs increased as managers occasionally traveled farther distances and influential clients requested specific personnel for in-person visits. However, team leader *visits to various sites* helped to improve communication as the manager serves as conduit to build trust and relationships among the virtual team members.

Finally, success in virtual teams and for a large-scale operational reorganization such as the one Thomson Reuters undertook requires strong, capable *Leadership* that is equipped for the challenges of a virtual team. As indicated, team leaders utilized *site visits* to introduce themselves to all team members and build the necessary interpersonal and social relationships. These actions served as an incentive for team members to build cross-functional trust and fostered team spirit. The company also committed to *80/20 listening* as virtual managers were provided training that included cultural dimensions, "what if" scenarios, and a coaching mind-set.

While the VTM is designed specifically to help NPD teams succeed with their formidable challenges in creating new solutions for customer problems, looking at the Thomson Reuters case study validates the model's effectiveness in routine business operations as well. Virtual teams can benefit from a focus on Initiation and Structure of the team, effective and appropriate Communication Practices, Meetings and Protocols, Knowledge Management, and Leadership.

References

Aguanno, K. (2005). Chapter 1: Introduction. In: *Managing Agile Projects* (ed. K. Aguanno). Lakefield, ON: Multi-Media Publications.

Connaughton, S. L. and Shuffler, M. (2007). Multinational and multicultural distributed teams. *Small Group Research* 38 (3): 387–412.

Hoegl, M. and Proserpio, L. (2004). Team member proximity and teamwork in innovative projects. *Research Policy* 33: 1153–1165.

Ivanaj, S. and Bozon, C. (2016). *Managing virtual teams*. Northampton, MA: Edward Elgar Publishing.

Jurgens-Kowal, T. 2016. Bridging communication gaps in virtual teams. In *Proceedings of the American Society for Engineering Management 2016 International Annual Conference*, ed. S. Long, E. -H. Ng, C. Downing, and B. Nepal. Red Hook, NY: Curran Associates, pp. 517–525.

Ketch, K. and Kennedy, J. 2004. *Unleashing the power of the group mind with dispersed teams*. White Paper, GroupMindExpress.com.

Lurey, J. S. and Raisinghani, M. S. (2001). An empirical study of best practices in virtual teams. *Information Management* 38: 523–544.

Monalisa, M., Daim, T., Mirani, F. et al. (2008). Managing global design teams. *Research Technology Management* 51 (4): 48–59.

Siebdrat, F., Hoegl, M., and Ernst, H. (2009). How to manage virtual teams. *MIT Sloan Management Review* 50 (4): 63–68.

Ward, A. C. and Sobek, D. K. II (2014). *Lean product and process development*, 2e. Cambridge, MA: Lean Enterprises Institute.

Zofi, Y. (2012). *A manager's guide to virtual teams*. New York: AMACOM.

Further Reading

Loehr, J. and Schwartz, T. (2001). The making of a corporate athlete. *Harvard Business Review* 79 (1): 120–128.

Project Management Institute (2013). *A guide to the Project Management Body of Knowledge (PMBOK Guide)*, 5e. Newton, PA: Project Management Institute.

Shah, H. (ed.) (2012). *A guide to the Engineering Management Body of Knowledge*. Rolla, MO: American Society for Engineering Management.

Smith, P. G. and Blanck, E. L. (2002). From experience: Leading dispersed teams. *Journal of Product Innovation Management* 19: 294–304.

Tuckman, B. W. (2001). Developmental sequence in small groups (reprint). *Group Facilitation: A Research and Applications Journal* 3: 66–81.

About the Authors

DONOVAN RAY HARDENBROOK, NPDP, PMP, MBA, MSEE, is the Director of Global Quality Management Systems at Littelfuse Incorporated in Chicago, IL. He is responsible for advocating and driving a "Zero Defects. Zero Excuses." quality culture and system across Littelfuse in the areas of product development and manufacturing operations. Mr. Hardenbrook is also responsible for standardizing quality systems and implementing product life cycle management. Prior to joining Littelfuse, Mr. Hardenbrook founded Leap Innovation Consulting in 2007 and has held previous management and engineering positions at Intel Corporation, Health Production Declaration Collaborative, Salt River Project, and Orbital Sciences. He is a 20-year member of the Product Development and Management Association (PDMA) and has served as the Book Review Editor for the Journal of Product Innovation and Management, Vice President of Association Development for PDMA, and founding President for the Arizona PDMA Chapter.

DR. TERESA JURGENS-KOWAL, PhD, PMP, NPDP, is the president of Global NP Solutions, LLC (GNPS), a boutique innovation training and consulting firm in Houston, Texas. GNPS helps companies achieve their strategic goals through new product development, product portfolio management, and project management best practices. Dr. Jurgens-Kowal has a passion for innovation and is a lifelong learner. She loves to help individuals and companies reach the highest levels of success in new product development and product portfolio management by gaining and maintaining their professional credentials, such as New Product Development Professional (NPDP), Project Management Professional (PMP), Scrum, and Lean Six Sigma. Dr. Jurgens-Kowal has a PhD in Chemical Engineering from the University of Washington, a BS in Chemical Engineering from the University of Idaho, and an MBA from West Texas A&M University. She has helped dozens of companies and individuals in diverse industries accomplish new product development goals of productivity and efficiency. Additionally, she has over 20 years of industrial experience and over five yeas' experience as adjunct faculty. She serves as PDMA's Book Review Editor and is a Registered Education Provider with PDMA.

Part 3

MARKET CONSTRAINTS

The chapters in Part 3 address market constraints, which we define as relating to particularities of specific markets that are targeted for the new product under development. Figure I.1 in the Introduction outlines the particular market-related constraints each chapter focuses on and indicates how these constraints typically arise in the new product development (NPD) process.

Chapter 7, by Ronny Reinhardt, acts as an overall organizing chapter for firms addressing low-end markets, which are defined as markets of customers with a low willingness or ability to pay. Their low willingness or ability to pay prevents them from purchasing currently available products. They typically go without or make do somehow. This chapter identifies eight capabilities that firms need to develop to adapt the standard NPD process (Introduction, Figure I.2) so that they can repeatedly develop low-end innovations. The chapter makes specific suggested changes for how to successfully adapt the standard NPD process to achieve each organizational or process capability.

Chapter 8, by Aruna Shekar and Andrew Drain, focuses on markets with a severe lack of resources, going beyond customers' low ability to pay. These markets also have customers with lower educational backgrounds, less mechanical knowledge, limited or nonexistent utilities, and other infrastructure holes. The chapter presents two specific adaptations necessary for more successfully innovating for low-resource markets and discusses how to implement them: new approaches to user interaction tasks to better understand the full implications of the low-resource context and partnering with local intermediaries for understanding the context and providing credence to both the innovation as a solution and the innovating firm as a provider.

Chapter 9, by Nivedita Agarwal and Alexander Brem, provides five specific inclusive strategies to further address markets constrained specifically by underdeveloped infrastructures, using the Indian healthcare market as the example in which explanations of the solutions to the constraints in these markets are embedded. The authors explicate how implementing these different adaptations can overcome infrastructure limitations in low-resource markets.

Low-end markets exhibit two additional cultural differences that frequently impede successful development and commercialization of new products. As covered in Chapter 10, these are the special considerations of status due to gender and social hierarchy, which can have detrimental effects on individuals and firms trying to sell into these markets. This chapter, by José Antonio Rosa and Shikha Upadhyaya, describes these constraints and presents five solutions for adapting the organization and its processes to address them successfully.

7

HOW TO DEVELOP LOW-END INNOVATION CAPABILITIES: ADAPTING CAPABILITIES TO OVERCOME CONSTRAINTS FOR CONSUMERS IN LOW-END MARKETS

Ronny Reinhardt

Friedrich-Schiller-University, Jena, Germany

Introduction

Low-end innovations are new products or services that expand a market by targeting consumers with a low willingness or ability to pay (WTP). Low-end innovations thus enable consumers who were previously unable or unwilling to buy due to high prices to buy the new product or the new service. For example, low-cost airlines such as Southwest or Ryanair expanded the air travel market for consumers who could not afford to fly. Similarly, GE's low-end medical devices enabled physicians in emerging economies to purchase medical technology to better diagnose and treat their patients.

Academics and practitioners use a range of related terms to describe innovations that address low-end customers. For example, the terms "resource-constrained innovation," "frugal innovation," "Base of the Pyramid innovation," "inclusive innovation," and "reverse innovation" are used by scholars and managers for low-end innovations in emerging markets. More general terms include "disruptive innovation," "cost innovation," and "low-end encroachment." All of these terms are relevant because they address new products and services that expand the market at the low end. However, none of these frameworks comprehensively addresses the capabilities, methods, and tools that firms need to develop low-end innovations successfully.

7.1 Why Are Low–End Innovations Important, and How Do They Differ from Standard Practice?

Managers should care about low-end innovation – and thus low-end innovation capabilities – for two reasons. First, low-end innovations are an important means to seize growth opportunities, make profits, and develop strategic assets. Estimates indicate that the 4 billion people at the base of the economic pyramid spend about $5 trillion annually. Another 1.4 billion mid-market consumers spend roughly $12.5 trillion (Hammond et al., 2007). A 2015 Nielson study covering 30,000 respondents from 60 countries also suggests that affordability is the most important attribute for new product purchase decisions in both developed and emerging markets. In addition, innovative technologies priced below the going rate can have substantial disruptive effects, highlighting the strategic value of low-end innovation. For example, Voice over Internet Protocol (VoIP) services such as Skype have essentially disrupted long-distance and international calling. Second, low-end innovations can make significant contributions to society, which is becoming increasingly important for stakeholders and consumers. For example, M-PESA, a mobile payment system developed in cooperation with Vodafone, has provided access for millions of Kenyans to the formal financial system.

However, low-end innovation faces specific constraints that require a capability set that differs from standard high-end innovation capabilities. Table 7.1 provides an overview of standard practices in eight different areas of innovation capabilities, constraints that low-end innovators face in these areas, and adaptations that help coping with these constraints. The chapter then briefly discusses the specific low-end innovation constraints and characteristics, providing an overview of the low-end capability dimensions and focusing on methods that can be used to adapt standard practice and develop a low-end innovation capability. Finally, the chapter outlines a process to help develop these capabilities.

7.2 Which Constraints Do Low–End Innovators Face?

If a firm is fit for innovation, does that mean it is automatically fit for low-end innovation? Not necessarily. Low-end innovation introduces additional constraints limiting success that firms need to overcome.

The primary constraint for low-end innovations, as indicated, is a low WTP. New products or services need to be affordable – and not just affordable for the average consumer but priced low enough to create a significantly large market at the low end,

Table 7.1: Innovation constraints and corresponding adaptions of standard NPD practice for low-end innovations.

Area	Standard	Constraint	Adaptation
Innovation culture and commitment	Focusing on high-end innovation ("higher, faster, further") Developing ambidexterity for incremental and radical innovation	Low-end market appears inherently less attractive (e.g. low WTP, low-end technical solutions)	Foster low-end and suppressing high-end aspirations Create high-end/low-end ambidexterity and a switching culture
Cost reduction	Using process innovation to reduce costs in later NPD stages (e.g. after testing or launch)	Low WTP	Integrated cost-reducing innovation from the outset
Scaling	Scaling capabilities often beneficial but not always required (e.g. very high-end products, niche products)	High number of customers Low WTP	High-volume scaling required from the beginning to reduce costs and serve low-end customers
Customer needs	Established and standardized methods for customer needs acquisition (e.g. Voice of the Customer) External providers of market research data	Large distance (geographically and psychologically) between developers and customers (e.g. different abilities to pay) Heterogeneous needs	Market immersion techniques to acquire distant customer needs
Innovation process	Using Stage-Gate–type processes Shortening NPD cycle times	Heterogeneous and ambiguous needs	Highly iterative processes to reduce ambiguity Longer NPD cycle times may be required
Innovation scope	Focused innovation efforts on core problems	Market constraints such as institutional voids and lack of infrastructure or training	Total solution development to overcome additional market constraints
Distribution	Relying on existing distribution channels	Distribution channels nonexistent or a large number of consumers unable to access the innovation Low-end products viewed as unattractive by channel gatekeepers (e.g. target consumers with a low WTP)	Develop distribution solutions that overcome access barriers Consider direct distribution
Networking	Collaborative efforts with upstream partners (e.g. universities) to solve technological problems	Infrastructural and institutional voids more important than technological problems Target customers' need for aid	Networking with downstream stakeholders and gatekeepers that support target customers

WTP – Willingness (and ability) to pay.

including consumers who previously have not been able to purchase comparable products. This constraint is unique because it requires cost-reducing innovation and high-volume scaling from the outset, which may make the market and innovation appear unattractive for the organization and its partners. In addition, this constraint can also create a disconnect in needs and context understanding between developers, who typically have a high ability to pay, and low-end consumers with a low ability to pay.

In addition, low-end markets typically contain secondary constraints. First, *market and consumer constraints* such as underdeveloped infrastructures, institutional voids, and a lack of training pose challenges not typically present in high-end markets. Second, low-end markets consist of a *high number of customers*, which creates challenges with regard to scaling and distribution. In contrast to high-end innovations, low-end innovations cannot diffuse from the top of the pyramid. Instead, low-end innovators need to produce products in large numbers from the beginning. Third, in contrast to general perceptions, low-end consumers are heterogeneous, and low-end needs and contexts are not uniform but heterogeneous. A consumer in Kenya has different needs and faces different obstacles from a consumer in South Africa, in addition to the presence of different individual needs within a region. This creates *ambiguity and fuzziness* regarding needs and product requirements. These primary and secondary constraints require developing capabilities that firms pursuing high-end innovation may lack or adapting current capabilities to operate in new ways.

7.3 Adaptations: Methods and Processes to Develop Low-End Innovation Capabilities

The following sections explain the eight different operational dimensions that make up a firm's low-end innovation capability. I briefly describe each dimension and provide an overview of methods, tools, or processes that can support firms in building each dimension. Using these general methods can serve as a starting point to developing unique routines, processes, and tools that create a competitive advantage for generating low-end innovations for firms.

Develop a Low-End Innovation Culture and Commitment

The objective here is to create and maintain an organizational environment that supports low-end innovation. Contingencies to consider are that if you produce low-end products only, you must suppress high-end product bias. If you produce high- and low-end products simultaneously, you must develop a switching culture.

Successful low-end innovation requires management commitment to low-end innovation as well as a culture that supports developing products for low-end consumers because low-end innovation appears less attractive than high-end innovation. Thus, firms need to create and maintain an organizational environment that supports low-end innovation. Depending on whether the firm aims at developing low-end products only or developing both low-end and high-end products, different strategies are required. Low-end-only firms need a culture and commitment strategy that suppresses aspirations for high-end projects because "high end" is associated with superior products and status (but not necessarily higher profits). In contrast, firms pursuing low-end and high-end innovation simultaneously need processes that support switching between these two innovation targets.

If firms solely develop low-end products, they need to establish a low-end culture and *suppress* aspirations toward high-end innovation. These firms need an organizational identity that centers on cost and low-end customers. For example, Ryanair is well known for its extreme cost orientation and its focus on eliminating any frills to lower prices and enable more consumers to fly. Founder and chief executive Michael Leary constantly emphasizes the firm's goal to remain the price leader and thus suppresses any aspirations for moving toward the higher end. In contrast, Volkswagen (the "people's car") did not suppress high-end ambitions when it introduced the Phaeton. However, the $100 000 flagship sedan never reached the sales targets, and the company reportedly lost $30 000 per car.

While an organization's culture may be the most difficult thing to change, three steps can support the process (DiDonato and Gill, 2015):

1. The first prerequisite is awareness, which managers can raise using communication tools ranging from personal communication (e.g. meetings, team events) to printed and visual communication (e.g. posters, newsletters, mouse pads).

2. After becoming aware of the desired low-end culture, the organization needs time to learn and adapt to the new culture. Learning requires in-depth understanding, which can be facilitated by workshops that cover different aspects of the intended low-end culture including successful examples such as Ryanair, GE, McDonald's, and Aravind Eye Hospitals.

3. Employees and managers then need to practice the newly learned behaviors before they are made accountable for their actions. For example, in a practice period, research and development teams are assessed depending on the time they have worked on low-end and high-end projects. After the practice period, funds can be awarded and withdrawn depending on whether team managers have reached the low-end innovation goals. Establishing goals related to the low-end strategy is important because managers may end up in an activity trap, implicitly fostering high-end projects in the day-to-day business. Thus, management by objectives using SMART – specific, measurable, achievable, relevant, time-bound – goals supports low-end innovation culture and commitment and thus avoids having the low-end strategy become a toothless paper tiger.

Switching between conflicting goals such as developing high-end and low-end innovations is an even more difficult task for organizations. Innovation research has coined the term "organizational ambidexterity" to describe an organization's ability to pursue two conflicting goals simultaneously. In particular, there are two ways to achieve ambidexterity: structural ambidexterity and contextual ambidexterity.

■ *Structural ambidexterity* means creating separate units each pursuing their specific goal. For example, the automaker Renault added Dacia as an independent brand to develop new models for the low-end market while Renault continued to serve the mid-range segment. This approach ensures that each unit can align the organization and the brand with the strategic goal. However, structural ambidexterity also impedes exploiting synergies because it may require parallel systems for research and development, production, marketing, and distribution.

■ *Contextual ambidexterity* requires that all members of the organization divide their time and attention between low-end and high-end projects according to the firm's strategy. However, if managers do not distinguish between high-end and low-end projects explicitly, the firm is more likely to neglect low-end projects because decision makers implicitly associate high-end with status and success. Therefore, contextual ambidexterity requires discipline and adequate management tools to maintain a low-end/high-end balance. First, firms need an overall strategy that differentiates between low-end and high-end markets and sets individual goals for each target market. Second, firms can adapt existing portfolio methods to balance low-end and high-end projects. Most firms already manage innovation portfolios that balance radical and incremental projects; they can use the same approach for managing low-end and high-end projects. A portfolio approach that illustrates both low-end and high-end projects in the new product development (NPD) process helps to uncover early on if the firm cuts back on switching and loses its balance.

Thus, depending on the specific situation, firms need to suppress high-end aspirations or manage a switching process between high-end and low-end innovation; neither capability is standard NPD practice. Thus, a structured process that emphasizes awareness, learning, practice, and accountability can help to establish a low-end culture. Structural or contextual ambidexterity that differentiates between high-end and low-end projects enables a switching culture.

Integrate Cost-Reducing Innovation Early

The objective here is to innovate inputs and processes during NPD to reduce costs significantly. There are no contingences to consider, as this is a necessary capability across all contexts.

In contrast to traditional innovation projects, where firms most typically launch cost-reduction initiatives after the product has found initial acceptance in the market, low-end innovation requires cost-reducing innovation as an integral part of NPD because the target customers have a low WTP. Therefore, the capability to innovate the design, inputs, and processes in early stages of the NPD process to reduce costs significantly is essential for firms targeting low-end markets.

Low-end NPD teams can use cost-oriented tools such as Design-to-Cost, target costing, value engineering, and Design for Manufacture and Assembly to structure cost-reduction efforts from the outset. As a first step, independent of which of these tools are used, low-end innovators need to identify the product cost drivers. Typically, this analysis separates product inputs and manufacturing process steps into the few items that account for a large percentage of the final costs versus a large number of items that contribute to only a small fraction of the final costs (cf. ABC analysis). In a second step, these cost drivers are analyzed to identify cost-reduction opportunities.

Cost-reducing approaches from project outset include (Meeker and McWilliams, 2003):

■ *(Re)design for low cost*. A large percentage of the final product's costs are determined in the design stage. Therefore, (re)design offers the largest potential for cost reductions. For example, both the Tata Nano and the Dacia Logan show that redesigning complex products like cars can lead to substantial cost reductions. In addition, Procter & Gamble redesigned the packaging of drugstore items and produced small sachets to make them affordable for low-income families in emerging markets, highlighting the cost-reduction potential of radical redesign even for relatively simple products. However, the multitude of starting points – ranging from changing the entire design or individual features, substituting input materials, to simplifying assembly steps – provides a challenge for low-cost innovators. Managers need to be aware that every design decision is a cost decision.

■ *Simplification*. Low-end products cannot offer all the features that high-end products offer. Therefore, a critical step in the cost-reduction process is simplifying the product or the service until only the essential features for this particular low-end target market are included. For example, low-cost cars (Suzuki Alto, Dacia Logan, Tata Nano) eliminate features customers in traditional markets expect (e.g. power steering, cup holders) to achieve a lower price at a "good-enough" overall performance level (Wang and Kimble 2010).

■ *Component substitution and sourcing*. Low-end innovators need to find new components that are cheaper and that better match the constraints in low-end markets. For example, GE designed a low-cost ultrasound device that uses commodity technologies such as notebook screens for imaging (Zeschky et al., 2011). Systematically screening for sourcing alternatives and the use of third-party solutions instead of internal procurement can reduce costs.

■ *Manufacturing and delivery*. In addition to design and input factors, manufacturing and service delivery processes contribute to cost-reducing efforts. For example, low-end airlines have increased labor utilization; Walmart has developed sophisticated, low-cost logistics systems; and low-end cars are typically assembled in low-income countries. Thus, including manufacturing and process considerations into the NPD process as suggested by Design for Manufacture and Assembly and related methods is paramount for low-end innovation.

Finally, and in addition to these process-oriented methods, firms can also benefit from cross-functional NPD teams that include experts for cost reduction, sourcing, and manufacturing. This may be particularly important to truly integrate cost-reducing innovation into the early stages of NPD, which is not standard practice.

Scale for High Volumes

The objective here is to grow volumes rapidly to lower costs and serve a large number of customers. The contingency to consider is that for a small firm, this capability dimension is highly relevant. For a large firm, the capability dimension is less relevant.

Low-end innovation means developing affordable products for a large population of consumers who were previously excluded due to their low WTP. Thus, low-end innovation requires scaling processes that allow firms to increase volumes rapidly and flawlessly from the beginning. While scaling is important in many different contexts, it is essential in a low-end context to reduce costs and serve a high number of customers.

Therefore, developing high-volume scaling capabilities requires a design-for-many mind-set. During NPD, the development team needs to be aware that the final product or service must scale to the large volumes required to be successful in low-end markets. Thus, including high-volume manufacturers in the NPD process is important for firms that do not have high-volume production facilities. For example, American Biophysics developed the Mosquito Magnet, a device to capture mosquitoes using carbon dioxide. Although the product was highly successful after launch, the firm was ill equipped to manage the transition of the production process from the small-scale facility in the United States to a high-volume plant in China. Quality levels dropped and the product almost went off the market (Schneider and Hall, 2011).

In addition, high-volume scaling for low-end markets typically requires overcoming the paradox of realizing economies of scale by producing more of the same product while also adapting the innovation to the heterogeneous low-end contexts found across the world. Using a modular design approach can help overcome this paradox by providing both the required number of parts to achieve economies of scale and the required differentiation for different needs. Designing standardized modules and parts for these modules increases scale economy advantages but also allows for adaptations.

To do high-volume scaling, firms can rely on closed or open modular systems (Wang and Kimble, 2010). For example, the Volkswagen Group successfully uses the same modular platform (Modularer Querbaukasten, or MQB) for a wide variety of different cars, creating internal economies of scale (closed system). In a service context, scaling may require turning different variations of a process into one uniform process. For example, low-cost airlines only use a single plane type to achieve lower inventory levels for spare parts and uniform maintenance processes (Raynor, 2011). When the personal computer industry moved from a closed to an open system, external economies of scale enabled cost reductions, which facilitated the development of lower-priced computers that significantly expanded the market at the low end.

Thus, developing a design-for-many mind-set and systematically exploiting economies of scale using a modular approach can support firms in developing high-volume scaling capabilities, which are particularly important to overcome the constraints of low WTP and high number of consumers.

Acquire Knowledge about Needs for Geographically and Culturally Distant Consumers

The objective here is to understand low-end consumer needs by overcoming the geographical and psychological distance between the NPD team and low-end consumers. The contingency to consider is the distance between the NPD team and the low-end market. The further they are apart psychologically and geographically, the higher the relevance of this capability dimension.

Low-end customers are often geographically, culturally, or psychologically distant from the NPD team. For example, engineers in Germany and the United States developing new low-end products for the emerging markets are geographically distant from those markets. In addition, engineers from developed countries typically live in a different world compared to low-income consumers in emerging countries, which adds cultural and psychological distance between innovation designers and users. Thus, firms need capabilities to systematically acquire knowledge about distant customer needs.

Methods that help the NPD team immerse itself in the market's needs and experience the constraints can help bridge the distance. Market immersion, ethnography, and empathic design allow a deep understanding of distant customers. During market immersion, the entire NPD team – not just one employee from the marketing department – obtains firsthand experience with customers and the market. Similarly, ethnographic market research centers on observing consumers in their own environment. This method typically uses notes, videos, and interviews as data for analyzing and understanding consumer needs. In a similar vein, for empathic design, innovators find methods to put themselves in the shoes of the customers. For example, suits that simulate the effects of aging by constraining and slowing movement can help the NPD team to develop senior-friendly products. In a low-end context, market immersion means living in the low-end context, visiting the low-end context regularly, or trying to experience the low-end context using storytelling or videos. For example, in Procter & Gamble's "Living It" program, employees lived with low-income consumers for several days to experience their needs and constraints firsthand. As a result, the company developed the Downy Single Rinse fabric softener that allowed Mexican mothers, for whom good-smelling and soft clothes were important, to rinse once instead of several times and thus overcome the "newly discovered" constraint of a limited water supply.

Immersion programs are important to bridge the worlds of high-income employees and low-income consumers. Programs that follow immersion techniques, ethnographic methods, or empathic design provide a basis to develop capabilities for acquiring distant consumer needs.

Iterate Between Product Development and Market Feedback

The objective here is to gather and process information to identify and test solutions that overcome ambiguity and constraints. The contingency to consider is the level of ambiguity in the target market. The more ambiguity there is in the market, the higher the relevance of this capability dimension.

Iteration processes use a large number of short development and feedback cycles instead of a few but longer cycles. Iteration supports firms in finding solutions for the constraints in low-end markets and resolving ambiguity associated with low-end market needs. For example, GE Healthcare relies on Fastworks – an iterative process to develop, test, and commercialize affordable healthcare devices for emerging markets.

Two specific support methods incorporate the iteration principle: the probe-and-learn method and the lean start-up approach. Both methods follow a similar procedure that firms can use to structure their iteration initiatives and develop capabilities in this dimension. The first step, probing, introduces an early-stage prototype, a minimum viable product, or an immature product to the market. The product does not need to be fully functional or meet all needs of low-end consumers initially. In the second step, learning, the firm collects real-world feedback and data to learn about the market and the initial solution. In this stage, it is important to gather qualitative data firsthand. Survey methods that are reliable in traditional markets do not provide reliable results in a low-end innovation context because low-end innovation addresses a large number of consumers who have no experience in this product category. This makes a direct, quantitative approach less reliable than in-person observation. The third component, iteration, refers to repeating the first two steps until the product meets low-end market needs and overcomes existing constraints. Managers should avoid trying to achieve everything in a single iteration but instead cautiously evolve toward the final solution. The rationale behind this process is that learning through experience is much more useful in low-end markets, which tend to be quite ambiguous.

It is important to understand that iteration and improvisation are different. While improvisation is a flexible and spontaneous process, iteration is a structured, goal-oriented process. Iteration uses structured experimentation to eliminate uncertainty.

Develop a Total Solution, Not Just a Product

The objective here is to develop holistic solution systems adapted to low-end market conditions and barriers that enable low-end consumers to buy and use the innovation. The contingency to consider is the number of constraints low-end consumers face. The more constraints there are, the higher the relevance of this capability dimension.

Innovation in low-end markets requires coping with more constraints than innovation in high-end markets. Developing a total solution and the business model around these constraints can take longer to develop than low-end products themselves (Chesbrough et al., 2006). For example, low-end medical device firms need to develop device-servicing networks already available in traditional markets. They may need to develop training materials, find partners that are able to provide the service, and establish a financial model to pay for these services.

To start, total solution development requires in-depth knowledge about all of the constraints target market members face. Low-end market immersion and iteration processes can provide this information. Two additional methods can help the NPD team to find a solution. First, a knowledge management system that contains blueprints for solutions that have successfully overcome constraints can be used to transfer existing solutions to the specific context. For example, Honda introduced a lottery system to finance low-cost diesel generators in India. Each customer in a predefined group pays a fixed amount of money each month. Every month, one randomly drawn customer receives a generator, until all customers have received a one. This solution is likely applicable in a different context as well.

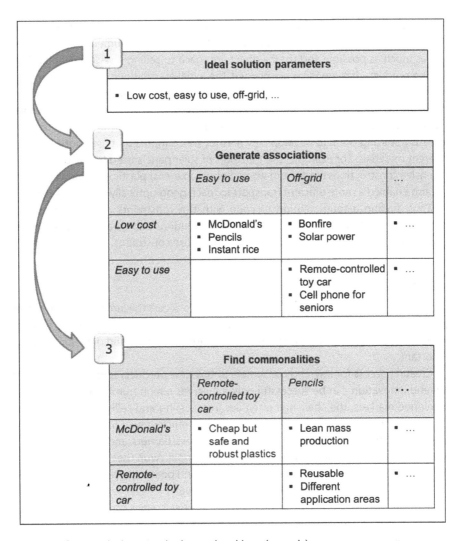

Figure 7.1: Creative thinking to solve low-end problems (example).

To develop entirely new solutions for existing constraints, this creative thinking technique can be helpful (see Figure 7.1 for an example). First, participants brainstorm five to 10 ideal solution parameters. For example, the product needs to be low cost, easy to use, and off-grid (i.e. not depending on public utilities). Second, these ideal parameters are combined to generate associations from each pair. For example, "low-cost" and "easy to use" can evoke diverse concepts like McDonald's, pencil, or instant rice. Combining "easy to use" and "off-grid" could evoke terms like "remote-controlled toy car" or "cellphone for seniors." These associations are the first opportunity to generate ideas by transferring them to the actual low-end context. For example, the principle of McDonald's self-service can be translated to business-to-business markets. Dow Corning launched the Xiameter brand that automated the consumer transaction process as much as possible and used a direct approach to selling low-cost, standardized silicone products. If more ideas are needed, the initial associations can be used in pairs in the "commonality matrix" to find a commonality that is transferable to the low-end innovation context. For example, combining McDonald's with the remote-controlled toy car could evoke the commonality "cheap but safe and robust plastic," which could serve as a starting point to develop new plastics-based inputs that previously relied on different materials. For example, the transport of solar panels used to rely on relatively expensive constructions made from wood. Robust, low-cost plastic edges lowered costs but also enabled a more efficient transport to reach geographically dispersed areas.

Thus, finding a total solution to cope with the constraints of low-end markets requires both systematic knowledge of existing solutions and creativity management to develop entirely new solutions that overcome those constraints.

Create Access for All

The objective here is to enable low-end consumers to access the innovation. The contingency to consider is the target market type. In emerging markets, firms need to focus on overcoming barriers; in developed markets, distribution access and diffusion are more important.

Creating access for low-end consumers to buy new products is important because low-end innovation can be successful only if it serves a high number of customers. In developed markets, the challenge often lies in accessing and selling the product into existing distribution systems and doing so in a cost-efficient way. In emerging markets, creating access refers to overcoming existing access barriers and institutional voids (e.g. lack of infrastructure or power supply). For example, Avon uses microfranchisees to reach people in the Amazon rain forest via canoes and boats, alleviating existing access barriers due to a lack of roads (Chesbrough et al. 2006).

In the face of barriers and institutional voids, three strategies can be used in isolation or combination (Khanna et al., 2005). First, the firm adapts its strategy to the low-end context and existing constraints. For example, while Dell was very successful using a build-to-order computer system in the United States and other developed markets, it used distributors and system integrators in China because internet usage was not as widespread and state-owned enterprises had unique requirements. Second, large multinationals may be able to change the context. For example, the Metro Group, a retail and wholesale company, established a cold-storage value chain that did not exist and therefore was able to sell fish and meats in urban areas in China. Third, if firms are unable to change or adapt to the low-end context, they may just have to stay away from the market. For example, Home Depot's business model relies on an efficient highway system to keep inventory costs low and enable low prices. Without certain systems and institutions like efficient highways, Home Depot may be unable to create a viable path for consumers in low-end emerging markets.

In developed markets, bringing the low-end product into existing distribution channels can be a challenge, because distributors may view low-end products as inferior and low margin. Changing the perspective toward total units and profits instead of profit per unit can help negotiate access. Alternatively, low-cost innovators can use direct distribution to ensure widespread diffusion at low cost. For example, DollarShaveClub.com and Ryanair were successful using a direct distribution approach. This approach, however, requires infrastructure, such as efficient postal systems and internet access as well as marketing capabilities to create consumer awareness. For example, DollarShaveClub.com was successful in creating viral marketing campaigns and Ryanair's chief executive, Michael Leary, continuously engages in publicity stunts, because creating brand awareness is an important success factor for direct distribution.

Thus, firms targeting emerging markets may face infrastructural and institutional voids. Adapting to or changing the context are two strategies that can help to create access. In a developed market, accessing existing distribution channels or establishing a direct channel are both viable but challenging alternatives to diffuse low-end innovations.

Network with Multiple Partners to Support Low-End Customers

The objective here is to connect with low-end consumers' stakeholders and gatekeepers to leverage existing distribution, protection, and support systems. The contingency to consider is the target market type. In emerging markets, firms need to connect with downstream stakeholders; in developed markets, engaging in strategic partnerships with gatekeepers is more important.

Strategic partnerships with stakeholders and gatekeepers help to access low-end markets. For example, Philips works with multiple partners to compensate for its lack of capabilities such as distribution knowledge for rural areas and marketing to the poor (Hens 2012). The Metro Group gained support from local governments for quality standards in exchange for bringing more food products into the tax net (Khanna et al. 2005). In general, research suggests that emerging-market low-end innovation projects benefit from government agency partnerships, because they often have social implications that are relevant to governments.

To structure stakeholder and gatekeeper integration for new product development, Vaquero Martín et al. (2016) provide a stakeholder model that is divided into three parts:

1. *Identification* refers to the capability to find and access all stakeholders that influence market acceptance and success. Mapping stakeholder groups and understanding their stakes and power can facilitate a comprehensive identification process that avoids biased stakeholder selection. For example, managers may have easy access to some stakeholders in higher-end markets and may integrate this stakeholder group while other more distant stakeholders in low-end markets may be more important for success.

2. *Interaction* refers to the capability to exchange information about the innovation with all relevant stakeholders. An open environment, using a common language, and adequate interactions methods such as face-to-face meetings all contribute to this capability.

3. *Integration* refers to integrating the information from the stakeholders in the internal NPD process. Internal resistance against external input and difficulty in finding a solution to address stakeholder needs are challenges, while formalization using tools, indicators, and incentives can help in the integration process.

Thus, firms need a structured process to connect with relevant downstream stakeholders and gatekeepers that can support the low-end innovation project. These processes differ from standard practice focusing on upstream partners such as universities to solve technological challenges.

7.4 Defining the Path for Developing Low-End Innovation Capabilities

Low-end innovation requires many different capability sets; so where should firms start? First, the firm needs to analyze internal and external contingencies as described in each of the earlier sections and define the target system for their specific low-end innovation capability. For example, is the target market an emerging or a developed market? Does the firm innovate for low-end markets only or for both high- and low-end markets? The answers to these questions define the configuration of the target system. Second, managers need to analyze the status quo for each capability dimension. To what extent does the firm fulfill the required capabilities? For example, does the firm have high-volume scaling capabilities? Does it lack a low-end innovation culture? Third, the firm needs to devise capability development plans considering the possible ways to develop each low-end capability dimension discussed earlier (see Figure 7.2).

In Step 1 of the low-end innovation capability development process, firms need to analyze their specific situation with regard to internal (firm) and external (market) characteristics. Figure 7.3 provides the most important contingency questions, describes the situation of Example Inc., and provides the results for the target system of Example Inc.

In Step 2 of the capability development process, firms need to analyze the status quo. Doing this requires determining several indicators for each capability dimension. Section 7.3 provides starting points for developing a coherent system of indicators. In addition, Step 2 requires finding a benchmark. For example, firms can use as benchmarks other firms that successfully serve the same or similarly constrained consumers,

Figure 7.2: Capability development process.

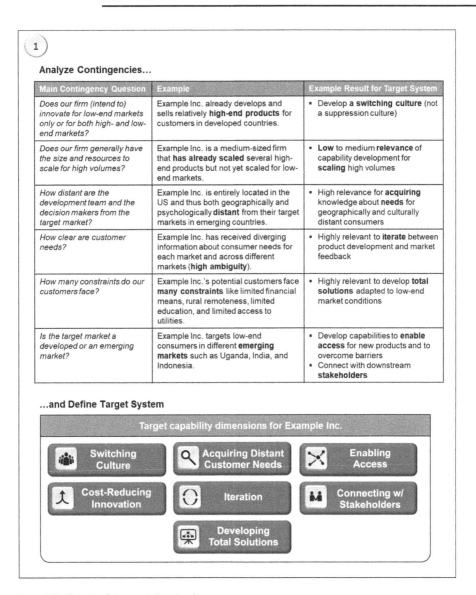

Figure 7.3: Step 1 of the capability development process.

or they can define their aspiration level internally. Subsequently, the firm needs to assess the status as compared with the benchmark or aspiration level. Figure 7.4 provides an example of an aggregated result of Step 2.

In Step 3, the firm needs to develop a specific action plan to improve inadequate capability dimensions. Section 7.3 of this chapter provides several examples for specific actions. The action plan needs to set objectives, define criteria for success, assign responsibilities and resources, and set target dates. Figure 7.5 provides an action plan excerpt for Example Inc.

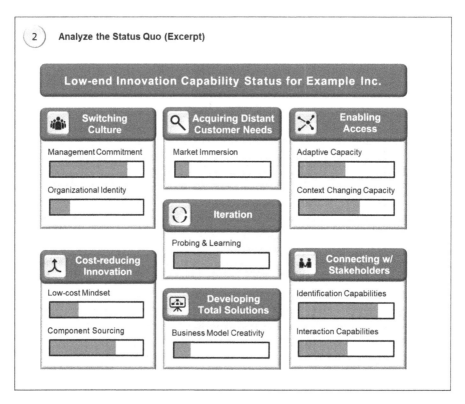

Figure 7.4: Step 2 of the capability development process.

3 Devise Capability Development Plan (Excerpt)

Aspect	Action Steps	Responsibility	Timeline
Management Commitment (Switching Culture)	• Communicate strategy	• John Smith	• Next month
	• Change accountability	• Marie Meyer	• End of year
	...	...	...
Organizational Identity	• Improve awareness	• Marc Coats	• End of year
	• Adapt performance metrics	• Toni Mueller	• End of year
	...	...	...
Market Immersion (Acquiring Distant Customer Needs)	• Conduct initial workshop	• Bo Johnson	• In 2 months
	• Train R&D in ethnography	• Zoey Barnes	• In 6 months
	• ...	• ...	• ...

Figure 7.5: Step 3 of the capability development process.

7.5 Conclusion

This chapter described low-end innovations and the constraints low-end innovators face. It also argued that low-end innovation requires a low-end innovation capability set that adapts standard NPD practice to cope with low-end constraints. This chapter explained adaptations in eight different low-end capability dimensions and provided ideas on how to develop a firm-level low-end innovation capability.

References

Chesbrough, H., Ahern, S., Finn, M., and Guerraz, S. (2006). Business models for technology in the developing world: the role of non-governmental organizations. *California Management Review* 48 (3): 47–62.

DiDonato, T. and N. Gill. 2015. Changing an organization's culture, without resistance or blame. Harvard Business Review 15 . https://hbr.org/2015/07/changing-an-organizations-culture-without-resistance-or-blame.

Hammond, A. L., Kramer, W. J., Katz, R. S. et al. (2007). *The next 4 billion: Market size and business strategy at the base of the pyramid.* Washington, DC: World Resources Institute.

Hens, L. (2012). Overcoming institutional distance: Expansion to base-of-the-pyramid markets. *Journal of Business Research* 65 (12): 1692–1699.

Khanna, T., Palepu, K. G., and Sinha, J. (2005). Strategies that fit emerging markets. *Harvard Business Review* 83 (6): 4–19.

Meeker, D. and McWilliams, F. J. 2003. Structured cost reduction: Value engineering by the numbers. Presented at The 18th Annual International Conference on DFMA. Newport, RI.

Nielsen. (2015). *Looking to achieve new product success?* The Nielsen Company: Listen to your consumers http://www.nielsen.com/content/dam/nielsenglobal/de/docs/Nielsen%20Global%20New%20Product%20Innovation%20Report%20June%202015.pdf.

Raynor, M. E. (2011). Disruptive innovation: The Southwest Airlines case revisited. *Strategy & Leadership* 39 (4): 31–34.

Schneider, J. and Hall, J. (2011). Why most product launches fail. *Harvard Business Review* 89 (4): 21–23.

Vaquero Martín, M., Reinhardt, R., and Gurtner, S. (2016). Stakeholder integration in new product development: a systematic analysis of drivers and firm capabilities. *R&D Management* 46 (S3): 1095–1112.

Wang, H. and Kimble, C. (2010). Low-cost strategy through product architecture: Lessons from China. *Journal of Business Strategy* 31 (3): 12–20.

Zeschky, M., Widenmayer, B., and Gassmann, O. (2011). Frugal innovation in emerging markets. *Research-Technology Management* 54 (4): 38–45.

About the Author

DR. RONNY REINHARDT is a Research Associate at the Chair of General Management and Marketing of the Friedrich-Schiller-University Jena, Germany. He received his PhD in Business Administration and Economics and his master's degree in Business Administration and Engineering from Technische Universität Dresden in Germany. His research focuses on innovation management with an emphasis on high-end and low-end innovation, decision making, and innovation adoption and resistance. Dr. Reinhardt has received numerous awards, such as the Academy of Management TIM Division Best Student Paper Award, the Innovation and Product Development Management Conference Thomas Hustad Best Paper Award, the Dr. Dietrich Fricke-Award, the Special Award of the Erich-Glowatzky-Foundation, and the Victor Klemperer-Certificate for his research and academic achievements. His research has been published in the *Journal of Product Innovation Management*, *Long Range Planning*, the *Journal of Business Research*, *R&D Management*, and *Technological Forecasting and Social Change,* among others.

8

DEVELOPING SOLUTIONS FOR UNDERRESOURCED MARKETS

Aruna Shekar

Massey University, Auckland, New Zealand

Andrew Drain

Massey University, Auckland, New Zealand

Introduction

This chapter provides guidelines on designing solutions for opportunities in underresourced markets. "Underresourced markets" are defined as communities in developing countries made up of resilient people who are not adequately served by currently available products, services, or infrastructure. While the literature uses many terms to describe this user group, such as base of the pyramid, emerging or developing market, or resource-constrained market, for clarity, the authors utilize a single term for clarity: underresourced market.

Underresourced markets offer many opportunities for innovators, but product developers must learn about the specific requirements of the users and market segments first. Traditional approaches are not suited to these resource-constrained environments, as they are based on Western ideology and assume the product developer has an implicit knowledge of the market and user group. This chapter begins by introducing the inadequacies of the traditional new product development (NPD) process for addressing underresourced market constraints. These constraints are then presented, discussed, and illustrated through project examples. Adaptations to the standard process are suggested as a way of leveraging these market constraints to improve product adoption. The chapter ends with some keys to success and pitfalls to avoid when looking to create products for under-resourced remote markets.

8.1 The Traditional New Product Development Process

Cooper's (2014) Stage-Gate® process provides structure to the development and commercialization of new products for developed markets. This model shows the clear focus expected at each stage in the process and provides process "gates" where particular deliverables are required. It also suggests user interaction at each stage in the process to assist in validating ideas as they transition toward physical products.

While many other design processes could be mentioned here, the underlying sentiment of all of them is similar: a large number of ideas, user interaction, and the ability to iterate early. However, while the utility of these principles is not disputed here, there is an obvious difference in success between projects in developed (resourced) versus underresourced markets (Chandra and Neelankavil, 2008). This is due to user and market constraints limiting a product developer's ability to meaningfully interact with underresourced market end users and understand the complexities of the sociocultural environments in which they live.

The reliance on traditional NPD processes, based on technology and internal capabilities, has resulted in the introduction of new products to global markets that have had limited penetration in developing countries, especially for the underresourced market demographic. While the single biggest constraint in developing products for underresourced contexts is affordability, affordability alone, at the expense of functionality and aspirational value, will not be successful. Many failures in underresourced markets are due to a lack of in-depth understanding of user needs and problems. This understanding has led to a greater focus on user-centered or codesign approaches to identify the factors related to key constraints. What are some of the key factors that need to be considered in NPD for underresourced markets?

8.2 Factors to Consider when Designing for Underresourced Markets

The examples given later highlight a number of factors that need to be considered very early in the design process. These factors are centered on identifying user and market constraints that will impact product requirements (see Table 8.1).

The three columns in Table 8.1 refer to particular factors relevant to users, market contexts, and products that need to be researched and considered before developing solutions. While studies have highlighted that most rural individuals have low incomes, low formal education levels, and generally engage in agricultural practices, it is important to not rely on these assumptions alone. As explained in the rice cooker example later in the chapter, ethnographic techniques and role-play are effective ways to learn about end user requirements that a product must address, specific to the

User (earns less than $2 a day)	Market context	Product
■ Education levels ■ Human resources and skills 　■ Culture, habits, attitudes 　■ Needs, goals, value 　■ Occupation 　■ Size of market ■ Financial resources 　■ Socioeconomic levels 　■ Disposable income ■ Language ■ Ethics	■ Reach, logistical access 　■ Natural resource 　■ Weather conditions 　■ Geography, terrain 　■ Humidity, temperature 　■ Access to electricity 　■ Local materials ■ Physical resources 　■ Electricity 　■ Transportation infrastructure 　■ Water supply 　■ Waste removal/recycling 　■ Communication systems 　■ Size and style of dwelling ■ Social resources 　■ Community power structures 　■ Existing relationships with organizations ■ Regulations ■ NGO and social enterprise networks ■ Government	■ Affordable ■ Robust ■ Locally available materials ■ Easy to maintain locally ■ Serves a core need ■ Caters to aspirations ■ Usable, desirable, and useful ■ Intuitive to use ■ Meets regulatory requirements ■ Competitive advantage

Table 8.1: Key factors to research in the specific underresourced market.

market in which it is to be used. Product developers should observe and learn how rural consumers go about their daily lives within their specific environment. They must talk to users and listen carefully to understand their goals, values, and attitudes and at the same time be open to user suggestions. Mutual learning and collaborations between the product developers and user communities must take place early in the NPD process.

Failures of medical products and of personal hygiene and home appliances that were targeted at rural markets in developing countries have shown that success is not as simple as transporting a product created in the West to a rural context (Shekar and Drain, 2016). NPD practitioners have found that establishing contacts with end users in remote rural villages in developing markets is challenging due to differences in languages spoken, the remoteness of some communities, and the lack of communication infrastructure.

The differences in market context conditions are so significant that they must explicitly be taken into consideration at the front end of NPD. Many new product entrants focus mainly on cost reduction of an existing product in order to enter these underresourced markets, which ignores much of the social and cultural value inherent in a new product. New approaches are required for a better understanding of unfamiliar markets, users, constraints, sociocultural issues, and infrastructures.

A useful framework for considering design for underresourced markets are the eight product indicators associated with success: affinity, desirability, reparability, durability, functionality, affordability, usability, and sustainability (Whitehead et al., 2014). These eight factors must be considered early in the product design process and verified through fieldwork. These indicators can help translate user and market constraints and requirements to product characteristics.

Rural areas in developing countries can have a number of constraints, such as lack of electricity, lack of road and transportation infrastructure, limited access to potable water, poor sanitation facilities and waste management, inefficient cooking methods, and labor-intensive methods of food preparation and transportation. However, no two areas are the same, meaning static assumptions about community deficiencies can be just as dangerous as no consideration at all. It is therefore clear that a new approach is needed to understanding the complex user and contextual constraints present in under-resourced markets.

Understanding people's lifestyles and their living conditions in specific rural com-munities has been shown to be critical, but how can companies or practitioners source in-depth information for NPD from a distance? Should they collaborate and, if so, with whom and how? How can they learn about the stakeholders and the needs of commu-nities? How can they carry out a field test for a product? These questions are addressed in next sections.

8.3 A New Approach for Underresourced Markets: Obtain User Knowledge and Partner with Local Organizations

Some companies have successfully developed products for markets in developing countries resulting in long-term profits. They have done so by shifting the focus from internal firm capabilities to utilizing organizational networks in underresourced markets and working closely with rural end users to truly understand the needs the product must address. A typical user approach that is undertaken in developed markets, where a company interacts directly with its users, is shown as a simple schematic diagram in Figure 8.1a. However, in an underresourced rural context (Figure 8.1b), this approach is not advisable due to the constraints listed in Table 8.1. Figure 8.1c highlights the new approach that is suggested when preparing to enter an underresourced mar-ket. Companies should work through an international nongovernment organization (NGO) such as Engineers Without Borders and partner with a local NGO and other key stakeholders to gain access to information and build trust within the community. Typically, rural villages have "chiefs" or village elders who are highly respected by the community. Getting their support can help with dissemination and adoption of social innovations within the community. Companies and product innovators can benefit by working closely in equal partnerships with user communities for mutual gains. Both parties can bring their perspectives and knowledge to the problem-solving and design discussions. Examples of these are given in the next two subsections. An examination of several unsuccessful and successful NPD projects aimed at underresourced markets have resulted in the following lessons learned.

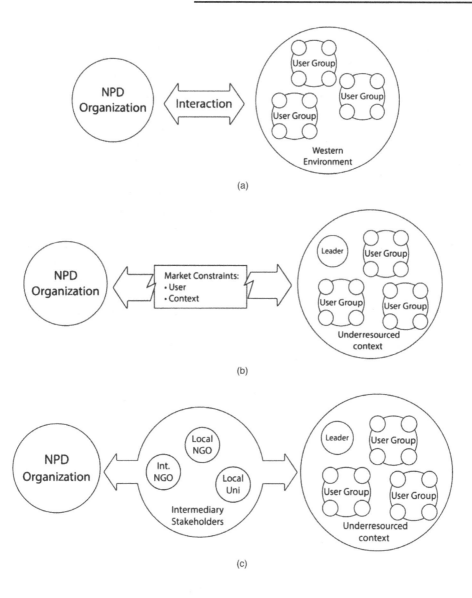

Figure 8.1: (a) Typical approach in a developed market. (b) Common challenges in underresourced markets. (c) New approach for underresourced markets.

Lessons from Unsuccessful Projects

Many product failures have resulted from designing solutions that were dependent on utilities that are taken for granted in Western markets, such as continuous electricity or potable water. Others have failed because designers did not communicate with the community or consider the cultural differences and implications of their solution.

For example, Bosch and Siemens Home Appliance Group's Protos plant oil stove initially failed because the product was rigidly designed for cooking in the home and involved the introduction of new technologies and the use of plant oil for fuel, which did not take into account the lack of a local stove service network or supply of the required plant oil. These contextual constraints were not identified until the field-testing stage, resulting in a waste of time and money.

In another example, providing infant formula to rural households in Bangladesh did not succeed because mothers did not know how to use it and could not differentiate between infant formula and milk powder. Huge amounts of foreign investments are wasted yearly due to failures to account for local customs, cultures, and behaviors by not consulting with individuals in the community about their specific context.

A project on shaving razors for men in rural India failed at first because the developers did not consider user access to running water, which was required during the product use stage. To avoid making a trip overseas, developers tested the product with international Indian students in the United States; however, these students had access to electricity and running water. Visits made to rural homes in India after initial failure discovered that men shave differently and their requirements were different too. For these users, safety in terms of not getting cut was more important than a close shave (as often they would shave in the early hours of the morning when it was still dark in their homes). After the razor was redesigned specifically for these emerging markets, it gained market share as it was relevant to the specific user needs and contextual constraints.

From these examples, it can be seen that it is important for product innovators to visit the specific market and interact closely with community members before and during product development.

Lessons from Successful Projects

An example of a successful product release is the approach Hindustan Unilever Limited (HUL) took to selling shampoo in 500,000 villages across remote parts of India. While entering this new market presented challenges, such as a lack of distribution infrastructure and a lack of disposable income among end users, the use of research information and market-specific product innovations ensured that the new product was a success. First, HUL developed a single-use shampoo sachet to address affordability within the target market. Second, sales training was provided to local women who then acted as product distributors.

Another example is the Tunsai, an innovative water filtration device distributed by iDE Global in Cambodia to rural communities in Southeast Asia. It utilizes locally manufacturable clay pots to filter contaminants from water as well as a simple design to ensure a low retail price. The product was successful, and it then allowed the company to identify an opportunity to provide a higher-quality product that contained more ergonomic and aesthetic considerations. The Super Tunsai was released to appeal to the emerging segment of users to provide a level of aspirational value to an otherwise inexpensive product.

The Norwegian University of Science and Technology (NUST) developed effective partnerships with multiple local organizations to design a new type of prosthetic aimed at being more appropriate for children and more effective in the wet and muddy farm-lands in Cambodia. The local organizations included the International Committee of Red Cross, Regional Physical Rehabilitation Centre, Phnom Penh Orthopaedic Component factory; and local Khmer villagers and children (Hussain et al. 2012). This collaboration helped NUST understand the product, user, and contextual constraints fully, resulting in prosthetics with molded toes and a wider base for walking through mud.

These successful examples show the importance of understanding users' abilities to purchase a product, from both a cost and a distribution perspective, as well as their aspirations and the social value of owning a product. The only way to learn about such complex requirements is through direct interactions with end users and meaningful fieldwork in collaboration with local organizations.

Next we describe in more detail a successful project example and explain how field-work was planned and implemented in a Cambodian village. The text highlights once again the importance of interacting with users in their environment and partnering with local organizations. It shows the importance of stakeholder engagement, hands-on field research, and product trials within the actual product environment.

The Cambodian Rice Cooker: An Example of Meaningful Fieldwork in Collaboration with Local Organizations

This project involved researching failure modes to develop of design improvements for a low-cost rice cooker fueled by methane-rich biogas. The authors worked on the project for a social enterprise based in Cambodia (referred to as Company A) and in a collabora-tive relationship with the international NGO, Engineers Without Borders.

The field research investigated why current rice cookers were failing during usage within homes and how design changes could be made to reduce or eliminate the iden-tified failures. While the collection of field data was instrumental to project success for a contextually appropriate solution, local manufacturing capabilities and user habits also were critical to improving the product.

Project Definition

The project was initiated by a Cambodian social organization based on feedback from rural development organizations and users that rice cookers were failing after an unac-ceptably short period of time. The rice cooker products initially were bought from an external supplier and distributed as an auxiliary product to Company A's main offering, a large organic material digester that produced biogas as a replacement for cooking over wood fires. Because of the cookers were bought externally, little was known about their detailed design or how they would operate in the rural Cambodian context. The main reasons for introducing biogas rice cookers were the heavy reliance on rice in the Cambodian diet and the opportunity to introduce a clean energy source for the cooking of rice. The project included four stages:

1. Background research
2. Contextual research
3. Failure mode analysis
4. Product redesign

This case study focuses on the importance of Stage 2 and the use of micro-ethnographic techniques to learn about how people interact with the product during usage and maintenance. The aim of this project was to "redesign an off-the-shelf biogas rice cooker to eliminate the current failures while being locally manufacturable, maintainable, and affordable." It was also within the scope of this project to define exactly what local manufacture and maintenance skills were available.

When this project was initiated, very little was known about how the rice cooker was used in context or why exactly the product was failing. Much of the feedback Company A had received was through word of mouth from their contacts in rural development organizations, with no empirical data or physical products to examine. What was believed was:

- Rice cookers were no longer functioning correctly after an unacceptably short period of time. This may have been due to corrosion or blockages in the gas flow.
- Rural users were not maintaining important components of the biogas system due to lack of knowledge and lack of access to spare parts.
- Hydrogen sulfide (a corrosive compound that is a by-product of the digestion process in the biodigester) was a contributing factor to failure, potentially due to a lack of required filtration.

While all of this information seemed plausible, it had been discovered through secondary sources and did not take into account user-centered design methods. Logistical constraints, such as access to the remote areas in which the product was used and limited staff resources, were the main reasons for this initial reliance on secondary sources.

Alignment with a Traditional Stage-Gate Development Process

The initial implementation of the rice cooker by Company A followed a traditional Stage-Gate process. The idea of introducing a rice cooker product was supported by a business case built around the relatively cheap cost of importing off-the-shelf units. While extensive technical development was completed on the biogas generator product, little attention was paid to the rice cooker as the complementary product supporting the biogas generator value proposition. It was assumed that adequate development had been completed by the manufacturer and that Cambodian market constraints would not require additional consideration.

Adaptation of a Traditional Stage-Gate Process

To ensure project success, a strong focus needed to be shifted from internal technology testing to user-focused usability and maintainability. This shift required obtaining access to multiple end users in rural areas of Cambodia as well as open discussions with them about the product. To facilitate this, a rural development organization was contacted and a partnership was formed between Company A and the rural organization.

Background Research

Before traveling to Cambodia, a number of areas needed to be researched in detail by the product developer to ensure that the fieldwork would be effective. First, a basic understanding of Cambodian culture, including community dynamics, language, and demographic information, was required. This was critical to interacting appropriately and effectively with end users, but also in interpreting findings and analyzing user behavior. To ensure this step was undertaken effectively, a number of training workshops were attended with NGOs and training providers in Phnom Penh, Cambodia. Second, technical research was undertaken on corrosion processes in biogas applications, chemicals, and materials as well as uncovering existing solutions to these problems in other applications.

Field Research: Fly-on-the-Wall Ethnography and Role-Playing

A development organization in the South Cambodian region of Takeo was used to schedule visits with rural families who had been provided with the biogas rice cookers. While a basic plan was developed, it was important to be flexible due to community priorities and environmental situations, such as monsoon rains. The plan involved accompanying two local technicians as they visited a number of biogas users in the community to discover failed or failing products. To assist with the natural discovery of local insights, two techniques were used: micro-ethnographic fly-on-the-wall research and role-playing.

Fly-on-the-wall ethnography is difficult because employees of the biogas firm are obvious outsiders and a translator must translate for them. It is therefore important to view the engineer's role in this activity as an observer who can be seen by all participants in the activity. Local facilitators should engage with participants and allow for natural interactions to occur between themselves and end users.

To encourage active participation from community end users and local technicians, a broken unit was used as a visual artifact for investigations and further discussions. The aim was to enable both end users and technicians to participate in active discussions about three areas:

1. Why did users believe the product was failing?
2. What, if anything, had they done to fix/minimize this failure mode?
3. How would they propose the product be changed?

The fly-on-the-wall activity involves three steps:

1. *Align with a locally known individual who will elicit interaction with others in the community.* In this case study, a local technician was chosen, as such technicians regularly interacted with families in the community.
2. *Focus interactions around a clear question about the product.* In this case study we focused on the failure modes (parts likely to fail) of the rice cooker.
3. *Firm employees attend as silent observers but are prepared to engage with the group.* It is important that the developer does not act as an "invisible" observer, as this may create a sense of unease in the group. The developer should attempt to withdraw from interactions but be ready to engage in a friendly manner.

While this ethnographic activity is helpful for documenting product change ideas from the technicians, it was harder to get information about product usage conditions that led to failure. To aid in this enquiry, the participatory design technique of role-play was employed.

The purpose of role-playing was to utilize live, acted-out scenes to learn about product aspects that did not naturally arise during conversation or the fly-on-the-wall method. To enable this to occur, a number of investigative questions were used to build a small amount of momentum in the session. Users were then asked to guide a tour of their kitchen and biodigester. This activity allowed the team to learn about the exact system the family had in place and also whether environmental factors, such as rain, dust, pests, or animals, were having a potential impact on the product.

The first role-play demonstrated users' cooking habits including meal preparation, cooking, and cleaning. The role-play activity implemented three steps:

1. *Explain a scenario to the participants.* In this case study the two scenarios explained were the use of the product for cooking rice and the diagnosis of faults if the rice cooker stopped working.
2. *Allow time for the activity to gain momentum.* Be prepared for this activity to start slowly as participants process the instructions and draw from their memory to form a scene. Facilitators may need to prompt participants at the beginning but should look to exit as soon as possible to avoid biasing the natural flow of the scene.
3. *Keep the scope of this activity wide and allow for the scene to transition into new areas.* It is important that facilitators do not enforce strict boundaries for this activity. Restricting scenes to a small scope may result in separate, but important, factors being missed. Facilitators should begin the activity with a small, clearly defined scenario but then allow for the activity to expand naturally.

Having learned that the technicians serviced a number of rice cookers a month, in a second role-play task, they were asked to role-play how they diagnose a fault and then list common issues and solutions. This role-play again took time to build momentum, with one of the facilitators starting the scene by dismantling a rice cooker. Once the technicians felt comfortable with what was expected, they spent two hours explaining in detail many issues faced and how they would usually rectify these issues. A number of scenarios were then proposed to the technicians as a way of investigating as wide a scope as possible. From this activity, corrosion of critical components was identified as a failure mode as well as seals breaking due to lubricants being removed during the maintenance process. A number of initial design ideas were also gathered from both the end users and technicians.

Failure Mode Analysis

The community visits resulted in two important outputs: Valuable information regarding product user interactions and maintenance issues was obtained, and physical broken rice cooker parts (shown in Figure 8.2) that could be analyzed to triangulate some of the information were gathered. The technical analysis is outside the scope of this chapter; however, spectral analysis and electron imaging were used to identify the types of corrosion present on the units and to analyze the gas flow from the biodigesters to identify potentially harmful components.

Figure 8.2: Biogas rice cooker: corroded parts.

Product Redesign

From both field research and technical analysis, a number of potential product changes were identified, including material and geometry changes of critical components, service training, and spare parts, as well as the potential for creating sealed units in the cooker to avoid the possibility of lubrication being removed accidentally.

The project helped to discover this important information:

1. The originally suspected failure modes (from secondary sources) were not accurate but did provide guidance for end user visits.
2. Product user interactions were different from what the organization originally anticipated.
3. The initial role of the local technician was underestimated and needed to be given more focus during both product design and servicing.

The field study identified the specific failure modes of the product and used these to suggest design improvements, based around the main constraints of being affordable and locally manufacturable. The redesigns reduced corrosion and prolong the life of the rice cookers.

8.4 Lessons from the Field Study

This section presents several lessons learned from undertaking the field study.

Partner with Intermediaries

Due to language and cultural differences, it is best to work with a local partner social enterprise, NGO, or university. These organizations are familiar with the behavior, needs, and practices of rural villagers. They generally have local networks and language translators they already have worked through and with.

Community chiefs or village heads are also key stakeholders to be consulted with early on in the process. It is beneficial to build a relationship with these leaders, as the community respects them. Their support can help with a roll-out of products into a new market. Local partners have also often built a relationship with these important community leaders.

Understand the Market and Users

Designers must be prepared to solve problems collaboratively with users, communities, and local organizations right from the very start. Involving key users throughout the process enables people to air their frustrations and voice their suggestions. End users often have a good knowledge of contextual factors, traditional practices, and insights into current local constraints and solutions.

In terms of market and environment constraints, the infrastructure, such as roads, power, water, and wireless communication, must be taken into consideration when looking to develop a product that may depend on such infrastructure. While many underresourced markets will be lacking in certain areas, there may well be opportunities related to infrastructure development. For example, Myanmar has transitioned from almost no telecommunication infrastructure to widespread 3G coverage and affordable internet-enabled smartphones in just a few years, partly due to large amounts of international investment. To assume that rural underserved communities in Myanmar have no mobile phone or internet access removes a potentially effective product launch communication tool.

It also is important to understand the sociocultural environment in which product testing occurs. For example, in some Asian cultures "saving face" is a strong custom that inhibits individuals from expressing critical opinion. This was witnessed firsthand while interacting with women in a small village during the rice cooker field study in Cambodia. Many commercial projects have failed because they do not take into account local behaviors and attitudes. In most cases the research appears to be carried out after the failure to determine why the product failed rather than research being done up front. Other causes for product failure include dependency on factors such as clean water supply, continuous access to electricity, expensive spare parts for maintenance, and other assumptions about infrastructure in underresourced markets.

In terms of product constraints, consideration must be given to the ease of construction, maintainability, robustness, effectiveness in addressing local needs, affordability, and simplicity. It is worth noting that in many underresourced cultures, people generally reuse or repair things, as they cannot afford to keep replacing items. Hence, products should be kept simple and modular so that only specific parts must be replaced. Expecting people to dispose of a single-use product is an assumption that needs to be verified through fieldwork. If in the users' eyes the product still functions, they are likely to reuse it for a longer period of time. Hence it is imperative to design products that are durable, rugged, and can be reused or have inexpensive parts that can be replaced easily by end users. Smaller portions or sachets have been successful for rural consumers as they allow them access to a product previously too expensive to purchase in bulk.

8.5 Adaptation of NPD Processes for Underresourced Markets

Based on the field study and examples, the authors propose the addition of two early stages (shown in Figure 8.3) to the standard NPD process:

1. Partnering with local organizations
2. Understanding the user and market

The addition of stages that explicitly guide the product developer toward partnership, empathy, and external knowledge is important as it ensures market knowledge is gained before the traditional testing stage. The "Partner with organization" stage involves research into the NGOs, social enterprises, and universities that best represent the target market (geographically, demographically, and in terms of values and goals). It also requires contacting and building relationships with those key organizations, which will take time. The benefits of this partnership will become apparent as development and testing in the actual environment becomes simpler and even more valuable.

The stage of "understand the user and market" already may have occurred informally during project scoping and idea generation. However, it is during the development and detailed design stage that in-depth knowledge of the market (as noted in Table 8.1) becomes critical to product success. It is at this stage that field

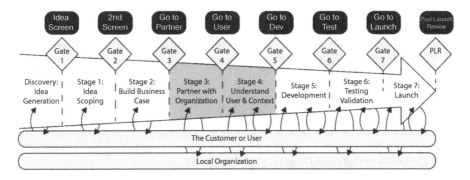

Figure 8.3: Adaptation of NPD process showing links with local organization.

trips into representative communities should be undertaken by product developers, in conjunction with local partners. As shown in the rice cooker field study, it was only through firsthand interaction with end users that the underlying issues could be uncovered. It is at this stage that Whitehead's eight product indicators – affinity, desirability, reparability, durability, functionality, affordability, usability, and sustainability – can be used to structure investigations.

NPD User Interactions in Underresourced Markets

Mutual learning and collaborations between the product development team and users are important, as local users have the best and most complete understanding of some of the contextual issues and problems. End users can offer some traditional solutions and methods based on their own knowledge that has been passed down from generation to generation. We have come across some clever indigenous solutions, such as adding crushed seeds to clarify water and using native plants to make containers and packages (to reduce or avoid the use of plastics). Empowering people with the confidence and abilities to solve some of their problems themselves may help produce sustainable solutions.

Keys to Success

1. *Market immersion.* A focus on the front end of the NPD process to research and learn about the users, product requirements, and contextual constraints is critical. Observe and understand the market environment in a more holistic manner. (See Chapter 7.)
2. *Empathy.* Having concern and care for the people, their lifestyles, needs, and wants, goes a long way in producing a better suited product. User-centered approaches facilitate this learning and ensure that the product meets user requirements.
3. *Field testing.* For any product or service to succeed in a new environment, it must be tested in the actual location by target users before implementation takes place. This testing is critical even if accessing that remote location is a challenge. Earlier simulated tests may be conducted in labs or with people from the target market. However, be aware that these conditions may not be identical to the actual rural market environment.
4. *Collaborations for success.* It is critical to involve key local partners, such as NGOs, community leaders and users, manufacturers, and universities. Clarify and define at the start what their capabilities and roles are.

Pitfalls to Avoid

1. Do not assume that the product will work in a new location without doing up-front research. Mere functionality of a product is not enough; it must function properly within the actual market context and conditions.
2. Do not assume that purchasing decisions of people in underresourced communities are driven only by initial cost.

3. Do not assume all underresourced communities are the same. Market constraints will differ based on sociocultural, economic, and geographical influences.

These guidelines are aimed at practitioners or companies looking to develop socially oriented solutions and consumer products for underresourced contexts.

8.6 Conclusions

This chapter has outlined some of the successful practices in developing solutions for underresourced contexts. Traditional NPD processes struggle to guide international companies to successfully establish themselves in underresourced contexts, because they are built on Western practices and markets. The chapter draws on examples in the literature as well as on project experiences and presents the factors to consider when designing for a community with extreme constraints. Questions such as whether to collaborate with a community partner, how to conduct field research, and what modifications need to be made to the standard process to design appropriate solutions are answered here.

In order to create solutions that are better suited to local needs, certain factors must be researched and taken into consideration early in the NPD process. Table 8.1 provides a list of key factors and constraints to be considered when designing for underresourced contexts. The rice cooker example described a method of investigating and incorporating field testing in a rural setting as a way of identifying some of these factors that are specific to a community or market context.

Solutions that are meant for rural villages must be better suited to the context and needs of people living there. Early collaborations with key local partners help clarify needs and issues and provide insights into contextual requirements. Community partnerships are vital enablers in designing appropriate products for these markets.

In summary, traditional approaches to social product innovation are inadequate in underresourced environments. Examples of a range of commercial endeavors highlighted the requirement for in-depth early research to identify market and user factors before designing solutions for underresourced contexts. These markets present different user needs and sociocultural habits that must be considered early in the NPD process. The adapted development process, keys to success, and pitfalls to avoid provide guidelines to help address some of the current issues of product failures in underresourced contexts and result in more appropriately designed solutions.

References

Chandra, M. and Neelankavil, J. (2008). Product development and innovation for developing countries: Potential and challenges. *Journal of Management Development* 27 (10): 1017–1025.

Cooper, R. G. (2014). What's next? After Stage-Gate. *Research-Technology Management* 51 (1): 20–31. doi: 10.5437/08956308X5606963.

Hussain, S., Sanders, E. B. -N., and Steinert, M. (2012). Participatory design with marginalized people in developing countries: Challenges and opportunities experienced in a field study in Cambodia. *International Journal of Design* 6 (2): 91–109.

Shekar, A. and Drain, A. (2016). Community engineering: Raising awareness, skills and knowledge to contribute towards sustainable development. *International Journal of Mechanical Engineering Education* 44 (4): 272–283.

Whitehead, T., Evans, M. and Bingham, G. (2014). A framework for design and assessment of products in developing countries. http://www.drs2014.org/media/654441/0313-file1.pdf.

About the Authors

DR. ARUNA SHEKAR is a Senior Lecturer and Major Leader in Product Development at Massey University, Auckland, New Zealand. She has taught at the university for more than two decades and has coordinated the final-year capstone projects with industry. She continues to champion the application of creativity and design skills to generating meaningful solutions that are strongly user focused and context appropriate. Dr. Shekar has led the first-year social innovation course in conjunction with Engineers Without Borders for four years, with her students winning national or Australasian awards every year. She has many publications to her credit in international peer-reviewed journals and refereed conference proceedings, including a chapter in the book *Open Innovation: New Product Development Essentials from PDMA*. She has presented keynote speeches and served as program chair at several conferences. Dr. Shekar is a Foundation Board member of the Product Development and Management Association in New Zealand. She was appointed Vice President for Global Affiliates of the Product Development and Management Association in the United States in 2016, and interacts with leaders and affiliates in the Asia-Pacific.

ANDREW DRAIN joined the Massey University School of Engineering and Advanced Technology at Massey University, New Zealand, in 2015 as a lecturer with a focus on product design and humanitarian engineering. His research focuses on the role of participatory design processes in the creation of technology with communities in developing countries. While his research includes a range of engineering applications such as sanitation, cooking, and domestic electronics, the design of assistive technologies with people with disability is the focus. This is due to the challenges individuals with disability face in rural areas of developing countries and their aspirations to be involved in local social, religious, and economic activities. He has worked as a product developer in the medical industry and more recently as a consultant in rural areas of Cambodia and India. He has published in creativity-focused journals such as *CoDesign* and has received a Red Dot Design Award for his humanitarian product development work.

9

OVERCOMING MARKET CONSTRAINTS IN EMERGING MARKETS: LESSONS FROM SOCIAL ENTERPRISES IN THE INDIAN HEALTHCARE SECTOR

Nivedita Agarwal

Friedrich-Alexander-Universität, Erlangen-Nürnberg, Germany

Alexander Brem

Friedrich-Alexander-Universität, Erlangen-Nürnberg, Germany

Introduction

Social enterprises are hybrid ventures that use innovative business models to address existing societal challenges in a financially sustainable way. Creating social impact is the main goal of such enterprises, and generating economic value is necessary for their sustainability. The immense success of these social enterprises in emerging markets has caught the attention of both business and academia. Blending business strategies with inclusive growth, these enterprises have reached unimaginable scale and inaccessible markets. Leading exemplars are the Grameen Bank and the Bangladesh Rehabilitation Assistance Committee in Bangladesh and Aravind Eye Care System (AECS) and Narayana Health in India. For example, Grameen Bank offers microfinancing opportunities to more than 97% of the villages in Bangladesh while the Bangladesh Rehabilitation

Assistance Committee has successfully delivered healthcare services to more than 90% of the households in hard-to-reach regions. Similarly, AECS and Narayan Health, accessing over 15 million blind people and around 2 million heart patients every year, have been successful in reaching the poor population in India who were cut off from traditional healthcare structures.

As indicated in Chapter 8, scaling and creating access to low-end consumers has always been a challenge for businesses commercializing at the low-income segment. Increasingly, businesses are adopting inclusive business models (including customers also as suppliers) and collaborating with local social enterprises, government, and stakeholders to reach the inaccessible markets. For example, Philips and GE have collaborated with local banks and other partners to generate a robust distribution network in resource-constrained regions. Telenor, in collaboration with both Grameen Bank and the Bangladesh Rehabilitation Assistance Committee, has started affordable Village Pay Phones services. Avon and Unilever have adopted inclusive models of microfranchising, a creative form of microcrediting to reach people far and wide. Unilever's Indian subsidiary provides training to local women in selling, commerce, and accounting and also simultaneously generates micro-entrepreneurs.

Given the growing focus of businesses that target inclusive growth, this chapter offers insights from successful social enterprises and their organizational adaptations that helped them overcome the specific constraints of emerging markets and sustain economic growth. Using specific examples from the Indian healthcare sector, five different adaptations to overcome infrastructure limitations in low-resource markets are illustrated and detailed.

9.1 Market and Innovation Constraints in Emerging Markets

There is no doubt that the role of emerging markets in the global economy is rising. In order to catch the core of innovation in emerging markets, there is a need to understand the particular market characteristics and innovation constraints. Emerging markets are often characterized by both market and societal constraints, including informal and underdeveloped regulatory infrastructures, high levels of poverty, unemployment, and high trade barriers. This implies that while emerging markets provide promising opportunities for firm revenue growth, they also represent a difficult business environment for organizations to navigate through.

The Indian healthcare market, where a majority of the population lacks basic healthcare services, is an appropriate example for understanding the market constraints of emerging markets. India currently suffers from a large healthcare service divide due to high rates of illiteracy, income disparity, low awareness, a fractured regulatory framework, and accessibility constraints. Although India is one of the largest producers of doctors in the world, it still suffers from an acute physician shortage. The physician/population ratio of India of 1 : 1700 is way below the worldwide average of 1 : 666 (Srivastava and Shainesh, 2015). Almost 70% of the Indian physicians reside in

Table 9.1: Market constraints in India's emerging healthcare markets.

Market constraints	Description
Environmental	Uncertain production environment due to unstable and weak political and regulatory structures
	Unavailability of resources in rural areas
	Creating rural access
Institutional	Lack of defined regulations
	Lack of trust in product offering
Customer	Low literacy rate
	Highly influenced by faith-based institutions
	Low disposable income
	Low willingness to pay
	Nonusers

urban areas that cater to only 30% of the total population. That means the medical requirements of almost 70% of the population living in rural areas go unattended due to inaccessible resources and poor healthcare services.

In such a scenario, the unavailability of a social security system further worsens the situation. Consumption of any kind of healthcare services thus directly impacts people's disposable income. Therefore, due to low awareness and income constraints, health-related problems are either reduced in priority or are never even considered by the majority of the population living under the subsistence level.

In these unique market conditions, where most of the population is still not consumers of healthcare services, the major challenge for healthcare companies is to convert these nonusers to first-time users and change their behavior toward healthcare. Table 9.1 summarizes the market constraints of the Indian healthcare sector at the environmental, institutional, and customer levels.

This chapter emphasizes organizational adaptations in the form of inclusive strategies that are necessary to overcome these specific healthcare market constraints and tap the economic potential for the bottom-of-pyramid (BoP) customer segment. It shows how businesses and practitioners can rethink and move beyond traditional marketing strategies toward shared value creation and purpose-driven branding to drive healthcare services access in these markets.

9.2 Inclusive Strategies of Social Enterprises

Extreme resource constraints not only affect people but also impact the business environment. Starting businesses in resource-constrained areas with extreme conditions forces companies to adopt innovative ways of doing business and often results in new organizational adaptations. Developing inclusive strategies is a major organizational adaptation firms can use to sustain economic growth in emerging markets. The term "inclusive" refers to moving from selling to customers to integrating them as suppliers within the value chain. Inclusive business models are about enabling participation of disenfranchised poor people into economic activities in the form of ownership, managerial control, employment, consumption, and supply-chain involvement. In markets where the majority of the population does not participate in or is excluded from economic activities, inclusive growth and proactive inclusion allow for firm success. Research has shown high relevance of this approach in the context of emerging markets, and the phenomenal success of social enterprises is a testimony to this trend.

Social enterprises are business ventures created to generate social value. They implement new business ideas for the well-being of the society and to enable the population to have access to basic services. While these enterprises are not profit oriented, inclusion of a sustainable business model that generates revenue is necessary for their long-term success. Social enterprises operate on a dual mission of financial sustainability and social value and strive toward creating economic value via societal development.

Social enterprises specifically in the Indian healthcare market have shown exceptional performance in delivering world-class healthcare services in an economically viable way to the masses. Delivering on the dual objectives of creating economic value and offering affordable healthcare services to the masses has required multiple organizational adaptations to overcome the constraints of emerging markets.

We take eye care in India as our example domain. Nearly 63% of the total vision impairment cases in India are due to cataract and diabetes. While 80% to –90% of cases of blindness can be cured, due to lack of awareness and unavailability of the basic healthcare infrastructure in the rural regions, most such cases go unattended, leading to a huge productivity loss. In such a scenario, successful proliferation of affordable eye care is not only important for the society but also inspiring for other businesses. The prominent examples delivering affordable eye care to the rural masses are AECS, Sankara Nethralaya, and Siliguri eye hospital.

AECS was set up in 1976 to offer quality eye care at no or low cost to the masses. Over the last 40 years it has overcome multiple constraints in the Indian market to run a profitable healthcare system. Dr. Govindappa Venkataswamy started AECS with a goal of replicating the standardization model of McDonald's for eye care within the healthcare delivery system. In order to use key resources efficiently and also to generate additional resources, AECS adopted several strategies for educating, employing, and engaging the local population that resulted in inclusive growth of society generally. AECS employed local women and provided them with basic training to perform non-critical tasks related to eye care so as to offload 60% to 70% of the doctors' work. AECS worked with local community workers to conduct outreach camps and started in-house academic institutions. These inclusive strategies not only increased the utilization rate of doctors but also offered educational and employment opportunities to the local population. The replication of AECS by several other social enterprises situated in emerging markets (across sectors and regions) further emphasized the importance and necessity of inclusive strategies.

Sankara Nethralaya and Siliguri eye hospital also were set up to offer affordable and quality eye care to the masses. Sankara maintains a self-sustainable status even after offering a free and highly efficient transportation network to customers, and Siliguri eye hospital is successful in sustaining its operation through actively engaging local community workers in the value chain.

Utilizing locally trained healthcare professionals (known as paramedics) and local community workers is a common phenomenon across different cases. Process standardization also emerged as an integral part of organizational adaptations, as in the case of AECS. Standardized and integrated processes ensure the provision of identical services and medications to patients, irrespective of location or paying capacity. This format built trust and provided the needed transparency in the healthcare structure. Formalizing educational institutes and collaboration with the government, in the case of AECS, also helped facilitate financial and operational stability and expansion opportunities.

These examples demonstrate a direct linkage between inclusiveness and business growth and show how including individuals from the BoP segment in the value chain is necessary to overcome specific constraints of emerging markets.

The remainder of this chapter focuses on the specific inclusive strategies of successful social enterprises from the Indian healthcare sector that enabled them to overcome emerging market constraints and sustain their operations over the long run. The intention is to provide guidance to businesses of all sizes seeking to engage commercially in emerging healthcare markets and looking for strategies for inclusive growth. The best practices offered in this chapter will help managers recalibrate their current strategies using a lens of inclusivity for long-term sustainability. Five key takeaways, summarized in Table 9.2 and presented next, are derived from cases of successful social enterprises in the Indian healthcare sector.

Table 9.2: Inclusive strategies and the key takeaways.

Inclusive strategies	Why	How-to
Involve intermediaries	To spread awareness and influence willingness to pay To build local reputation and brand	Include social and opinion leaders, local volunteers having high community influence Personalized one-to-one marketing through outreach camps Collaboration with government, NGOs, insurance companies
Social embedding	To target heterogeneous customer base For higher user acceptance	Narrow geographical focus Customized offering Respecting social norms and settings
Internalizing resources	To overcome resource constraints and create own resources	Establishing academic and training institutes Localizing manufacturing Skilling/reskilling local population
Local delivery models	To create access through local distribution network	Hub-and-spoke model with spokes spread in far-off locations Utilize advanced technologies like telemedicine
Purpose-driven marketing	To build local reputation and brand	Collaborating with government, NGOs Bringing standardized and transparent healthcare practices to the BoP Shared value creation

Takeaway 1: Involve Intermediaries in the Healthcare Value Chain

Emerging markets typically are communal societies with strong social relationships. People have low literacy rates and are highly influenced by faith-based institutions. In such settings, involvement of intermediaries in the value chain is considered an influential marketing and distribution tactic for BoP-targeted services or products. These intermediaries may range from community workers or opinion leaders to teenage stars on YouTube. They play an important role in creating awareness, shaping customer preferences, and building local brand and reputation for the enterprise.

Relationship building through intermediaries emerges as a key marketing activity across all social enterprises. Facilitating one-to-one interactions with the patients, these intermediaries are influential in setting expectations and willingness to pay. Such personalized marketing efforts increase awareness of the available services as well as influence the buying behavior of patients. Collaboration with government and local nongovernment organizations (NGOs) are often used to identify and involve these intermediaries.

AECS, Sankara, and Siliguri each have a strong regional focus. AECS and Sankara are based out of Tamil Nadu (a state capital of India) and target customers situated in and around cities of Madurai and Chennai, respectively. Siliguri hospital is located in the city of Siliguri in northwestern India and focuses specifically on the local community of tea farmers.

A narrow regional focus ensures homogeneity of the target customer segment in terms of language, culture, and buying behavior and also makes it relatively easier for service providers to identify relevant intermediaries and establish personalized relationships. Eye care providers identified that local community workers such as mailmen, school teachers, political leaders, and grocery shopkeepers have a high influence on the buying behavior of the local community. Therefore, in order to reach and influence the end customers, it was important for the providers to first educate these intermediaries about the need and availability of affordable eye care and then integrate them into the value chain to further spread awareness. Eye care providers, along with these intermediaries, also employed and trained school graduates with basic medical skills to do door-to-door marketing and establish one-to-one relationships with the local population. This allowed a deeper penetration into the target region and also influenced willingness to pay for eye care services within the target segment.

Apart from these direct intermediaries, eye care providers also collaborated with NGOs, insurance companies, and government, which gave them credibility and created trust for their brand.

Takeaway 2: Ensure Social Embeddedness of the Business Strategies

Social embedding to create deep understanding of the local environment and adapt to local customs is crucial in heterogeneous emerging markets to gain social acceptance and increase willingness to buy in the target customer segment. Business success in emerging markets depends on the ability to reflect the local conditions and build trust with the target population. Respecting the societal norms is highly important in emerging markets like India where customers come from varied political and regulatory backgrounds and have different beliefs based on religion and culture.

Organizations need to ensure social embeddedness for each of their strategies. To be more in tune with the market, in-depth understanding of the implicit factors that impact a patient's buying decision, such as local norms, religious beliefs, cultural practices, and employment sources, is necessary.

Social enterprises show the potential benefits of customizing strategies with respect to social norms and local settings in a heterogeneous market such as India. Sankara Nethralaya optimizes its customer flow and year-round resource utilization based on cultural and religious settings. It plans outreach camps according to regional festivals and do patient segmentation based on religious beliefs. In the months of October and November, where most of the Hindu festivals fall, Sankara Nethralaya plans more out-reach camps in Christian communities, where patients are more willing to have oper-ations during that time. This helps Sankara maintain a year-round, continuous flow of patients.

AECS chooses locations for its clinics that are natural centers of several neighboring villages. AECS selects not only geographically but also in terms of practices, like preferred locations for weekly shopping or regular purchase.

Takeaway 3: Internalizing Resources

As mentioned earlier, India suffers from a huge service challenge in offering high-quality, affordable, and accessible healthcare services. To offer healthcare services, organiza-tions in the Indian market have to deal not only with infrastructural but also with human resource challenges. Generating local human resource capabilities by enhanc-ing the skills and productivity of the local population is necessary to overcome these healthcare challenges and ensure a steady flow of skilled workers. Investing in the local environment by establishing local training and/or academic institutes or manufacturing facilities can be fruitful for businesses entering the Indian healthcare market with a long-term horizon.

Across all of the enterprises studied, a strong focus on education is evident. Paramedics (emphasis on the "para" in this context) form the backbone of these healthcare sector social enterprises. Social enterprises train local school graduates in basic medical skills and employ them to offload the noncritical tasks from the medical doctors. This training is done largely through internal programs.

AECS, in particular, exemplifies the long-term benefits of investing in the local environment. AECS established Lions Aravind Institute of Community Ophthalmology, a training and consulting center, in 1992 to build capacity and train individuals involved in the eye care sector. Apart from offering various ophthalmology programs at different levels (for paramedics, doctors, administrative staff, etc.), the institute also supports other eye care hospitals, agencies, and eye care policy makers in the government.

AECS also started a local research and development facility at Madurai called Aurolab for manufacturing optical lenses, blades, and sutures. Aurolab not only provides significant employment opportunities for the local population, it also reduces the cost of optical lenses by 80% for AECS. Such internalization of resources has enabled AECS to bypass the human resource challenge and offer affordable eye care services to the Indian BoP market.

Takeaway 4: Local Delivery Models

Creating access to healthcare services is an ongoing challenge in emerging markets. It is even more of a challenge in rural areas due to the lack of basic infrastructure and nonexistent distribution network. Therefore, businesses need to explore new or alternate service delivery approaches to be successful in emerging markets like India. Adoption of innovative delivery models, such as creating a local sales force of community workers, utilizing advanced technologies like telemedicine, or adopting hub-and-spoke business models, can help businesses reach inaccessible patient bases in the BoP. Social enterprises in the eye care sector demonstrate several different innovative delivery models that enable easy access to healthcare services even in hard-to-reach regions.

AECS has adopted a hub-and-spoke model and uses telemedicine technology to reach patients in far-flung areas. AECS operates a main center, or "hub," at Madurai. All sophisticated equipment and high-quality talent are centralized at this hub. Different spokes (clinics) connected through technologies like telemedicine are then established around this hub. Situated in far-flung areas and staffed with local paramedics, these spokes are able to offer eye care services nearly at patients' doorsteps, so that patients can avail themselves of the services without any travel.

Takeaway 5: Purpose-Driven Branding

Emerging markets often suffer from corruption and bureaucracy. Due to unregulated healthcare practices, countries like India have a relatively high number of unqualified doctors (known as quacks), which instills a high amount of insecurity and mistrust among patients receiving medication. Therefore, offering transparent and standardized healthcare services is important to create trust and a reliable reputation in the Indian healthcare market. This can be realized through partnerships with renowned local or Western medical institutes, collaboration with the government and NGOs, and by offering transparent pricing structures to patients. In particular, engagement in cross-sector partnerships and long-term alliances with local NGOs and other civil society organizations ensures a direct linkage of businesses to the social cause to help create a purpose-driven brand.

Social enterprises in the Indian healthcare market can successfully leverage this purpose-driven branding to create a special reputation and brand value. Their strong focus on inclusive growth and social objectives provides them with a competitive edge over other for-profit businesses.

AECS, one of the oldest (40 year) social enterprises in the Indian healthcare segment, is a leading example of such purpose-driven branding. The company has benefited greatly from the trust and word of mouth created by collaboration with the government over the years, and its dedication to social healthcare causes has led it to become an endorsement brand. In the absence of strong institutional and regulatory structures, new (both nonprofit and for-profit) healthcare providers use their association with AECS as an endorsement of their their credibility and interest in social causes. The developed brand and provision of standardized healthcare services, irrespective of paying capacity, has helped AECS to attract not only BoP customers but also those from other income segments, gradually increasing its ratio of paid to free customers.

9.3 Conclusion and Outlook

Over the past two decades, there has been a tremendous growth in emerging markets (Agarwal and Brem, 2012). Countries like India have become a breeding ground for inclusive innovation successes. These innovations have shown phenomenal success, economically as well as in terms of societal impact (Sheth, 2011). Using specific cases of social enterprises that were successful in diffusing accessible and affordable innovations, this chapter discussed several inclusive strategies that are deemed important in sustaining economic activities in an emerging market context.

The chapter aimed to inspire business leaders to rethink their business strategies and apply "inclusive" strategies for commercializing at BoP. Drawing insights from the success of social enterprises in the Indian healthcare sector, this chapter emphasized the need for shared value creation through involving intermediaries, social embedding, and internalizing resources. Adopting innovative delivery models and purpose-driven branding also have shown high influence in reaching customers across the last mile of service delivery and influencing their service choice preferences.

Table 9.2 details the different inclusive strategies and implementation examples to overcome specific constraints of emerging markets covered in this chapter. In a communal society, relationship building and engineering the customer's social network is a crucial dimension in shaping customer preferences and building product meaning and reliability. Local alliances and social embedding provide in-depth understanding of the market and help in targeting a heterogeneous customer base, which is specific to emerging markets. In a society of strong social relationships, with influential faith-based and sociopolitical institutions (such as religion, social community, and government), acclimatizing to the societal norms and behavior is a necessary condition. Businesses that are sensitive to local customs and more congruent to the societal setting of the markets in which they are operating have greater chances of success. Contrary to advanced economies, considering emerging markets as homogeneous markets could prove to be disadvantageous for a company.

The example of internalizing resources or absorbing local population into the value chain shows multiple benefits for sustaining business operations over the long term. Investment in the local environment on the one hand helps businesses bypass resource constraints by generating their own local resources and on the other hand facilitates societal acceptance. The importance of cross-sector partnership is also highlighted for purpose-driven branding.

This chapter drew attention to an increasing need of reviewing current business strategies in the context of emerging markets and offered inclusivity as an optimal lens. Current business strategies primarily developed in the context of advanced economies have largely ignored the inclusion of nonviable customers and have also undermined the significance of inclusive marketing. However, the rise of emerging markets, where most of the population is still at the BoP, has reinstated the focus on inclusive growth and necessitated the inclusion of societal value creation into company goals for long-term survival. Therefore, the takeaways are to assist business managers in this transformation and provide them with several nontraditional and innovative practices from the social enterprise that appears to be leading this transformation.

References

Agarwal, N. and Brem, A. 2012. Frugal and reverse innovation – Literature overview and case study insights from a German MNC in India and China. In *18th International Conference on Engineering, Technology and Innovation: ICE 2012—Conference Proceedings*, ed. B. Katzy, T. Holzmann, K. Sailer, and K. D. Thoben (Red Hook, NY: Curran Associates), pp. 1–11.

Sheth, J. N. (2011). Impact of emerging markets on marketing: Rethinking existing perspectives and practices. *Journal of Marketing* 75 (4): 166–182. doi: 10.1509/jmkg.75.4.166.

Srivastava, S. C. and Shainesh, G. (2015). Bridging the service divide through digitally enabled service innovations: Evidence from Indian healthcare service providers. *MIS Quarterly* 39 (1): 245–267.

About the Authors

DR. NIVEDITA AGARWAL is an Assistant Professor at the Chair of Technology Management at the Friedrich-Alexander-Universität Erlangen-Nürnberg, Germany. Her research focuses on new product development, social entrepreneurship, and constraint-based innovation especially in context of emerging markets. Inspired by the existing challenges at the bottom of the pyramid, her research highlights the role of innovation and entrepreneurship enabled by disruptive technologies in shaping the complex ecosystem at the bottom of the pyramid. She has reviewed and published articles in several peer-reviewed academic journals, such as the *Journal of Business Research*, *IEEE Transactions on Engineering Management*, and *International Journal of Technology Management* and is an Associate Editor of *International Journal of Entrepreneurial Venturing*.

DR. ALEXANDER BREM holds the Chair of Technology Management at the Friedrich-Alexander-Universität Erlangen in Nürnberg, Germany, which is located at the Nuremberg Campus of Technology. He is a Children's Commissioning Support Resource International Research Associate at DeMontfort University, in the United

Kingdom, a Visiting Professor at the EADA Business School in Barcelona, Spain, and the HHL Graduate School of Management in Leipzig, Germany. Moreover, he serves as an Academic Committee Member of the Center of Technological Innovation, Tsinghua University, Beijing, China. In addition, he was appointed Honorary Professor at the University of Southern Denmark in May 2017. His research activities are focused on the management of research and development in high-tech firms, which involves research fields like idea management, constraint-based innovation, user innovation, and technology entrepreneurship.

10

AMBIGUITY AND MISDIRECTION? BRING IT ON! LESSONS ABOUT OVERCOMING FROM WOMEN MARKET TRADERS

José Antonio Rosa
Iowa State University, Ames, IA, USA

Shikha Upadhyaya
California State University, Los Angeles, CA, USA

Introduction

A recurring theme in this book is that innovation has many manifestations and that alongside highly publicized breakthrough technologies and magical experiences, hundreds of innovative and yet simple artifacts and processes come to light every day. Equally pervasive ideas are that innovation can arise from unlikely sources and that market and environmental constraints can lead to greater innovation. Constraints force us to adopt and modify current approaches just to overcome them, and they often also elicit hope and persistence that wear away the hindrances. One additional idea, albeit perhaps not as strongly argued in this book, is that creativity under constraints often involves some level of rule breaking on the part of companies and individuals. When socially accepted pathways to market gains are not accessible, rule-breaking solutions are likely to emerge in firms that wish to succeed.

This chapter looks to an unlikely source – women market traders in subsistence marketplaces – for practical insights into innovation under constraints. Examining how women market traders innovatively navigate uncertain and hostile environments, and how they sometimes break rules to take advantage of ambiguity and misdirection in market environments, makes a strong case for companies to allow similar behaviors when business constraints exist and intersect. The constraints these women face – exclusion and sometimes ill treatment on account of gender and social class – are enduring and seemingly immutable in many societies with large, untapped markets. For companies in similarly hostile and unchanging situations, innovative rule breaking may be a means to survival, if not growth. Insights into the functioning of marketplaces in subsistence markets can also help companies that want to serve the 4-billion-strong emerging economy consumer segment. Consultants and business leaders worldwide agree that it is among these 4 billion that most future market growth can be expected. Moreover, bridging the last mile in the producer-to-consumer value chain in subsistence markets presents significant challenge to producers and retailers globally and continues to require the involvement of market traders like those described in this chapter. The practical suggestions presented here will help companies develop low-end innovation capabilities by adding resilience and market responsiveness to that indispensable last-mile distribution support network.

10.1 Innovation and Rule Breaking

The criminal is the creative artist; the detective only the critic.

G. K. Chesterton

Seeing innovation as violating behavioral norms is intuitively plausible when one stops to consider what is involved. Creativity takes place when existing knowledge is recombined into unusual arrays, and unusual most often means that rules were violated. Children are inherently creative (we call it play) because they are still learning society's rules, and many criminals are creative because they disregard social norms. Sociologist Robert K. Merton (1957) proposed that, in most societies, rules exist about what should be pursued (goals) and how to pursue it (means), and that when people follow rules about goals but disregard rules about means, they are innovative (see Figure 10.1). In general, Merton advocated for societies where goals and means align so people will conform. Modern companies and organizations, however, encourage employees to break rules, or at least some rules, especially in the name of innovation. Many encourage innovation (pursuing company goals through alternative means), and others encourage rebellion (i.e. overthrowing industry and market conventions).

It can also be argued that tendencies toward innovative rule breaking are easiest to find in social contexts where constraints are most severe, as they typically are in subsistence markets. Prahalad (2006) argued that the poor are an unexplored business opportunity. His perspective was in itself innovative, one that inspired others to look at the poor through different lenses. He illustrated through case studies that poor consumers and merchants are clever because of constraints and life factors that they endure daily. He also proposed that we can learn from the poor about creativity under constraints. This chapter builds on that tradition.

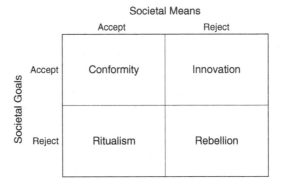

Figure 10.1: Societal goals and means typology.

This chapter stems from a large investigative project that has taken us into subsistence markets in India, Colombia, Guatemala, and Fiji, exposing us to dozens of examples of innovation under constraints being carried out by poor people living in subsistence contexts. Some of them involve unique approaches to products such as soaps and hand tools, and others to processes such as hammock weaving and milk retail sales. Innovative rule breaking is amply evident, since in many instances subsistence innovators are involved in raw material reuse and repurposing that people in most developed societies would consider unsafe or unorthodox (e.g. home-crafted hair gel packaged in sandwich bags) and in the continual adjustment of products and processes in response to fast-changing market conditions (e.g. dynamic pricing in response to demand fluctuations throughout the day). Among the poor, innovations have a short half-life because constraints are recurring and their day-to-day implications are unpredictable.

10.2 Constraints Arising from Gender, Social Class, and Their Intersection

This chapter focuses on women market traders, who operate market kiosks and sell door-to-door around the world, and on the gender and social class constraints that they endure and overcome. Gender and social class constraints are inescapable aspects of social identity in all countries and are very much present among the poor. They shape self-image and how others treat us in social encounters. They are also often used by people in power as grounds for exclusion or the withholding of important resources. For women market traders, gender, social class, and their intersection are a continual source of business challenges and hence a trigger for innovation under constraints from which we can learn.

Gender

Gender-based threats and consequences faced by poor women traders are summarized in Table 10.1. The recurring and seemingly unresolvable problem is the inferior status

Table 10.1: Threats women market traders face.		
Threats	**Consequences**	**What companies can do about it**
Inadequate literacy and numeracy skills	*Finances*: The women resist joining savings plan that would help them invest better and manage their personal lives.	Provide women with employment-based savings plans and educate them on cash management.
	Further, financial decisions are made by older family members or male members, which affirms the women's lack of autonomy.	Provide technology (e.g. calculators, mobile devices) and training (e.g. basic math courses) to help enhance numeracy and literacy.
	Managing exchange processes: Women are disadvantaged in daily buying and selling.	Give the women credentials that will enhance their social standing with abusive males.
Infrastructure Deficiencies	*Physical safety*: Transportation and public space deficiencies (e.g. illumination) put women at risk of physical violence, particularly those who work at night or have to travel long distances.	Invest in sustainable and safe infrastructure that provides women privacy (i.e. lighting, bathrooms, access to clean water, nursing/changing rooms).
	Hygiene and sanitation: Lack of access to reliable sanitary facilities causes women to postpone their hygiene needs, which has severe health consequences.	Implement a shuttle service that ensures women working late hours have a reliable and safe transportation.
Pressure to comply with gender/ethnic norms	*Gender norms*: Women are under pressure to balance economic and domestic responsibilities to preserve social standing and access. Engagement in the formal or informal economy is part of their caretaking responsibility, but often they are mocked for focusing on money making.	Align workplace policies and conditions with local cultural and gender norms, such as providing time for prayer, allowing women to wear clothes that fit with their local culture, and allowing women to bring their children to work.
	Ethnic norms: Market traders face ethnically grounded demands such as contributing to community funds without regard to their financial situation and selling at a discount to family members and others related by ethnicity.	
Inconsistent implementation of marketplace policies	*Inequities*: Market administrative practices guided by social class and ethnic biases contribute to invisibility and systemic exclusion of women operating in formal and informal economies.	Provide periodic training to merchant relationship managers to clearly communicate policy goals and mechanisms. Create open communication channels with law enforcement officers to ensure all voices are heard and avoid instances of policy-based exclusion.

of women in most subsistence societies and how that status impacts marketplace functioning. Because of family needs, low-income women have to contribute to household income while also meeting marriage and parenting responsibilities. When children are ill, it is the woman who tends to their needs without neglecting other duties, such as preparing meals and maintaining a welcoming household for her husband and other family members. The demands are many, and sometimes incompatible, such as when tending the market kiosk conflicts with caring for sick children. Shakuntala (all names are disguised), an Indo-Fijian market trader, exemplifies the daily routines of women market traders in her homeland. Six days per week, she gets up very early (3:00 a.m.), completes daily household chores with no help from family members, travels one hour by bus into the city, sources produce (e.g. jackfruit) from wholesalers before 8:00, works 8–5 in the marketplace, and returns home to cook for the family and complete end-of-day tasks. She goes to bed around 10:00 and starts over in the morning. There are millions of women worldwide just like her.

Lack of sleep, difficult work schedules, and incessant demands notwithstanding, many women market traders are ridiculed incessantly for not being "good mothers" and for "worrying too much about money." Such remarks put considerable pressure on women to comply with irreconcilable gender ideals as they work in the marketplace, and many share that they feel "bad" because of the adverse social perceptions.

Additional complications may arise from women's role in managing family finances. In some societies, such as India and most Latin American countries, women have some latitude when managing family income and expenditures. In other societies, such as Bangladesh and Pakistan, only husbands or other dominant males (e.g. older brothers) manage money and make purchases. And even in societies where women have some latitude, dominant males generally rule the household and have final say on how family income is used. Moreover, violations of family income and spending norms are swiftly and brutally punished, suggesting that many women live with some level of fear day in and day out.

Gender factors are important when serving subsistence markets because retail sales – those important last-mile transactions that take place in open markets and door-to-door – are beneath the dignity and social standing of men in most subsistence societies and are hence what anthropologists call feminized labor. Women doing retail distribution work in subsistence markets share common concerns, such as husbands or brothers appropriating daily sales receipts for their own use (e.g. paying off gambling debts, partying with friends, other business ventures) and male customers refusing to pay for goods. Among women who operate in municipal markets, differential implementation of rules and regulations by the men who also work there also occurs.

Even when women market traders are successful and achieve relatively high levels of income, they remain vulnerable to the men both in their homes and workplaces. For instance, because of dominant males stealing their hard-earned cash, women market traders find innovative ways to safeguard their money, given that commercial banking is not a viable option for most of them. Some "roll the money" by reinvesting cash into gold jewelry and other nondepreciating assets that they can protect on their bodies, while others invest in savings circles and other forms of community savings plans to ensure their money is secure.

Also affecting women market traders are social norms that define how they should behave toward family or clan members. In some societies – in South India, for example – young married women must be deferential to mothers-in-law as much as to their husbands and, by association, to older women members of the husband's family. Many of the women traders talk about family members making fun of them on account of missing family functions and community ceremonies because of working in the marketplace and using those social norm violations as an excuse to demand money and special favors.

In some societies, such as Fiji, expectations may also involve deference to higher-status members of the clan or village. Demands from such people cannot be ignored, and may create significant problems for a woman market trader who is trying to maintain adequate inventory levels and pay for delivered inventory on a timely basis. High-status people, such as village elders and family matriarchs, asking for handouts mostly happens to Native Fijian traders. Not surprisingly, it is primarily those traders who highlight the social and communal aspect of their ethnic identities. Giving back to the society through *soli* events (charity), donations to the church, drinking kava,[1] weaving mats with other women for free, and interest-free loans (seldom fully repaid) to family members and friends are common social practices that define Indigenous Fijian identity, irrespective of people's personal needs and level of income. Not surprisingly, saving money and aspiring to social and economic mobility and independence become a huge concern for many women market traders.

Women market traders find innovative workarounds for gender constraints. One example is embodied in Janaki, who has three children, a "not useful" husband, and sells milk door-to-door in Chennai, India (Viswanathan et al., 2010). She involves her children in milk deliveries while making sure they stay up-to-date in their studies; by utilizing her children, she violates her milk distributor's rules and local regulations. In addition, she has elaborate verbal arrangements with customers by which she sets daily prices based on clients' ability to pay on the spot and their past purchase loyalty. Janaki maintains a running balance of who received what concessions and when, which she uses to sustain equity among her customers while also being able to sell her daily milk quota. On a somewhat regular basis, she brings accounts up-to-date, demanding rectifying payments from customers who are in arrears and giving price breaks to customers who have in effect been subsidizing other customers by making full payments. Because Janaki's milk distributor frowns on price breaks and expects daily payments from her, she cleverly manages this complex retail system on her own, relying mostly on memory because she both is illiterate and cannot do even simple arithmetic. Her children help with the accounting, and she deals with a local loan shark when client payments fail to cover the daily payment that the milk distributor expects.

Gender factors create recurring constraints in the development and implementation of the small businesses that these women operate. Given the ways in which these factors are manifest, they should be the focus of ongoing monitoring and adaptation by companies. One example is the easing of credit and collection practices that has been implemented by companies such as Hindustan Unilever Limited in India. Initially, the company expected prompt payment from its (women) distributors and wanted them to adopt cash-only sales practices. Both constraints had to be eased in response to the behaviors of husbands and other family members, male clients, and corrupt law enforcement officers, which led the company to place adaption authority over company policies in the hands of merchant relationship managers – the people who personally provide inventory and collect payments from the market traders. Relationship managers are almost always local male merchants who are economically only one step above

---

[1] Derived from a plant root, it is consumed in many Pacific island nations as an astringent and has a relaxing effect.

the women market traders and hence well versed in the nuances of the local market. Relationship managers understand how factors such as harvest cycles in rural areas or waves of police corruption after local elections in cities can broadly affect consumers' ability to pay; and more pointedly, they understand the frequency and intensity of demands for additional money from husbands and families of market traders. And these managers can allow women market traders the flexibility they need to deal with such unpredictable constraints. Giving relationship managers flexibility makes it possible to retain market traders, but it has also introduced operating rule breaking into the system and may affect profits adversely. Given that the likely outcomes from not allowing adaptation are a loss of market trader engagement and innovativeness and reduced market access to consumers in remote villages and urban slums, some companies working with market traders have chosen a rule-breaking approach. Similar flexibility in business practices seem advisable even when market traders are not women and constraints are not based on gender, but instead on other chronic constraints.

Social Class

Alongside the gender-based vulnerabilities affecting women market traders are social class inequities that lead to differences in access to resources and to unequal treatment. Practically all societies have some form of social hierarchy. In the United States, for example, people from low socioeconomic levels tend to have limited access to education, healthcare, and even retail shopping alternatives. Similar distinctions can be found in many European countries, and they may be related to ethnicity (e.g. the Romani) or religion (e.g. Muslims). In India, social class distinctions emerge from a centuries-old caste system that was affirmed by colonial powers until the 1940s. The caste system was constitutionally abolished in India, but caste distinctions remain embedded in the social norms that tacitly structure life within Indian within Indian communities worldwide. The caste system is interesting in that the correlation between caste level and wealth or income is not as high as in Western countries. High-class Indians can be poor, and low-caste Indians can be affluent.

Under socially enduring Indian caste distinctions, poor high-caste market traders (e.g. Brahmins) will likely have more access to resources and information than low-caste market traders (e.g. Shudras), and more latitude in their actions. If a Brahmin market trader complains to the market administrator, she may get more respect and responsiveness than if the complainer is from a lower caste. Similarly, higher-caste market traders will be listened to more attentively and respectfully when they speak on marketplace issues, and they may be given preferential access to government aid. In Fiji, social class differences exist between Native Fijians, who either own land or are members of a landowning clan, and Indo-Fijians (Fijians of Indian origin) whose ancestors came to the islands as indentured laborers and who are prevented by law from owning land.

Differences also exist between rural and urban dwellers. Indigenous Fijians from rural areas may actually enjoy higher social status than city-dwelling ones because their work upholds the Fijian cultural heritage. The same does not hold for Indo-Fijians. An interesting aspect of Fijian marketplaces is that caste-based distinctions that may have once been present among Indo-Fijians have virtually disappeared, likely because all Indo-Fijian share second-class status. Because Indo-Fijians cannot own land, they are overrepresented in the urban population, although some Indo-Fijians lease land for agriculture and live in rural areas. Because rural-dwelling Indo-Fijians almost never own their land, however, they are little more than indentured servants, and to the extent that urban dwellers have higher status than rural dwellers, Indo-Fijians who live in rural areas are at the bottom of the social class order.

In Fiji, Native and Indo-Fijian women market traders use ethnic differences to gain political power and cultural autonomy in the marketplace. For instance, the marketplace has formal or informal associations by which women market traders collectively voice concerns about working conditions and other issues (e.g. bathroom cleanliness). However, the voices of some women remain unheard primarily because of their ethnic identity. This insight came from an Indo-Fijian market trader who complained bitterly about the Native Fijian women switching conversations from English to Fijian whenever it was expedient to exclude the Indo-Fijians. Other Indo-Fijian women echoed the sentiment. In Fiji, English is understood by all ethnicities, albeit with different levels of proficiency. However, women belonging to one ethnicity may use their language in meetings to establish ethnic separation that enhances their political power and sense of superiority. This ethnically grounded separation tactic is possible in part because Native Fijians are overrepresented in market administrative positions.

In subsistence environments such as India and Fiji, social class distinctions are long standing, complex, and hard to change, and they can have a significant effect on how women market traders operate their businesses. In Fijian municipal markets, for example, Native Fijian and Indo-Fijian women market traders have side-by-side stalls and sell similar products, but market administrators respond differently to complaints based on the trader's social class status. Similarly, urban-dwelling market traders operate stalls inside the market building, while rural dwellers operate temporary stalls outside the building; market administrators enforce different rules for the two groups. Rural Native Fijians and Indo-Fijians who work the land are allotted special cultural capital in Fiji and are given permission to sell outside municipal markets buildings (not allowed otherwise) on Saturdays. They are expected, however, to observe market stall rules and pay market fees. Many market traders reported, however, that although technically against the rules, market administrators regularly allow rural traders to freely occupy open market stalls even inside the building and do not require them to pay marketplace fees. In effect, administrators are discriminating against urban market traders in violation of Fijian laws, and they defend the practices because of the importance of agriculture in Fiji's history and society.

As with gender-caused constraints, monitoring and responding to constraints caused by social class is important for companies, but for different reasons. Whereas gender-based constraints will likely apply equally to traders in a particular location, constraints based on social class create inequities within markets, and they can lead to radically different rule-breaking responses by traders. In Fijian markets, for example, Native Fijian women market traders seldom experience social class constraints, except for those created by market administrators implementing different rules for rural and urban traders. Constraints caused by social class, consequently, tend to elicit surprise, anger, and possibly open rebellion among the Native Fijian market traders. Rule breaking and innovation among Native Fijians is often very visible.

Indian Fijian women market traders, in contrast, are used to social class discrimination everywhere and hence respond to constraints caused by social class with covert workarounds and silent determination. Rule breaking and innovation among Indo-Fijian market traders is seldom overt or admitted to when exposed. Louisa (a Native Fijian trader) and Anita (Indo-Fijian woman market trader) exemplify these differences. Louisa openly (and loudly) highlighted how market traders have repeatedly complained at city council meetings about market administrators who allow violations of market stall regulations by some traders on account of their political connections or rural status. Anita, in contrast, was circumspect in her narrative and alluded in general terms to the Indo-Fijian women keeping a low profile and avoiding public conflict while working through coercive back channels to get more equitable administration of market rules.

Companies wanting to work in subsistence markets where social class constraints are present and wishing to identify the innovative behaviors that can be emulated elsewhere need to be assiduously observant of market trader behaviors. Moreover, they need to establish trust with market traders from different social classes in order to fully grasp how they are operating their businesses and innovating in response to constraints.

When Gender and Social Class Intersect

Additional complications from which we can learn arise when gender and social class intersect. When women market traders face constraints that differ from those facing males and women in lower social classes face constraints different from those in higher classes, the adaptations required are challenging. Gender and social class intersecting escalate the scope and speed of challenges, and adding other social identity dimensions, such as age, income, and education, to the mix places even more pressure on market traders.

When identity dimensions intersect, the constraints and pressures experienced by a person can be more than the sum of pressures coming from each constraint. Our research shows women market traders overcome the intersection of gender and social class constraints by embracing (and even encouraging) marketplace ambiguity and misdirection – which we define as a state of affairs where the changeability and inconsistency of social norms leave market traders with a sense of things being neither true nor false. Typically, Western firms view ambiguity and misdirection as detrimental to successful business practices. Among women market traders, however, they are a mixed blessing, because they create threatening conditions from which good things can arise.

Operationally, marketplace ambiguity and misdirection arise when norms are unclear, such as when administrators and other market traders forget the rules or misapply them, or perhaps falter in their applications because situations are unusual or novel. Market administrators are not more educated than the women traders (i.e. they have basic reading and arithmetic skills) and can be confused by new government regulations or by the entry of new market vendors. When marketplace ambiguity and misdirection are at play, women market traders often behave erratically, and they fluctuate between being highly energized or listless. Not surprisingly, marketplace ambiguity and misdirection is mentally and emotional taxing and likely contributes to the noted listlessness. Because marketplace ambiguity and misdirection can involve lapses in the application of discriminatory gender and social class constraints, however, they can alternatively create moments in which traders feel liberated, even if for short time periods; and that sense of liberation can be inspiring and energizing. A market trader experiencing momentary empowerment induced by an episode of ambiguity and misdirection might engage in highly innovative (and risky) experimenting with pricing, credit practices, and product delivery or presentation, experimentation that could alter her market reputation or reach.

An Indo-Fijian market trader named Krishna, for example, reported how she and others practice what amounts to dynamic pricing in order to manage the rate at which products sell throughout the day. The objective is to run out of stock at the same time that the market closes, instead of experiencing stock-out conditions or selling any remaining product at the end of the business day to vendors selling (illegally) outside the market after 5:00 p.m. Krishna experiments with her prices to accelerate or slow down demand for her products. Doing this requires constant monitoring of prices for the same product throughout the market, however, which is cognitively and emotionally draining because it triggers high levels of social disapproval (as she seeks pricing information from competitors) and is hence not something she can do every day. On days that ambiguity and misdirection leave her feeling energized, she engages aggressively in dynamic pricing. Other days she sadly accepts her business losses and the possibility that her children will go hungry that night. Krishna's story, similar to that of other market traders, makes clear that marketplace ambiguity and misdirection can trigger debilitating anxiety and marketing mistakes. Nevertheless, many women market traders take advantage of marketplace ambiguity and misdirection, in spite of its potential detrimental effects, because of the psychological comfort it can afford. They sometimes go as far as promoting ambiguity and misdirection by engaging in unexpected and disruptive behaviors, such as encouraging raucous complaining about bathrooms or engaging in loud arguing that forces market administrators out of their comfort zones.

When companies respond aggressively to innovation (rule breaking) that stems from marketplace ambiguity and misdirection, it can lead to mistakes, such as granting promotions to temporarily hyperproductive market traders who are otherwise mediocre in skills or terminating women market traders who are momentarily suffering but will be effective in the long run. Dealing with unpredictability in marketplaces is difficult, and having to manage women market traders who are made even more unpredictable by marketplace ambiguity and misdirection further complicates matters. Hence, it seems important for companies that rely on women market traders to accept the idea that traders may be more unpredictable, less emotionally stable, and more likely to break rules than retailers and individual salespeople might be. Concurrently they should expect greater and unexpected innovation, and they are hence encouraged to have processes that allow practice adaptation in different ways from how it may be implemented in other contexts.

10.3 Five Practical Suggestions

Table 10.2 offers five practical suggestions based on our examination of the innovative practices of women market traders, as we believe that understanding their approaches can be valuable to companies. Unique constraints, such as low literacy and numeracy, deprivation, unhygienic work conditions, and compromised legal and administrative systems, give rise to unique innovative thinking. It seems plausible, in fact, that the people best equipped to arrive at innovative solutions for subsistence markets are the women market traders who operate in those environments.

As seen elsewhere in this book, adaptation readiness can be achieved through organizational development, design thinking, individual championing, and other approaches. In the case of subsistence markets, adaptation may be best carried out by the person or team who has direct managerial contact with the women market traders. We call those people *merchant relationship managers*. Their duties include recruiting women market traders, helping them manage cash flow and inventory, and coordinating across a disparate and unusual retailer group.

Because of subsistence market complexities, it seems wise that merchant relationship managers operate as autonomous distributors. When companies rely on

Table 10.2: Five practical suggestions for emerging market adaptation readiness.		
Practical suggestions	**It will work because …**	**Look out for …**
1. Provide merchant relationship managers with graduated immersion experiences (e.g. single-week, multiweek, multimonth as needed).	Market rules and processes are sustained through stories. Immersion helps managers capture emotional and cultural nuances. Graduated immersion facilitates knowledge internalization.	Information or experiential overload. Relationship managers identifying too closely with specific market players or market factions (i.e. going native).
2. Provide merchant relationship managers with training grounded in psychology and anthropology.	Mental models through which relationship managers can position and interpret market developments help maintain a balance operational consistency and situational sensitivity.	Relationship managers using mental model details prescriptively with merchants and other market actors. Models are frameworks and seldom are complete or fully accurate.
3. Establish communities of practice for merchant relationship managers.	Idea sharing and peer conversation serve to encourage participants and broaden their grasp of constraints and opportunities in subsistence markets.	Overstructuring community of practice exchanges.
4. Equip merchant relationship managers with information technologies (e.g. video capture equipment, cell- or satellite-based internet access) that facilitate quick problem resolution and information sharing.	Relationship managers will be better able to solve problems and provide answers locally while accessing global resources. In addition, such access will accelerate the logging of innovative ideas emerging from subsistence markets.	Equipment value becoming a crime endangerment factor for merchant relationship managers.
5. Allow merchant relationship managers some latitude with individual merchant inventory levels and credit practices.	Relationship managers will have more flexibility to address individual-level and community-level cash flow constraints.	Reliance on hard-to-track cash transactions. Use mobile banking technologies whenever possible.

distributors in developed economies, they leave most aspects of reselling (e.g. physical distribution, financing, returns, etc.) to distributors. In subsistence markets, merchant relationship managers will likely be employed by the firm and be responsible for administering company policies and processes. It is important, however, that they also be sufficiently trained and independent to deal with the localized and unique constraints that gender, social class, and marketplace ambiguity and misdirection can create. Next we expand on the five practical suggestions to achieve such ends.

Immersion Experiences

Firms should provide merchant relationship managers with graduated immersion experiences with the markets they serve, starting with weeklong introductions and building to multiweek or multimonth immersion as needed. Immersion duration depends on the trainee's background and familiarity with the target subsistence population. An example of extreme immersion is how Boo (2012) attained her award-winning grasp of life in the slums of Mumbai, India. Boo lived among the slum dwellers for a year, and she engaged in many of the same activities as her informants. Her goal was to grasp the physical and emotional effort required to deal with environmentally dangerous living conditions, corrupt law enforcement, and unemployment. Similar goals should be adopted by company immersion programs. It is important that individuals and teams dealing with women market traders be familiar with how the traders live and the demands they face. Boo achieved her insights by living with informants. Likewise, companies should promote to merchant relationship manager status people who have done market trader work, lived in their villages, walked in the slums, and traveled overnight from rural villages on buses and trucks. Shared nationality and cultural bonds are not enough, given that someone sufficiently educated to attain proficiency with corporate processes is not likely to have emerged from a subsistence environment where marketplace innovation is expected to arise. At least 30- to 90-day immersion experiences, however, are advisable.

Training Workshops on Related Consumer Behavior Concepts

At the same time, however, it is important for companies to protect their merchant relationship managers from identifying too closely with market traders. A second related suggestion, therefore, is for companies to provide relationship managers with structured training in consumer behavior and on how social and cultural factors shape human thinking and behaviors. Such training need not be formal classroom instruction but can instead be provided through self-administered instruction regimens of audio, digital, and print articles and books on topics like how the mind works, the role of emotions in decision making, and the importance of conversation and socialization to innovation. Training in the specific culture or cultures with which they will work is also advisable, and this involves not only the history and cultural profiles published in popular sources but also revisionist accounts that provide counterpoints to mainstream historical and cultural perspectives. In subsistence markets, likely many historical perspectives are shared across the generations and in the day-to-day verbal interactions of families and friends; relatively few if any historical accounts may be dominant. Many subsistence consumers and consumer merchants are illiterate, and even if they can read, they may not have had access to documented histories of their people and cultures. The goal is for merchant relationship managers to have detailed knowledge of how their clients think, feel, and behave – knowledge that help them understand what may be behind listlessness one day and euphoric experimentation the next – and know how to respond. Well-trained merchant relationship managers will be better able to consistently marshal and channel the women market traders' energies and innovative tendencies, to recognize when rule breaking may be allowed or must be curtailed, and to move between exerting control and giving latitude.

Communities of Practice

A third recommendation is to facilitate communities of practice for merchant relationship managers. Communities of practice are informal groups bound by shared expertise and passion for a joint enterprise. In most communities of practice, membership is voluntary, and whatever coordination arises is emergent and group driven. Communities of practice are deliberately unstructured and nonhierarchical, and they receive no formal charges from company management. Companies make them possible, however, because they help build member capabilities and shared knowledge. In companies serving subsistence markets, communities of practice would likely provide a setting where relationship managers can share insights and challenges pertinent to their market traders, help one another solve problems and identity innovation opportunities, and encourage one another. It is likely that community-of-practice participation by companies involved with subsistence markets will ebb and flow depending on local and global factors. It is also likely that participation will depend on information technologies and involve limited face-to-face interaction between members. Making such communities possible, however, can generate value. Companies can facilitate communities of practice by providing physical or virtual (see the next subsection) space where relationship managers can meet regularly. The space should provide some degree of confidentiality, sufficient for managers to share insights and discuss concerns openly. Further, companies can invest in low-cost computers, tablets, and possibly printing capabilities to help ensure adequate distribution of community-of-practice insights and recommendations throughout the organization.

Access to Information Technology

A fourth recommendation is to provide merchant relationship managers with information technologies such as video-capture equipment, and cell- or satellite-based internet access. As mentioned, one advantage from such technologies is to support virtual communities of practice when geographic and cultural distances make them necessary. An even more important benefit from such technologies comes from relationship managers having access to aggregated company knowledge while framing and solving problems at the local level.

Merchant relationship managers have to sustain trusting relationships with women market traders, and doing that requires sensitivity to local factors and norms. Relationship managers need to be both respected and appreciated, serve as both business sages and confidants, and have access to suggestions and solutions in the moment while not losing track of company objectives. Because women market traders are generally familiar with mobile information technologies, a relationship manager pulling out a smartphone to access distant databases will not likely seem scary or exclusionary to the women and hence may help maintain the all-important personal trust that relationship managers must treasure. One additional advantage is that it will greatly facilitate the sharing of innovative ideas (or unusual and thorny problems) that merchant relationship managers will likely encounter when working with women market traders.

Having systems that facilitate the logging and archiving of innovation successes and failures is a tried-and-true practice in companies that value creativity. To the extent that subsistence markets may be sources of unique thinking and solutions, companies should equip the most immersed and knowledgeable people to contribute promptly and easily to such archives. One word on caution with information technologies is to avoid brands and products that attract thieves and potentially place merchant relationship managers and market traders at risk.

Operational and Policy Autonomy

One final suggestion is to allow operational and policy autonomy to merchant relationship managers in subsistence markets. Even if companies expend the resources needed to produce subsistence market responsiveness as described, leaving reporting structures left unchanged will likely have these well-trained and equipped people working for supervisors and executives who would find it difficult to grasp the thinking behind relationship managers' decisions and points of view. With such a mismatch, it seems inevitable that at some point supervisor discomfort will rise to unmanageable levels and that the adaptation required to advance innovative solutions and best serve subsistence markets will be compromised or curtailed. As in other contexts, commitment to successful adaption in response to market idiosyncrasies should not be compromised by managerial ineptitude or inadequate organizational reporting structures. It may be good, in fact, to generally hold relationship managers accountable for business outcomes but not necessarily for compliance with documented business procedures. Such an approach admittedly opens the door to rule-breaking (deliberate or accidental) behaviors and possibly adverse outcomes. Given the seemingly intractable nature of constraints in subsistence marketplaces, however, they may be risks worth taking.

10.4 Conclusion

This chapter, based on explorations of women market traders in subsistence markets, provides unique insights into rule-breaking innovation under severe constraints and into some of the factors that contribute to such innovation. It also leads to practical recommendations for companies wanting to do business in subsistence markets and to rely on market traders to close the last-mile distribution gap endemic to subsistence economies. The insights arise from identifying discrimination factors pervasive in subsistence markets, such as gender and social class, and shown to disrupt the smooth functioning of business operations in subsistence societies. Market traders are further found to overcome such discrimination by engaging in clever rule-breaking behaviors and to embrace and sometimes encourage market ambiguities and inconsistencies that accidentally and temporarily allow them otherwise inaccessible opportunities. The chapter showed how intentional rule breaking is integral to day-to-day subsistence market practices and hence should be taken into account when designing, implementing, and managing business initiatives in subsistence contexts.

References

Boo, K. (2012). *Behind the beautiful forevers: Life, death, and hope in a Mumbai undercity.* New York: Random House.

Merton, R. K. (1957). *Social theory and social structure.* New York: Free Press.

Prahalad, C. K. (2006). *Fortune at the bottom of the pyramid: Eradicating poverty through profits.* Philadelphia: Wharton School Publishing.

Viswanathan, M., Rosa, J. A., and Ruth, J. A. (2010). Exchanges in marketing systems: The case of subsistence consumer-merchants in Chennai, India. *Journal of Marketing* 74 (3): 1–17.

About the Authors

DR. JOSÉ ANTONIO ROSA is Professor in Marketing and John and Deborah Ganoe Faculty Fellow at Iowa State University. He has studied topics such as the role of hope on innovation among poor consumers, boundaries between creativity and deviance among the poor, and how poor consumers use creative pursuits to cope with forced displacement due to natural disasters and violence. He has also investigated behaviors and decision making by low-literacy consumers, the social construction of product markets, and the role of embodied knowledge in consumer and managerial thinking. Dr. Rosa has taught marketing management, consumer behavior, and managing for innovation to undergraduate, professional graduate, and doctoral students and mentored doctoral students throughout his career. He holds degrees from University of Michigan, the Tuck School at Dartmouth College, and General Motors Institute (Kettering University). In his professional career, he held management positions in marketing and manufacturing in the automotive and banking industries.

DR. SHIKHA UPADHYAYA is an Assistant Professor of Marketing at California State University, Los Angeles College of Business and Economics. Her research focuses on the identity projects and multidimensional experiences of economically disadvantaged consumers in different consumption and marketplace settings. Her research provides important insights on consumption-related discrimination and disadvantage with implications in the areas of public policy and transformative consumer research. Dr. Upadhyaya teaches consumer behavior and social marketing courses and has held a range of marketing and business development roles at leading consumer and nonprofit organizations.

Index

Page numbers followed by *f* and *t* refer to figures and tables, respectively.